Varieties of Resilience

Resilience refers to the ability of individuals, groups and societies to withstand and recover from external shocks. This pioneering, book-length comparative study examines resilience as it is experienced across different countries, such as the United Kingdom, the United States, France, Germany and European Union. Furthermore it considers cases from policy sectors including national security, counter-terrorism, civil protection, disaster risk reduction, critical infrastructure protection and overseas interventions. In doing so, Joseph provides an account of why it is that resilience has become such a popular policy topic, looking at its focus on complexity, the human and the role of resilient individuals and communities.

Arguing that resilience has risen to prominence because it fits with a particularly Anglo-Saxon and neoliberal form of governance, Joseph discovers differing results across policy domains and national contexts, fomenting variations and tensions in the international discourse of resilience in policy-making.

JONATHAN JOSEPH is Professor of Politics and International Relations at The University of Sheffield and a former Senior Fellow at Käte Hamburger Kolleg/Centre for Global Cooperation Research, University of Duisburg-Essen. He is the author of *The Social in the Global: Social Theory, Governmentality and Global Politics* (Cambridge University Press, 2012).

Varieties of Resilience

Studies in Governmentality

JONATHAN JOSEPH
University of Sheffield

CAMBRIDGE
UNIVERSITY PRESS

CAMBRIDGE
UNIVERSITY PRESS

University Printing House, Cambridge CB2 8BS, United Kingdom

One Liberty Plaza, 20th Floor, New York, NY 10006, USA

477 Williamstown Road, Port Melbourne, VIC 3207, Australia

314–321, 3rd Floor, Plot 3, Splendor Forum, Jasola District Centre, New Delhi – 110025, India

79 Anson Road, #06-04/06, Singapore 079906

Cambridge University Press is part of the University of Cambridge.

It furthers the University's mission by disseminating knowledge in the pursuit of education, learning, and research at the highest international levels of excellence.

www.cambridge.org
Information on this title: www.cambridge.org/9781107146570
DOI: 10.1017/9781316551028

First published 2018

Printed and bound in Great Britain by Clays Ltd, Elcograf S.p.A.

A catalogue record for this publication is available from the British Library.

ISBN 978-1-107-14657-0 Hardback
ISBN 978-1-316-60157-0 Paperback

Contents

Acknowledgements

I have benefited significantly from discussions with various resilience scholars, certainly with David Chandler most of all. Thanks must also go to Philippe Bourbeau, Léo Bourcart, Martin Endreβ, Ana Juncos, Kristian Krieger, Claudia Morsut, Marie Naumann, Jan Pospisil, Benjamin Rampp and Tudor Vilcan. A glance at this list of names shows how they have helped me understand the European 'varieties' of resilience. Also, much appreciation goes to Jan Orbie and Valérie Rosoux who went out of their way to help fix me up with visiting positions at the Universiteit Gent and the Université catholique de Louvain respectively, although sadly I have not reciprocated in covering the understanding of resilience in Belgium.

A fellowship at the Käte Hamburger Kolleg/Centre for Global Cooperation Research at the University of Duisburg-Essen allowed me the valuable time to finish off the manuscript. I am particularly grateful to the Centre and to the German Federal Ministry of Education and Research for funding and resources and to colleagues, notably Frank Gadinger, Katja Freistein, Matthias Schuler, Pol Bargúes-Pedreny and Peter Finkenbusch.

Thanks also to colleagues at the University of Sheffield and to John Haslam at Cambridge who is always great to work with.

Finally, thanks to Ai, Hannah and Léo, particularly during the times when I am away at work.

Introduction: Resilience in Context

Resilience is a word that feels like it should have been around for a long time, but in fact it has only entered into contemporary political discourse very recently. It has made up for lost time by spreading rapidly through a whole range of policy areas from development policy to counter-terrorism strategy. Indeed the proliferation of the term has been so rapid that, like the revolutions in communications and digital technology, we are left with a sense of being overwhelmed and wondering how we managed before the idea emerged. It seems as if before we started using the term, we were left exposed to such shocks and traumas as terrorist attacks, economic crises, civil wars, droughts, floods, hurricanes and earthquakes, cyber threats, power blackouts and other infrastructure failures. A major purpose of this book, therefore, is to take stock and to step back. It seeks to raise questions about the rise of resilience and to query both whether the idea is useful, and also whether the spread of the idea really is as widespread or significant as it at first seems. There are two principal ways in which this can be done: by looking at the influence of resilience across a range of different policy areas, and by looking at whether this influence is evenly spread across a number of different countries.

If this were a book on a major philosophical issue we might expect a lengthy discussion of the meaning of the idea as well as a likely refusal to attempt to provide a simple definition for a very complex notion. In the case of resilience, this book, while opening with a chapter on the meaning of the term, sees more to be learned from its use than from engaging in a thorough philosophical investigation. Surveys of the literature (Manyena 2006; Martin-Breen and Anderies 2011; emBRACE 2012; Bourbeau 2015) commonly note the absence of any agreed concept of resilience, or even a general agreement of approach, either among academics or policy makers. The emphasis of this book is, therefore, on exploring varieties of understanding and differences

1

in approach. It does this by shifting attention to the contexts within which resilience operates.

While possible contexts are wide and varied, this book is concerned with the social, political and international contexts of resilience. In particular, the argument is concerned with resilience as it relates to societies and people and the particular ways in which these are managed, regulated and governed. Notwithstanding the problems of definition, resilience might be understood in its simplest sense as the ability of societies and people to manage, withstand and recover from shocks. This understanding – based on how the majority of policy papers and strategy documents use the term[1] – is focused on the socio-political aspects of resilience or what might be termed societal resilience. The following chapters will provide a comparative analysis of socio-political contexts and will consider varieties of resilience in the shifting contexts of different societies and different forms of societal consciousness and awareness. A societal approach points to how the practices of resilience vary according to their different social, political and cultural environments, as well as various political traditions and historical legacies. The more-political dynamics of societal resilience are highlighted through a focus on the processes and mechanisms of governance.

Conceptual Framework

Chapter 1 will briefly trace some of the origins of the idea of resilience, starting with influential ecology literature and examining how this relates to particular understandings of society. These understandings are, in turn, related to certain ontological assumptions that are sometimes implicit, but often explicit, in arguments about societal resilience, its wider context and the nature of various key actors and institutions. Ecology literature introduces the idea of complex systems that are in constant motion with no one stable state, and subject to multiple externally imposed crises and shocks (Holling 1973). Resilience comes to refer to the ability to 'bounce back', to withstand, or to evolve and adapt to a constantly changing equilibrium. These arguments relate to major trends in contemporary social and political discourse, for example, ideas about social and system complexity, non-linear causality,

[1] E.g., DFID 2011a: 7, European Commission 2012b: 5.

emergent states, relationality, social embeddedness, reflexivity and adaptability (see Chandler 2014). Resilience is also associated with wider philosophical notions such as post-humanism, non-cognitive functioning and emergent complexity.

The aim here is not to write a philosophical book that closely interrogates these assumptions, but to look at how these work in relation to strategies of governance insofar as they constitute something of a discursive shift in how we understand the world, our societies, the nature of the social, and the role of human action and consequently the means of governing our behaviour and environment. Our concern, thus, shifts away from a philosophical account of deeper human or social conditions to a more strategic-focused argument about how these ideas support certain forms of behaviour, preparing us for the subsequent chapters which examine the influence resilience and its associated notions have on a range of policy areas and across different countries and organisations. Hence the argument is sceptical of the claim that resilience, in itself, represents a fundamental shift in late-modern, post-modern or post-liberal thinking (see Chandler 2014; Evans and Reid 2014) and instead is concentrated on the way that resilience-thinking accompanies and supports various practices, tactics, strategies and interventions.

Key to the conceptual framework for understanding resilience, and why this book fits within the field of politics and international relations, is the claim that *resilience derives its meaningful character from its relation to governance strategies that have various populations as their target.* For this reason, the conceptual framework is organised around the concept of governmentality. This approach, as will be outlined in the next section, argues that contemporary governance relates to the mechanisms for the management of populations, a concern for their health and welfare and an attempt to direct their conduct from a distance (Foucault 2007: 108). What is distinctively liberal about governmentality is the attempt to appeal to the freedom of the governed. Liberal governmentality seeks to limit direct forms of governance by appealing to the governed to govern themselves (Foucault 2008: 319). This becomes embedded in a set of normative assumptions about individual conduct and responsible behaviour. Applying this to a study of resilience means looking at how a resilience strategy works 'from a distance' (Miller and Rose 1990: 9) by appealing to responsible behaviour and in particular, placing emphasis on strategies of learning, awareness and adaptability. In terms of governance, it is about shifting responsibility away from states and institutions and on to populations and communities. Governmentality draws attention to the way resilience goes beyond a reactive approach that teaches us how to 'bounce back' but is, in O'Malley's (2010) view, a new way of creating adaptable subjects capable of responding to, and even taking advantage of, situations of radical uncertainty.

For now, the point to emphasise is that the emergence of resilience in policy discourse has to be understood as related to, and dependent on, strategies of governance that seek to shape human conduct in particular ways. Indeed, it will be argued that resilience is derivative of these governance approaches. The book refrains from calling resilience a concept in its own right and instead sees it as a particularly useful *tool of governance*. Its usefulness to policy makers derives from its ability to play a certain role, particularly in its societal resilience guise, in managing or governing populations. As this book progresses, the case will be made for *why* resilience is being used by policy makers and *how* it works in particular policy contexts. However, the scope of resilience must be somewhat wider than this in order to justify extensive examination. Hence the starting focus on some key ontological and epistemological assumptions that render resilience a significant contemporary idea. While a strong argument of the book is that resilience fits with contemporary forms of governance (or governmentality), it is also the case that resilience offers a slightly different way of thinking about important questions relating to the nature of the social, the human, our context and our capacities, that challenges some of the essential assumptions of classical liberalism while enhancing the technologies and techniques of governance.

Comparative Approach

An effort will be made to determine whether resilience has more influence in some fields than others and, perhaps more significantly, whether it has greater impact in certain cultures and societies than others. It will soon become clear that resilience fits very well with an Anglo-Saxon way of thinking and that it is more prominent in these cultures or policy spheres. An important puzzle for this book is why it does not enjoy quite the same success in different European contexts. This unevenness of influence also has an impact of the way the argument is presented, since in studying the uptake of resilience we are not comparing like with like. By comparative approach, therefore, we do not mean the use of a 'scientific method' to discover an empirical relationship between variables (Lijphart 1971: 683), nor do we engage in a full cross-societal institutional comparison. If resilience is far less prominent in French policy making, then there is little point writing a full chapter on French resilience-thinking. The United Kingdom is therefore taken as the baseline by which to compare the influence of resilience in other countries as the United Kingdom is the country where resilience discourse is most-developed and most-influential. In each of the policy fields, the UK position will be outlined in most detail, with other countries brought in by way of comparison and contrast. This focus reflects the reality of the situation as described above, rather than any intended UK-centric bias on the part of the author. It is hoped that such a focus is nevertheless illuminating of other countries' approaches as well as illustrative of the leading position the United Kingdom has in resilience thinking.[2]

The method of analysis is to examine the most important policy documents produced by national governments and leading departments. Resilience is clearly a diverse notion to be found in an array of non-governmental domains. The book does not try to cover this wide area of things, like community-based projects or private initiatives. Instead, it concentrates on the idea of resilience as governance and looks at the leading policy documents that support this view. It is recognised that this contradicts those governmentality approaches that would start from the bottom up and look at the emergence of resilience among a set of everyday micro practices. Instead, it takes the view that such practices – even if they 'come into play at the lowest levels' – acquire the most influence when they are 'displaced, extended and modified' and how they are 'invested or annexed' by powers at the macro level (Foucault 2004: 30–1). The study therefore seeks to trace dominant trends rather than trying to cover every instance of the idea's presence. These trends are discernible from the main policy

[2] Of course it can still be argued that the focus of the book is Eurocentric if not UK-centric. This is a reasonable point since, in keeping with much Foucauldian scholarship, the discussion is limited to questions of governance and power within Western countries. An account of non-Western forms of resilience is of course of pressing concern, but this study at least shows that the idea of a coherent Western or European perspective is itself something of a myth.

documents, even if this does not indicate the possible differences and difficulties in translating these into action on the ground. The focus is more on revealing the extent to which resilience is shaping, or is shaped, by policy discourse and as such, a focus on the main documents is sufficient for such a purpose. The book's analysis is informed by critical approaches to discourse (Fairclough 2003), but is not an exercise in detailed textual analysis. It is enough to determine the dominant trends and influences.

This book seeks to address two key questions about resilience in this policy context. The first is whether resilience means the same thing and is playing the same role across different policy domains. The second is whether resilience is understood in the same way and is used for similar purposes in the policy making of the different countries studied. For example, resilience is often seen as a security concept because of its close relationship to civil-defence strategies. But, is the way the concept works in this area similar to the way it works in development policy? When resilience is applied to natural disaster management, does it retain the same security focus? And is the way that resilience is understood in French security strategy the same as in UK security strategy? Such questions raise the issue of the relationship between meaning and context. To examine context is to look at dominant culture, discourse, political traditions, institutional arrangements, legal frameworks and historical path dependencies, among others.

The brief argument above suggests that the answer to these questions is that resilience means different things in different contexts, but this has to be empirically demonstrated. Such a project never starts from a neutral ground and the assumptions driving this particular research are based on an understanding of the relationship between governmentality and neo-liberalism. As Chapter 1 argues, governmentality, while not an exclusively neo-liberal form of governance, takes neo-liberalism as its dominant form in this contemporary period. This is due to the dominance of particular states in the world system, and particular socio-economic models in those dominant states.

However, if this is the case, it is equally true that taking this as our framework might lull us into the sense that resilience is spreading everywhere across the globe due to its relationship to dominant socio-economic models. If, however, this dominant discourse is predominantly Anglo-Saxon in character, then we would expect resilience to face significant challenges when encountering other national or cultural contexts. The researcher has to be careful not to confuse the views from the United Kingdom and the United States as representative of the rest of the world, even if this view carries a particular weight within international relations. This book argues that the Anglo-Saxon view of the world is not quite as prevalent as it first appears and that consequently, resilience cannot be considered to have achieved the status of an all-conquering idea, reflective of Anglo-Saxon hegemony. In many parts of the world, and indeed, across Europe, resilience is nowhere near as prevalent as it is, for example, in the United Kingdom. In Europe, in particular, different social and political traditions and different ways of understanding the role of the state, make it difficult for the idea to spread in an unconstrained or uncontested way.

The politics of the EU and its member states is particularly interesting because the EU is an evolving project whose direction is still being debated. Different member states have different socio-economic models as well as different political traditions relating to the role of the state, legal system, civil society and private sphere. This leads to differences not only between member states such as France, Germany and the United Kingdom, but within the EU as well. The discussion that follows intends to reveal these differences across a range of policy areas. There may, for example, be significant differences in how civil defence and counter-terrorism are understood in various countries because of different understandings of the relationship between state and society, or state and legal system. However, in other areas – such as overseas development and humanitarian aid policy – we may find that there is much more consensus between countries. Likewise, EU policy in various areas may reflect strong divisions between different socio-economic models, while development policy may appear to be much more coherent or have a greater degree of consensus. It is suggested that this is due to a closer fit with what is going on among other international organisations – like the International Monetary Fund (IMF), World Bank, United Nations Development Programme (UNDP) and the Organisation for Economic Co-operation and Development (OECD) Development Assistance Committee – where an Anglo-Saxon consensus is much more evident. There is also less pressure on the EU in this area of policy making because of its external focus. So, the development of ideas like resilience depends on context, whether this is national, regional or international, or to do with policy context and the prevalent socio-economic discourse. While studies of resilience might be tempted to claim that its influence is spreading rapidly across these different areas, the task of the rest of this book is to draw attention to the particularity of context and to highlight the unevenness of the idea's development.

I will now briefly conclude by summarising the issues at stake and outline the plan of the book in going about drawing out the different policy and country contexts.

Structure of the Book

The main issue that this book addresses is the degree to which resilience is becoming a widespread part of policy making across a significant number of areas and within a range of countries – and to search for varieties of resilience that might be on offer.[3] Because the focus is on policy making, the book only looks at the resilience strategies of governments or departments and not at independent resilience-building projects carried out locally, within communities or by private initiatives. The survey is focused on Western countries and is not an attempt to assess whether resilience-building projects can succeed in poorer countries, or indeed whether poor countries can develop their own approaches to resilience. However, the following pages should indicate areas or agreement and disagreement and variations in interpretation, understanding and implementation across Western countries based on distinct political cultures and traditions. Clearly an issue to address is whether resilience is mainly a neo-liberal discourse or Anglo-Saxon phenomenon, or whether it has resonance elsewhere.

This is the main issue of the book and therefore a more empirical, policy-oriented approach is deployed. However, underpinning this is a particular conceptual agenda. By focusing on actual policy, and the degree of influence resilience has in different areas, certain core conceptual issues can start to be addressed. Clearly the issue of neo-liberalism is paramount, alongside a particular understanding of new forms of governance. Behind this lie further issues that the book's analysis will address, notably, the issue of governing from a distance, the use of monitoring and surveillance, the use of benchmarking and

---

[3] It should be noted that the book was largely written prior to Brexit and the Trump victory which will clearly have an impact on some of the issues discussed in the following pages.

performance indicators, the notion of reflexive governance, awareness of coordination problems, the role of government as a facilitator, the promotion of the private sector, models of socio-economic development, welfare and security issues, risk and insurance and the changing role of the state and international organisations. From an International Relations perspective, the book raises questions about the main global actors, power relations and inequality in world politics, bureaucracy and norm diffusion, global governance and the promotion of good governance, partnership approaches and local ownership. Clearly many of these issues are overlapping and co-dependent, so the perspective of the book is holistic, looking for continuities and discontinuities within dominant discourses of governance.

The chapters that follow are structured according to policy areas. Within these areas the approaches of different countries as well as the EU will be considered and compared with the dominant UK approach. The first policy chapter (Chapter 2) looks at security policy and counter-terrorism strategy and compares the approaches of the United Kingdom, United States, France, Germany and the EU. It aims to tease out differences between Anglo-Saxon approaches and the more statist and legalist approaches of France and Germany. It also focuses on issues such as prevention versus preparedness, and whether the state has an obligation to provide protection. It argues that approaches such as the UK's, place more emphasis on populations and how they respond to crises. Tensions between different approaches is evident in EU policy and practice.

Chapter 3 provides an analysis of disaster management and critical infrastructure protection, continuing many of the policy themes given that these are closely related to security strategy. It looks, for example, at US disaster management post-Katrina as well as European strategy in the wake of disasters like flooding and earthquakes. This chapter focuses on internal disaster management (Chapter 4 looks at overseas policy in these areas), again teasing out differences between more the statist and legal approaches of some countries, and the population-focused approaches of others. It notes that at a European level, a more Anglo-Saxon view is being pushed by the European Commission.

Chapter 4, focusing on resilience and development strategy, notes that while EU policy is divided on internal matters, there is more coherence on overseas development and humanitarian policy because the neo-liberal approach is widely accepted in this policy area and is to be found across other international organisations. A comparison between European and American (e.g., United States Agency for International Development – USAID) approaches finds remarkable similarity. The new development agenda is discussed and related to the governmentality approach. This is developed in Chapter 5 and the Conclusion which tie together the issues of resilience, governance and governmentality. These final two chapters are more conceptual, but draw on the empirical evidence of the previous sections. The Conclusion summarises the main findings and suggests possible future research agendas.

1 | *The Development of Resilience*

Introduction

This book is concerned with resilience as it relates to societies and people. In its simplest sense, resilience might be defined as the ability of societies and people to withstand and recover from shocks. However, interpretation of this is a more complicated matter. It is widely noted now that thinking on resilience has evolved from an initial emphasis on coping, or restoring functioning, to the view that adaptation is necessary, to the more radical argument that social and agential transformation is required in the face of global change (Keck and Sakdapolrak 2013). Therefore, this chapter traces some of the origins of resilience thinking, starting with its use in the ecology literature and examining how this has influenced understandings of society and human action. Underpinning these developments are certain ontological assumptions that are discussed here in relation to contemporary social and political discourse. These theoretical concerns will prepare us for the following chapters which examine the influence that resilience is having across a range of policy areas. As mentioned, an effort will be made to determine whether resilience has more influence in some fields than others and, perhaps more significantly, whether it has greater impact in certain cultures and societies than others. In starting with conceptual discussions, as well as highlighting its contested nature, the ground will be prepared for the examination of resilience in a variety of contexts with the emphasis shifting from how resilience is conceptually debated, to a focus on the social and political context within which resilience operates.

The Origins and Development of the Idea of Resilience

Resilience has a number of origins. In psychology work dating as far back as the 1950s, the idea ranges from issues of child development and personality adaption to trauma and risk exposure. Here resilience is understood as successful adaptation and avoidance of a pathological outcome following exposure to stressful or traumatic life events or circumstances, maintaining a healthy outcome and the capacity to rebound (Seery, Holman and Silver 2010: 1025). While this approach may be concerned with returning to a pre-trauma state, avoiding further harm and encouraging full recovery, a distinction can be made between recovery back to 'baseline functioning' and drawing from negative events greater capacity for future resilience with exposure to stress having a positive toughening effect (Seery, Holman and Silver 2010: 1026). Whereas high levels of adversity may overwhelm, lack of exposure means we are not challenged to manage stress and develop toughness. Alongside toughness, stress management and coping mechanisms, resilience might be enhanced by positive emotions and ability or willingness to effectively adjust to a new situation (emBRACE 2012: 3).

This literature continues to have an influence, particularly in French understanding of resilience (e.g., Cyrulnik 1999) and also in response to traumatic events such as 9/11. In contrast to the psychological approach, a more systems-oriented understanding of resilience develops out of the ecology literature of the 1970s. Some of this literature draws on models from mathematics and engineering, although the following discussion will raise questions about whether such a focus on formal models is really that significant when translated into policy documents. Engineering resilience follows the model of classical physics in emphasising the return to a state of equilibrium following a disturbance. The ecological literature at first embraced this approach, but later started to challenge this view in two ways – first by emphasising multiple equilibria and tipping points, and second by examining the ability of a system to reorganise itself in the face of shocks and stresses (transformation) (Gunderson, Holling, Pritchard and Peterson 2002). Whereas engineering resilience is focused on the return to one stable state or global equilibrium, ecological resilience looks at how systems might reorganise and, indeed, change their states. Initially focused on the renewal cycles of forest ecosystems, the work of C. S. Holling argued that instead of returning to a stable-ready state, ecological resilience needs to examine how instabilities can change a system through reorganisation and renewal (Holling 1973). Disturbance is seen in relation to its ability to change a system, change the structures of the system and alter behaviour within these – often in unpredictable ways. Ecological resilience therefore looks at the movement from one form of stability to another and raises the possibility of multiple states and continuous transformation (Gunderson, Holling, Pritchard and Peterson 2002: 530).

Holling's work shifts attention from the life and death of aspects of a system to the endurance of the system as a whole. His famous 1973 article 'Resilience and Stability of Ecological Systems' argues that when faced with unexpected external shocks, the constancy of a system is less important than the ability of its essential relationships to withstand these shocks and persist (1973: 1). Holling draws a contrast between equilibrium states and resilience, with the latter understood as a capacity for relationships to persist within a system and for these systems to absorb changes. In contrast to an approach promoting stability as a return to an equilibrium state, the resilience approach emphasises change and heterogeneity (Holling 1973: 17). This sounds radical, but should be tempered by an understanding of what it is being contrasted with. Resilience, therefore, is about the capacity of a system to undergo change and to reorganise in the face of external shocks while retaining essentially the same function, structure, identity and feedbacks (Walker, Holling, Carpenter and Kinzig 2004). This might be understood as resilience as the capacity to persist (Keck and Sakdapolrak 2013).

The development of more social approaches to resilience have challenged this view somewhat. Indeed, Brand and Jax argue that the original ecological dimension of resilience is disappearing and being replaced with an emphasis on the social, political and institutional dimensions of resilience.

Applying resilience to societies means placing emphasis on such things as complexity, self-organisation, functional diversity and non-linear ways of behaving (Gunderson, Holling, Pritchard and Peterson 2002: 530). Ecological and social components are linked by complex resource systems such as economic systems, institutions and organisations. Resilience focuses on how complex systems develop the ability to withstand and survive shocks and disturbance with a particular emphasis on the capacity for renewal (Gunderson 2003). The adaptive capacity of social systems depends on the nature of their institutions and their ability to absorb external shocks (Berkes, Colding and Folke 2003). While the ecology literature looks at external shocks as global

environmental change, a focus on societal resilience can be extended
to include such things as pandemics, economic shocks, terrorist threats
and new security challenges. This places resilience in cultural and
political context and gives it a stronger normative element in terms of
assessments and judgements on what ought or ought not to be, as well
as the promotion of resilience as a desirable thing.

For Adger, social resilience can be defined as the ability of communities to withstand external shocks to their social infrastructure and
that this will inevitably require innovation, social learning and coping
with change (Adger 2000: 361). Institutions are here understood both
as formal structures of governance or law and in the broader sense of
norms and socialised behaviour.

Berkes and Ross make an interesting argument that the two strands
of resilience thinking – psychological and ecological – can be combined in an integrated concept of community resilience (Berkes and
Ross 2015: 6). Adaptive capacity is understood as spanning different
levels from individuals through to communities, societies and social-
ecological systems. It is defined as the capacity to thrive in an environment characterised by change. Extending the psychological capacity
of individuals to interact with their social environment means looking at how communities can draw on such things as social networks,
communications, sense of belonging, learning and readiness to accept
change and is connected to the notion of social capital (Berkes and
Ross 2015: 10–11).

Community resilience looks at how people work together to survive. Aldrich and Meyer use the idea of social capital to understand
the dynamics of individuals and their means of accessing resources
through networks and communities and their levels of trust, collective action and other public goods. The communities in which we
live are the source of financial and non-financial resources, access
to information, emotional support and social cohesion (Aldrich and
Meyer 2015: 259).

Community resilience can also be linked to the idea of wellness and
well-being, connecting psychological and social capital approaches.
Norris, Stevens, Pfefferbaum, Wyche and Pfefferbaum understand
community-level adaptation as 'population wellness' understood in
terms of mental and behavioural health, role functioning and quality of life among the populations (Norris, Stevens, Pfefferbaum,
Wyche and Pfefferbaum 2008: 133). Community resilience draws on

networked adaptive capacities and dynamic resources such as robustness, redundancy and rapidity (Norris, Stevens, Pfefferbaum, Wyche and Pfefferbaum 2008: 135).

Crises can actually be said to bring the best out of societies, communities, institutions and individuals and helps explain why resilience is attractive to policy makers. Berkes, Colding and Folke argue that crises can actually play a constructive role in resource management because they force us to consider issues of learning, adapting and renewal (Berkes, Colding and Folke 2003: 20). This is particularly the focus of the Stockholm Resilience Centre, the Resilience Alliance and the network of scholars grouped about the journal *Ecology and Society*. Resilience thus understood comes to recognise both systemic capacities to reorganise in the face of shocks and disturbances, and social capacity to learn and adapt. Societal issues connected to the latter might include social capital, social learning, anticipatory action, organisational capacities, social vulnerabilities and freedom, entitlements and choices (emBRACE 2012: 2).

The emphasis on instability of systems and the need for restructuring is appealing to policy makers because, whether or not this is emphasised in the original literature, the consequence in the political realm is an argument for human adaptability. We find resilience being used to justify this approach in a wide range of policy documents and strategy papers. For example, the British think tank Demos argues that resilience should be seen not only as the ability of a society or community to 'bounce back', but as a process of learning and adaptation (Edwards 2009: 11). The Global Resilience Partnership, of which United States Agency for International Development (USAID) is a member, also talks of learning and transformative capacity in the face of shocks and stresses. Like Berkes, Colding and Folke, it suggests that people can mitigate, adapt to, recover from and even thrive in the face of challenges.[1]

One of the key arguments to be developed in this book is that resilience ought to be seen first and foremost in relation to forms of governance. Because it is present in a range of policy areas, it is tempting to regard resilience as essentially related to that area. In particular, it is tempting to see resilience as primarily to do with security strategy because of its connection to such things as protection, preparedness

---

[1] www.rockefellerfoundation.org/our-work/initiatives/global-resilience-partnership/ [Accessed 25 May 2018].

and survival. But an examination of security strategy reveals its use to be uneven. It is prevalent in a certain area of security strategy, namely the area relating to civil protection and preparedness, but less so – if at all – in more strategic areas of foreign and defence policy. Likewise, we will see how resilience relates to certain areas of development strategy, but not to others. In both these cases, whether or not resilience is appropriate is derived from its relation to the governance of populations. The newness of these forms of governance relate to their promotion of strategies of learning and adaptation and is about the resilience of people, not of things. The emphasis on learning and adaptation leads to a view of resilience as *transformative*, something we will highlight as we progress through the chapters. The aim of a transformative approach is no longer to return to a previous state, or even perhaps to protect or prevent, but rather to encourage change in our ways of organising and behaving.

The primary conceptual claim made in this book is that resilience derives its meaningful character from its relation to governance strategies that have various populations as their target. For this reason, the conceptual framework is set out in relation to the concept of governmentality. This approach would emphasise how resilience promotes strategies of learning and adaptation that shifts responsibility on to populations so that they are better able to govern themselves. Its usefulness to policy makers derives from its ability to play a certain role in managing or governing populations from a distance, through the conduct of conduct. As this book progresses, the case will be made for *why* resilience is being used by policy makers and *how* it works in particular policy contexts. For now, it can be suggested that the rising popularity of resilience derives, to a large extent, from its usefulness and usability as a tool of governance. However, its scope must be somewhat wider than this in order to justify extensive examination. The next section will link the usage of resilience to a particular type of governance discourse and draw out some key ontological and epistemological assumptions that render resilience a significant contemporary idea that helps to frame complex problems in certain ways.

The Philosophical Assumptions of Resilience

It should be evident by now that a main argument of this book is that resilience has to be understood in relation to new approaches to governance. This follows previous work that argues that there are close synergies between new forms of governance and a wide range of contemporary social theory (Joseph 2012). This is not to say that social theory necessarily has a great impact on policy making nor that policy making always directly influences the arguments of social theory. Rather, they both develop within the same broad discursive framework and make similar ontological and epistemological assumptions about the nature of the world and the changes it is undergoing. The argument is that resilience has found its place within a broader discourse of governance because of the ontological assumptions that underpin it. These are consistent with the assumptions of contemporary forms of governance and they help render the world governable in certain ways. Before one can govern or, indeed, use particular tools of governance, one has to see the world in a particular way and make certain assumptions about its nature and the types of activities that take place within it. There are also epistemological questions about the nature and status of the knowledge we acquire and whether this knowledge is useful in relation to various social practices. The idea of resilience fits fairly comfortably with the prevailing ontological and epistemological commitments of both contemporary social theory and contemporary practices of governance.

A survey of the most influential arguments in contemporary social theory tends to find a similar set of ontological commitments. In contrast to the rather pessimistic stance of earlier postmodern approaches, these new ideas are usually given a positive slant. Complexity is probably the most obvious term that has acquired a positive meaning in and of itself. There is not a lot of sense in this since the world has always been complex regardless of whether this is recognised by theorists. Yet, this is now promoted by contemporary theory and in so doing, as with previous debates about risk, there tends to be a conflation of two different issues – that of whether the world actually is more complex and that of whether our theories now better recognise this. However, this conflation serves to promote the idea of complexity in a positive way so that it is seen as progressive to regard the world as having little by way of coherent structure or enduring processes. This allows a further conflation between the idea of complexity and that of contingency. It may now be the case that we are seen as inhabiting a world based on uncertainty, but this is regarded as preferable to a world of necessity (Chandler 2014). It may be that there are no enduring social relations, but this frees us to become more individualistic and enterprising. Things like predictability and durability are regarded negatively. Against this is the positive promotion of such things as contingent assemblages, the fluidity of social processes, networked connectivity, individualisation and the reflexive monitoring of our situation and life options – particularly in relation to risk.

The notion of resilience shares most of these ontological assumptions. It too regards the world as increasingly complex, but also radically contingent. It rejects the idea that there are stable and enduring social relations or steady states. Even in the earlier ecology literature we found a rejection of stable equilibrium in favour of the view that there are multiple states. As this literature blended with sociology in order to examine socio-ecological systems, emphasis is placed on continuous change and disturbance. For Folke (2006: 259) this issue is no longer one of looking for robustness or capacity to absorb disturbance, but that of examining dynamic adaptive interplay. Applied to societies, these arguments question the notion that there are stable social roles, identities and functions as well as suggesting a move away from collective identities and actions based around such things as class or nation-state. These are said to have given way to complex networks of actors, each with their own individual trajectories. As Folke puts it, these networks 'serve as the web that seems to tie together the adaptive governance system' (2006: 267). Our social engagements have no necessity to them, but are a convergence of diverse elements that blend together with our own particular narratives. And in order to survive the uncertainties of complex systems, people have to show their own initiative as active and reflexive agents capable of adaptive behaviour. The problem for resilience, as Chandler (2014: 67) argues, is shifted to the human and away from the social relations in which we are embedded. It is at the micro level where people are in touch with reality, something confirmed by resilience embracing a form of 'life politics' (Chandler 2014: 41). This is an important reason for looking at resilience through the lens of governmentality.

Resilience is appealing as a policy tool because it urges a turn to ourselves and suggests a need for people to show initiative, enterprise and adaptability. The next section will link this to a set of neo-liberal beliefs and ontological commitments. In a more general sense, resilience is significant because it refocuses on subjectivity. However, this occurs in a paradoxical sense because this active conception of the subject is founded on a passive conception of its relation to the wider social condition. Indeed, the ontological assumptions behind resilience might be said to be fatalistic. Resilience discourse is usually found arguing that the complex and uncertain nature of systems and macro-level processes means that there is little we can do in the face of catastrophic threats. But it is precisely for this reason that individuals, communities and governments need to become more proactive in order to live with such conditions. Hence, resilience fits with a social ontology that urges us to turn from a concern with controlling the outside world to a concern with our own subjectivity, our adaptability, our reflexive understanding, our knowledge acquisition, our decision-making, our life-choices and our risk assessments. Various approaches agree on the need to see resilience in relation to ways of governing through risk and uncertainty. Wildavsky (1988) notably argues that we need a more risk-oriented and market-oriented approach to resilience and anticipation. Although we started with ontological assumptions about the bigger social world, we arrive at a view by which the best way to govern society is through a greater awareness of our own behaviour in relation to the challenges we face. Indeed, a major claim here is that the way resilience works, certainly in Anglo-Saxon approaches, is to move fairly swiftly from thinking about the dynamics of systems to emphasising individual responsibility, adaptability and preparedness. For all the systemic arguments of the ecology literature, as far as policy makers are concerned, governance works more through the adaptation of subjects rather than systems.

These arguments are not that dissimilar from some of the claims made about globalisation, most notably in the work of Anthony Giddens. Rather than being a process that we can control, globalisation was seen as something that we have to learn from and adapt to. Behind the resilience point of view is a similar, but slightly different, ontological picture with the world seen as being beyond us not so much because of some inherent characteristic of modernity working its way through (Giddens 1990), but due to the inherent complexity of social systems. This is combined with a blurring of the boundary between the social and the natural and a post-humanist (and therefore anti-Enlightenment) perspective as might be found in approaches such as complexity theory, actor network theory and new materialism (see Chandler 2014). This approach lacks the idea of progress or development as might be found in sociological approaches to modernity and is more pragmatic or realist insofar as it takes the social world as it finds it rather than viewing it according to some general liberal norms.

Contemporary social theory matches the blurring of boundaries between the social and the natural with the conflation of ontological and epistemological issues so that we can no longer distinguish between the social world and our (lack of) understanding of it. Writers on resilience embrace the conceptual vagueness and malleability of the idea as better able to 'grasp the ambivalent character of boundary objects' (Brand and Jax 2007). But the sudden popularity of certain ideas that have long been advocated by constructivist and poststructuralist scholars should not necessarily be welcomed with open arms, especially given their implicit fatalism and lack of a more progressive vision of the world and our place within it. Indeed it might even be suggested that certain ideas previously associated with constructivism, poststructuralism and various critical approaches to the social world have now been incorporated into a particular view of the world that renders it beyond our control while simultaneously co-opting these ideas into a more realist political strategy that utilises them as tools of governance. If, as some critical approaches suggest, the lines between reality and discourse are blurred, then why try to understand or act upon anything? The only answer is to take a more pragmatic approach.

Resilience is a key part of a wider social ontology that is now dominant among mainstream thinkers and policy makers. It constructs the world as one that is beyond our control and also beyond our comprehension. Traditional methods of analysis are no longer adequate to understand this world in all its new-found fuzziness. But, rather than rejecting the usefulness of social knowledge, this contributes to the instrumentalisation of different techniques of analysis. The paradox of contemporary understandings of the world is that the more uncertain we are of the bigger (global) picture, the more we must rely on the small details of the little picture. Resilience-thinking fits with the return of the everyday. It turns from the grand projects of social engineering and the big 'L' liberalism of universal rights to take a much more pragmatist view of social life. Resilience resigns us to the view that the increasingly complex bigger picture is beyond both control and compression, that the human-centred project of modernity is an illusion and that we must instead pay attention to our place within the system. Rather than trying to change the world, we have to learn how to adapt our behaviour. The less certain we are of the wider world whose problems are considered too complex to control, the more we need detailed knowledge of the micro-level in order to better understand what we need to do in order to survive. The fuzzy macro reinforces the detailed micro picture.

Resilience-thinking is consistent with this view insofar as it emphasises preparedness and adaptation rather than prevention and intervention. However, preparedness and adaptation still need to be carefully planned and monitored. In effect, as the global picture becomes increasingly fuzzy, with blurred boundaries between the social and natural and the human and non-human, this legitimates greater concern with implementing and following the correct techniques and procedures at the micro level. The ontology and epistemology of resilience is uncertainty and diversity, but the methodology is more precise and standardised. We will see that this is particularly the case with overseas interventions in poorer countries. Hence, while resilience might seem like it is rejecting a number of significant liberal interventionist assumptions, it should still be understood through a governance paradigm that in the next section will be characterised as neo-liberal governmentality.

Governmentality and Neo-liberalism

Michel Foucault's concept of governmentality argues that modes of governing have shifted dramatically from more direct forms of coercion to greater regulation of populations through disciplinary techniques, monitoring and surveillance. While this means that modern techniques have an unparalleled capacity to regulate all aspects of our lives – enhanced by technological innovations such as computerisation, big data gathering and electronic and biometric databases – Foucault's theory of governmentality suggests that this is achieved while simultaneously becoming the type of governance that operates from a distance through encouragement, persuasion and facilitation.

While the type of disciplinary power outlined in Foucault's (1979) accounts of prisons and hospitals works directly on the body to place it under constant supervision and surveillance, a new form of power, governmentality, works in a less direct way by shaping conduct from a distance. Although there are debates about different types of governmentality (see Walters 2012), Foucault's main focus in his writings is on the development of a liberal rationality of governance, something that will inform the analysis of this book. Governmentality has a liberal rationality insofar as it works through the principles of freedom of conduct and limited government (Foucault 2008: 10). Effective liberal governance claims to respect the freedom of the governed through the deliberate self-limiting of government and a legitimacy of rule derived from the principle of letting things take their natural course. *Laissez-faire* governance, based on the liberal principles of political economy, finds its true expression in civil society and is legitimated through the liberal concern that one must not 'govern too much' (Foucault 2008: 319). This can be contrasted with sovereign power, with its concern for territory, and disciplinary power, which functions in a more coercive and preventive way (Foucault 2007: 45).

Governmentality does not replace other forms of authority, but emerges alongside established forms of sovereignty and discipline. It is distinctive in taking population as its main target, political economy its means of knowledge and apparatuses of security its main technical instrument (Foucault 2007: 108). The distinctively liberal nature of governmentality is expressed through its appeal to the freedom and autonomy of the governed. This works through the promotion of responsibility, self-awareness and self-regulation. Liberal governmentality works through a continual assessment of government's need to impose limitations on itself, by respecting the 'natural' laws of the market, and leaving things to other social institutions, to civil society and to the private sphere. It addresses populations from a distance and, in an indirect way, as a means of influencing the actions of others (the conduct of conduct).

Foucault develops an account of neo-liberal governmentality by showing how this conduct of conduct is achieved through the disciplinary mechanisms of the market. This is presented as an exercise in freedom with citizens or consumers encouraged to take responsibility for their life choices. Neo-liberalism is understood by Foucault as a form of governance where conduct is 'subject to the dynamic of competition' and 'regulated by reference to the market' (Foucault 2008: 147) which is not a natural process, but artificially contrived. This is recognised in the work of early neo-liberal and ordoliberal thinkers (for an interesting analysis of Hayek in relation to resilience see Cooper and Walker 2011 and Zebrowski 2013). And as it was historically enacted, it was first concerned with the dismantling of the institutional architecture of the post-war socio-economic system, then was required to aggressively promote of a new set of norms and values based on the often-forceful introduction of competition and commodification into ever more spheres of social life. In the historical context of dismantling the post-war institutional settlement, neo-liberal governmentality emerges as a rationality intent on devolving power away from centralised state power in favour of working through a network of private and quasi-private bodies that is based on belief in the superiority of market forces and competition. Embedding a new set of norms of conduct, the logic of the market is 'normalised' through softer ideas like public–private partnerships, networked governance and a civil society of active citizens. This is presented as a positive liberation from statist governance. Foucault, however, understands it not as the retreat of the state, but the governmentalisation of the state according to the mechanisms of the market (Foucault 2004: 109). Powers appear to be devolved downwards. In reality, this devolution amounts to a form of responsibilisation of conduct with the state continuing to play a directing role, albeit from a distance.

This new form of governance appeals to people as citizens or consumers who are 'free' to take responsibility for their own life choices, but who are expected to follow competitive rules of conduct and not rely on support from the state. Governmentality works by telling us to be enterprising, active and responsible citizens. It is the process of constructing, shaping and guiding 'free conduct' so that it can be responsibly exercised (see Dean 1999: 165). It is in this context that we can understand resilience, at least as it appears in certain policy discourse. Certainly the approach that is prevalent in the United Kingdom constitutes an active intervention by the state into civil society and the private sphere. The UK's counter-terrorism strategy, for example, talks not just of protecting physical infrastructure, but building more resilient communities through cohesion-building, education, sharing information, planning for business continuity and working with the private sector (Home Office 2011). All this is premised on a certain view of the relationship between state, society and its citizens, of the duties and responsibilities of each, of the role of government, civil society and the private sector, of the means by which information is shared, the public informed and their roles understood. From a governmentality perspective, it can be seen why a resilience-based approach should place such emphasis on things such as awareness, preparedness, information sharing, informed decision-making, understanding our roles and responsibilities, showing adaptability to our situation and having the psychological ability to 'bounce back' if things go wrong. These fit with neo-liberal approaches that put emphasis on us as having the freedom, but also the responsibility, that comes with governing ourselves in appropriate ways. Resilience, seen in relation to governance, is about encouraging active citizenship where people, rather than being dependent on the state, take responsibility for (if not necessarily control of) their own well-being. In particular, this relates to the risk and security aspects of governance (which is why resilience might be mistaken as a security concept) and it operates through an appeal for preparedness, awareness and reflexive monitoring of our situation and our ability to respond.

This explains why resilience has entered the political vocabulary, at least in certain places like the United Kingdom where a neo-liberal rationality is strong. Moreover, by employing a Foucauldian understanding of governing we can better understand what the concept of resilience is actually doing. Some scholars have started to develop this line of argument. For example, O'Malley (2010) argues that resilience is not just a reactive model that teaches people how to 'bounce back', but also acts as a means to create adaptable subjects capable of adapting to, and exploiting situations of, radical uncertainty. Zebrowski talks of resilience as an enframing of life correlated to neo-liberal governance and looks at 'the politics constitutive of resilient populations as a referent of governance' (2013: 170). Resilience, therefore, is part of a process that not only frames the world in a certain way, but also helps construct a particular type of subject that operates according to the norms and values of such a framing. This subject will be evaluated according to its resourcefulness and ability to cope in the face of adversity. As noted by MacKinnon and Derickson, 'this places the onus squarely on local actors and communities to further adapt to the logics and implications of global capitalism and climate change' (MacKinnon and Derickson 2012: 266).

There are problems with the governmentality approach as developed by some poststructuralist scholars who concentrate on the construction and framing processes at the expense of a study of the wider social field, and the conditions that make this possible. But, governmentality is the most appealing of Foucault's concepts precisely because it can be prised away from a poststructuralist framework and set within a wider social ontology (see Jessop 2007; Joseph 2012; Kurki 2013). Without re-running these debates here, it can be suggested that governmentality be used to explain *how* governance works by emphasising the various procedures, tactics, methods and technologies of governance. It is not so good at explaining the reasons behind the emergence of different forms of governmentality or the conditions of possibility that are required if governmentality is to work effectively. This leads some governmentality scholars to overstate the degree to which governmentality emerges as a dominant form of rule (for more on these debates see Selby 2007; Joseph 2010; Death 2013; Vrasti 2013), something this book addresses in an empirical manner by investigating the limits to governmentality through the variations in the appeal of resilience across political cultures and policy areas. Linking governmentality to neo-liberalism goes some way in indicating why it is that ideas like resilience emerge more strongly in certain places or policy areas. This, of course, still begs the question of why neo-liberalism itself should arise in certain areas, something that requires a move beyond an analysis of governmentality to look at underlying developments in capitalist production, political systems, class relations and the kinds of hegemonic projects that Marxist and Gramscian approaches, among others, might identify (Joseph 2012; Sum and Jessop 2013). What is certain is that governmentality is not a realm of its own that somehow stands in its own discursive sphere independent of, or autonomous from, an array of other, perhaps deeper or more enduring, social relations and historical processes. Rather than starting from the idealist view that a change in discourse or episteme leads to a change in social reality, a study of the emergence of resilience discourse should look at social context and the embeddedness of resilience-thinking in a set of social practices and deeper social structures.

Conclusion

Having outlined an appropriate conceptual framework, discussed some of the relevant academic literature and set out some key questions, the next three chapters will be more concerned with exploring the complexities of resilience *in practice*. This is not to turn away from conceptual matters, indeed each chapter will summarise the conceptual issues that are at stake. However, some of these issues can only be understood by looking at actual policy-making and strategic planning. It is easy to get caught up in theoretical debates, especially with an idea that is new to political analysis. Indeed it is arguable whether the notion of resilience is developed enough even to enjoy the status of a concept. Instead, it is suggested here that its dominant meaning derives from its position within a broader discourse of governance – or specifically, governance from a distance – as well as wider conceptions of the social and natural worlds based on ideas of complexity and uncertainty. These broader conceptions of governance and complexity (or indeed the governance of complexity) have a firmer and more established basis and resilience fits in with these ideas, rather than the other way round. Resilience also reflects – even if it is not reducible to – a neo-liberal view that has been described here as a form of contemporary governmentality. This, of course, needs to be shown in the rest of this book.

This is not, however, to suggest a one-way relationship where the meaning and role of resilience is wholly determined by the discourse and practices of governance. Clearly, resilience is doing something different to merit our attention. Although resilience fits neatly into contemporary discourse and practices of governance, it does offer something new to these practices that makes it an important tool in the governance of populations. We have emphasised this in negative terms as a fatalistic philosophy of adaptation and a fine-tuning of strategies promoting self-governance through learning and self-awareness. These place limits on the possibilities of action, but there is also an enabling aspect of resilience reflected in the recognition that human activity is embedded within a social context. It looks for ways of drawing on societal resources in order to strengthen our ability to face challenges. It takes a more human approach to the social world, albeit one focused on our essential vulnerabilities, and invokes various human qualities that cannot be reduced to a rational, calculative logic. Whether this in fact challenges neo-liberalism and recognises the limits of a market logic (Bevir 2013: 162), enhances neo-liberalism through adding a more reflexive approach to social or human capacities, or represents some form of variegated governance that combines different elements are matters to be investigated. We will return to these conceptual issues in Chapter 5, but the following three chapters, in examining different policy areas in different countries, first seek to understand resilience by looking at what resilience is actually doing.

2 | Resilience in National Security and Counter-Terrorism Strategy

Introduction

In the last decade security discourse has started to engage with the notion of resilience, both in terms of making nations more resilient, and making communities and citizens more resilient. The national angle includes the societal and relates to communities and citizens. However, it might also include national infrastructure, border control, transport and service provision. An approach that places greater emphasis on communities and citizens might be said to be focused on civil protection and is more in line with the type of governance approach outlined in the first chapter. Having given a brief sketch of resilience, the purpose of the next three chapters is to examine what the idea means in practice. This chapter on security and counter-terrorism starts with the appearance of resilience in the 2010 United States National Security Strategy (NSS) and goes on to examine how American and British approaches to security and counter-terrorism emphasise the vital role of resilient communities and citizens. This will be compared with other countries in order to determine whether this discourse is peculiarly Anglo-Saxon, or has a wider resonance across national borders. It is the case, for example, that resilience has started to be used in French security discourse. However, it needs to be examined whether this notion is working in the same way as in the United States or United Kingdom, or whether there is a specifically French meaning attached to the term. If, as Chapter 1 suggested, resilience discourse is of a more Anglo-Saxon character, then we might expect resilience to be less significant in, say, French or German security discourse, compared to equivalent British or American strategy. This chapter will go some way to suggesting that while this may be a tendency, matters are not always this straightforward.

Chapter 2 starts with an examination of security discourse in the United States before comparing with other countries. While the chapter concentrates on security and counter-terrorism discourse, it should be noted that in reality such distinctions are not so clear-cut since counter-terrorism strategy is a part of the wider security strategy and relates to issues like community cohesion and education. It also relates to issues covered in the next section on disasters and emergency response. Indeed, it is part of this book's argument that these policy areas cannot be so easily separated from one another, so the following discussions should be read as part of a more holistic approach rather than as setting out distinct arguments about particular policy areas. The idea of security itself needs to be understood in a flexible way. In International Relations, ideas of security and 'securitisation' have been applied to a wide range of issues going well beyond the confines of 'traditional security' studies. However, while it is possible to be sympathetic to the social constructivist and post-structuralist motivations behind this move, the result for a book such as this would be to turn every page into a page on security. Therefore, security is understood in this chapter as focused on arguments around national security, homeland security and counter-terrorism, while recognising the difficulties present in trying to limit the discussion of security to such areas. It should also be stressed that this chapter is not an exercise in presenting the security strategies of the different cases. This in itself would require an entire volume. Instead, the focus here is on the intersection of security issues and resilience. If German security strategy does not engage much with resilience, then there is little need for us to engage much with German security strategy. Likewise, the focus of the next section will be limited to those areas of US national and homeland security where resilience is discussed. The chapter is not attempting to provide a complete account of US national security strategy, something which, in any case, has just got a whole lot more complicated.

Hence, another note on the method of comparison for this, and subsequent chapters, should be made. The purpose of Chapter 2 is to examine the different contexts where the notion of resilience is prominent – this is very much the case in relation to the United States and United Kingdom and also, to a large degree, in EU discussions, although resilience is not evenly spread across all areas of security policy. It is also possible to discuss the presence of resilience in the past two French White Papers on defence and national security, and here it is compared to the Anglo-Saxon approaches. However, there is little to discuss in French counter-terrorism strategy where the idea of resilience is absent. The chapter contains a short discussion of German national security where resilience only emerged in the 2016 White Paper on National Security. As a general method, therefore, each chapter identifies those countries and those policy areas where resilience is present while offering some explanation for why these arguments are missing in other areas. This will be done in the analysis section where the arguments will also be examined in relation to arguments about neo-liberalism and governmentality in order to assess how resilience relates to strategies of governance.

Resilience and American Global Security

Although the latter part of this chapter focuses on the United Kingdom, we start the discussion with the US approach to resilience. The reason should be obvious to scholars of international relations. In what is deemed to be a changing global environment with increasing threats and challenges, rising uncertainty and questions over leadership and values, what goes on in US National Security Strategy (NSS) is of primary importance for the rest of the world. Indeed, what is distinctive about the US approach to national security in comparison to the others discussed in this chapter is the emphasis on the need to maintain strong and sustainable leadership in a complex and changing global environment. We start, therefore, with the wider global context and how US security strategy seeks to understand this. We note how the idea of resilience was first introduced in the 2010 NSS, arguing that resilience is the ability to adapt to changing conditions and prepare for, withstand, and rapidly recover from disruption (United States Government 2010: 18). The 2010 NSS contains a number of references to resilience that will be discussed in this section and the next. It appears with less frequency in the 2015 NSS, but is elaborated on in detail in documents such as the 2014 Quadrennial Homeland Security Review and the arguments setting out the National Preparedness Goal. These latter arguments relating to homeland security will be discussed later, while this section briefly reviews some issues in US foreign policy and looks at US government thinking on resilience in the broader global context. It is this broader understanding of the changing global context that frames both the US approach to resilience and security and that of the EU and other countries discussed in this chapter.

The Obama Presidency's first NSS in 2010 starts with the pragmatic advice that we must 'face the world as it is'. Positively, there is a much-reduced threat of nuclear war, major powers are at peace, the global economy has grown (although this was written in the middle of the financial crisis), commerce has brought people together, and we are better able, as people, to determine our destiny. However, alongside such promise are the 'perils' of change. Firstly, ideological wars are seen to have been replaced by religious, ethnic and tribal conflicts of identity. There is growing economic inequality and instability. The environment is threatened and there is food insecurity and public health dangers that are increasingly shared across nations. Rather vaguely, it is claimed that the very things that empower us may also destroy us (United States Government 2010: 1).

Forward to 2015 and the new global challenges are mainly focused on violent extremism including the remaining networks of al-Qa'ida and more significantly ISIL (Islamic State of Iraq and the Levant) and affiliated groups. These groups are seen as exploiting the fragility of the Middle East and North Africa – which, it might be added was largely a product of previous US and Western intervention. In addition, such conflict-prone regions and fragile states may produce weapons and drug smuggling, infectious diseases and destabilising refugee flows. Rather than blaming Western intervention, these are seen as internal problems caused by poor governance and endemic corruption. The 'nexus of weak governance and widespread grievance' gives rise to extremism and violent non-state actors. The United States thus prefers to work with those fragile states with 'a genuine political commitment to establishing legitimate governance and providing for their people'. The document talks of areas of proven need and impact – inclusive politics, effective and equitable service delivery, reform of security and rule of law fighting corruption and organised crime and promoting economic opportunity (United States Government 2015: 10). These are issues that we will explore in detail in Chapter 4 when discussing resilience building in the Sahel and Horn of Africa.

The NSS stresses the need for the United States to work with the international community to confront these issues, alongside other serious concerns such as nuclear proliferation, cyber-attack and the risk of another global economic slowdown (United States Government 2015: 1).

However, whereas other countries talk of partnership, the United States talks of leadership:

These complex times have made clear the power and centrality of America's indispensable leadership in the world. We mobilized and are leading global efforts to impose costs to counter Russian aggression, to degrade and ultimately defeat ISIL, to squelch the Ebola virus at its source, to stop the spread of nuclear weapons materials, and to turn the corner on global carbon emissions. A strong consensus endures across our political spectrum that the question is not *whether* America will lead, but *how* we will lead into the future. (United States Government 2015: 2)

The NSS makes the case for 'strong and sustainable leadership' as the best means to safeguard national interests and sets out the principles that will guide the use of US power and influence. American leadership, it is argued, is founded on economic and technological strength as well as the values of the American people. In a new global context, US leadership is presented with new challenges and also new opportunities. Claiming to redouble commitment to existing allies and partners as well as constructively engaging with 'responsible' rising powers, the 2015 NSS affirms US leadership of a rules-based international order 'that works best through empowered citizens, responsible states and effective regional and international organizations' (United States Government 2015: 1). We now have the opportunity to reshape some of these rules and norms, powers and obligations. These passages provide the context for ideas like resilience to develop. They continue to emphasise institutions, rules and norms as the basis for peace, security and prosperity also see a shift away from the post-war international system towards a more fluid global environment that calls for new, more intuitive, strategy and policy-making. The 2010 NSS summarises the situation thus:

Now, the very fluidity within the international system that breeds new challenges must be approached as an opportunity to forge new international cooperation. We must rebalance our long-term priorities so that we successfully move beyond today's wars, and focus our attention and resources on a broader set of countries and challenges. We must seize on the opportunities afforded by the world's interconnection, while responding effectively and comprehensively to its dangers. And we must take advantage of the unparalleled connections that America's Government, private sector, and citizens have around the globe. (United States Government 2010: 9)

In this more fluid global system, economic power and individual opportunity are described as being more diffuse. The United States retains the strengths that allowed it to dominate, but these are now understood in a slightly different way. Fundamental strengths should no longer be taken for granted. Instead:

We must be innovative and judicious in how we use our resources to build up our national power. Going forward, we will strengthen our foundation by growing our economy, modernizing our defense, upholding our values, enhancing the resilience of our homeland, and promoting talent and diversity in our national security workforce. (United States Government 2015: 3)

In these statements from the two most recent NSSs the link between global leadership and national resilience and capacities starts to become clearer. Leadership abroad comes from strengths at home. American society is described as exceptional in its openness and diversity. It has resilient and engaged citizens. Civil society and the private sector embody ingenuity and innovation (United States Government 2010: 9). Resilience links efforts to integrate national security with homeland security. Commitment to 'secure a more resilient nation includes rebuilding infrastructure and making it more reliable in the face of terrorism and natural disasters, supporting education and science, developing new sources of energy and better coordinating between Federal, state and local government in response to possible threats (United States Government 2010: 2). In short, resilience acts as a powerful framing device for a set of identity-forming values in relation to the United States and its relationship to a changing global environment (Selchow 2016: 13).

It is true that the case for resilience is made much more forcibly in the 2010 NSS where it appears for the first time. By 2015, the term is somewhat taken for granted and reads more like a buzzword, being attached to a number of areas such as cyber resilience, economic resilience, the resilience of space capabilities, climate resilience and agricultural resilience without the resilience element ever being explained or elaborated. However, the 2015 NSS does provide a detailed explanation of the framework within which resilience emerges as a key idea and strategy and this is useful in explaining the connection between international relations and homeland security. First is the aforementioned belief that we must be innovative and judicious in the use of resources. Second is the view that power 'is shifting below and beyond the nation–state' so that governments need to be more accountable to sub-state and non-state actors. Citizens are seen as more empowered, with higher expectations for governance. Thirdly, the interdependence of the global economy, combined with rapid technological development is creating new linkages between individuals, groups and governments. This creates new incentives for cooperation across security, trade and investment, but also produces shared vulnerabilities to such things as climate change, pandemics, cyber threats, terrorism and crime (United States Government 2015: 4).

The idea of resilience is emerging in relation to perceived new challenges facing the United States both globally and at home. In Chapter 4 we will look at how resilience is being integrated into overseas strategies, particularly as a bridge between short-term intervention and longer-term development and capacity-building strategy. The next section deals with resilience at home and how it informs homeland security and national preparedness.

Resilience and National Preparedness in US Homeland Security

Recent US security strategy talks of moving beyond the traditional distinction between homeland and national security. Indeed, national security is based on the strength and resilience of American citizens, communities and economy. Counter-terrorism strategy, for example, must coordinate between actions abroad and precautions taken at home. A more secure and resilient nation is built through better developing the capacity to deal with the threats and hazards we face (United States Government 2010: 10).

The roots of homeland security are to be found in the 'traditional and historic functions of government and society, such as civil defense, emergency response, law enforcement, customs, border patrol, and immigration' (2010: 15), however, the Department of Homeland Security was only founded in the aftermath of 9/11. This catastrophic event, and the perceived need to confront new threats and evolving hazards, resulted in a reorganisation of cabinet departments and the creation of a body primarily responsible for protection against domestic and civil emergencies. Homeland security strategy sets the context by noting how the nation is more secure, but that its people must continue to learn and adapt to evolving threats and hazards, to guard against terrorism, to improve information sharing, aviation and border security and, above all, to develop community-based efforts, particularly in relation to extremism – something we shall discuss at the end of this section. Thus, as the 2010 NSS goes on to argue:

> It is not simply about government action alone, but rather about the collective strength of the entire country. Our approach relies on our shared efforts to identify and interdict threats; deny hostile actors the ability to operate within our borders; maintain effective control of our physical borders; safeguard lawful trade and travel into and out of the United States; disrupt and dismantle transnational terrorist, and criminal organizations; and ensure our national resilience in the face of the threat and hazards. Taken together, these efforts must support a homeland that is safe and secure from terrorism and other hazards and in which American interests, aspirations, and way of life can thrive. (United States Government 2010: 15)

What is evident from these arguments is a strong societal element. The above passage talks about shared efforts and collective strength as well as American interests, aspirations and way of life. It is important to secure and ensure the function of those essential services which are said to underpin American society. The latest NSS advocates a 'Whole of Community approach, bringing together all elements of our society – individuals, local communities, the private and non-profit sectors, faith-based organizations, and all levels of government – to make sure America is resilient in the face of adversity' (United States Government 2015: 8).

The US Government seeks to decrease vulnerabilities and enhance resilience across a range of sectors – energy, finance, transportation, health, information technology – and build preparedness against climate change and pandemics. This is to be achieved through strategic partnerships. It means partnering with states and local communities as well as working with the owners and operators of the main physical and cyber infrastructure (United States Government 2015: 9). Here we address two of the most distinctive aspects of US resilience strategy – the orientation towards the private sector, and the appeal to individuals and communities. It is these two aspects that give domestic resilience strategy a distinctive Anglo-Saxon character. This attitude towards the merits of human resourcefulness and ingenuity is summed up in the following passage from the 2010 NSS:

> The American People and the Private Sector: The ideas, values, energy, creativity, and resilience of our citizens are America's greatest resource. We will support the development of prepared, vigilant, and engaged communities and underscore that our citizens are the heart of a resilient country. And we must tap the ingenuity outside government through strategic partnerships with the private sector, nongovernmental organizations, foundations, and community-based organizations. Such partnerships are critical to US success at home and abroad, and we will support them through enhanced opportunities for engagement, coordination, transparency, and information sharing. (United States Government 2010: 16)

The Anglo-Saxon belief in the merits of private initiative is reflected in the strong endorsement of public–private partnerships. Of course, it is the case that much of the US critical infrastructure is owned and operated by the private sector and the 'naturalness' of this is taken for granted. Public–private partnerships are assumed to be the best way to ensure the security and resilience of critical infrastructure, now guaranteed by a National Infrastructure Protection Plan. Strengthening public–private partnerships requires incentivising the private sector to develop structures and systems that can withstand disruptions, mitigate consequences and maintain the ability to function. When incidents do occur, a resilience approach emphasises the need to maintain critical operations and return as soon as possible to normal life, making pragmatic changes where necessary (United States Government 2010: 19). Where possible, government will help with investment in maintenance and improvements and in testing continuity plans.

The US approach places emphasis on 'shared efforts' to protect infrastructure, identify threats and deter attacks. It talks of 'across Federal, state, local, tribal, territorial, nongovernmental, and private-sector partners, as well as individuals and communities' (United States Government 2010: 18). Part of the resilience strategies lies in this emphasis on better coordination and integration at all levels of government and with private and non-profit sectors. The US strategy encourages regional planning, integrated preparedness programmes and for all levels of government to engage in long-term recovery planning. A particularly important element of this approach is the emphasis on engagement with communities and citizens:

> We will emphasize individual and community preparedness and resilience through frequent engagement that provides clear and reliable risk and emergency information to the public. A key part of this effort is providing practical steps that all Americans can take to protect themselves, their families, and their neighbours. This includes transmitting information through multiple pathways and to those with special needs. In addition, we support efforts to develop a nationwide public safety broadband network. Our efforts to inform and empower Americans and their communities recognize that resilience has always been at the heart of the American spirit. (United States Government 2010: 19)

Homeland security strategy emphasises the threats and hazards faced by communities at home. It is recognised that not all of these threats – terrorism, natural disasters, pandemics and cyber-attacks – can be prevented or deterred. Hence communities must also enhance their resilience. They must be capable of adapting to changing conditions and prepare for, and withstand, disruption (United States Government 2010: 18).

As this point from the 2010 NSS makes clear, if resilience in US homeland security is focused on communities, individuals and private companies, then the key elements of the strategy are adaptation and preparedness. The issue of preparedness has had particular attention and is emphasised, for example, in the 2014 Quadrennial Homeland Security Review which draws lessons from Hurricane Katrina to 'strengthen the Nation's ability to respond to disasters in a quick and robust fashion' (United States Government 2014: 8). Launching a Campaign to Build and Sustain Preparedness, it lists four main elements:

> (1) [A] comprehensive campaign, including public outreach and community-based and private sector programs; (2) federal preparedness efforts; (3) grants, technical assistance, and other federal preparedness support; and (4) research and development. This initiative provides a structure for integrating new and existing community-based, nonprofit, and private sector preparedness programs, research and development activities, and preparedness assistance. (United States Government 2014: 74)

The strategy uses the term 'Whole Community approach' to describe how government helps different communities 'make smart decisions' about community needs, involving a diverse array of actors: residents, emergency managers, organisational and community leaders, government officials, private and nonprofit sectors, faith-based and disability organisations and the general public (United States Government 2014: 74).

This holistic approach is also evident in the National Preparedness Goal, a notable 2015 exercise in building community preparedness. Launched by the Department of Homeland Security and its special agency, the Federal Emergency Management Agency (FEMA) it defines the preparedness goal as: 'A secure and resilient Nation with the capabilities required across the whole community to prevent, protect against, mitigate, respond to, and recover from the threats and hazards that pose the greatest risk' (FEMA 2015: 2). The whole community approach starts with the individual and ranges through to the government sector. Security and resilience are understood through core capabilities and these are listed as:

Preventing, avoiding, or stopping a threatened or an actual act of terrorism.

Protecting our citizens, residents, visitors, assets, systems, and networks against the greatest threats and hazards in a manner that allows our interests, aspirations, and way of life to thrive.

Mitigating the loss of life and property by lessening the impact of future disasters.

Responding quickly to save lives, protect property and the environment, and meet basic human needs in the aftermath of an incident.

Recovering through a focus on the timely restoration, strengthening, and revitalization of infrastructure, housing, and the economy, as well as the health, social, cultural, historic, and environmental fabric of communities affected by an incident. (FEMA 2015: 2)

Core capabilities are considered highly interdependent, requiring the need to coordinate and unify existing networks and activities, improve training and exercises, promote innovation, enhance scientific capacities and ensure sound financial, administrative and logistical systems are in place (FEMA 2015: 1).

The resilience approach therefore starts with the community and talks of how preparedness 'is the shared responsibility of our entire nation', that the whole community contributes to this approach and that 'individual and community preparedness is fundamental to our

National success' (FEMA 2015: 2). It then defines the responsibilities relating to security and resilience in terms of sustaining core capabilities. Individuals and communities will be assisted in this regard by the provision of necessary information and resources as well as a pragmatic orientation to existing networks and practices. The approach seeks coordination around five mission areas which are related to these capabilities. These mission areas are: Prevention, Protection, Mitigation, Response and Recovery. We shall see that similar classifications are present in UK and EU approaches to security resilience.

To summarise these points, Prevention relates to terrorism and the capabilities necessary to avoid, prevent or stop a threatened action (FEMA 2015: 5). Protection deals with the capabilities necessary to safeguard against both human and natural disasters and is focused 'on actions to protect our people, our vital interests, and our way of life' (FEMA 2015: 8). Mitigation links capabilities to the ability to reduce the impact of disasters (FEMA 2015: 10). Response deals with the measures to be taken after an incident has occurred to protect and meet basic needs and restore services and 'community functionality' (FEMA 2015: 12). Recovery relates to the capabilities necessary to assist communities' recovery effectively, ranging from care of individuals through to public health, safety and restoration of livelihoods (FEMA 2015: 17). The focus throughout the National Preparedness Goal is on communities and their ability to prepare for, and recover from, disasters in an effective manner. This is based on increasing resilience and fostering key capabilities.

Moving on to briefly consider specific counter-terrorism strategy, it is important to again emphasise the focus placed on community, particularly in relation to counter-radicalisation. There is also an emphasis on such things as secure, well-managed borders and strong enforcement of immigration laws – traditional features of US policy-making. But the best defence against violent extremists, particularly individuals radicalised at home is to 'empower communities to counter radicalisation' through well-informed families, local communities and institutions. These will be supported by Federal Government investment in intelligence and the facilitation of community engagement and development programmes. Combatting radicalisation and disrupting recruitment requires community-based problem-solving and local law enforcement programmes, community-oriented policing efforts and more effective information-sharing (FEMA 2015: 36).

It is noticeable that the United States does not have a single counter-terrorism strategy document like the UK's CONTEST (Lowe 2016: 26). However, the 2011 National Strategy for Counterterrorism, like the UK approach, does set out a clear role for resilience in the struggle against terrorism and radicalisation. Counter-terrorism objectives, it argues, are best served by fostering a culture of preparedness and resilience that will allow the United States to prevent, respond to and successfully recover from acts of terror. While many of the arguments here are similar to the ones already covered, with terrorism it is worth considering the strong psychological element present in American thinking.

Resilience is, therefore, seen very much as a psychological attitude towards terrorism. Denying success to groups like al-Qa'ida requires a demonstration that the United States can protect its vital assets, its people and its way of life. It is argued: 'The United States also contributes to its collective resilience by demonstrating to al-Qa'ida that we have the individual, community, and economic strength to absorb, rebuild, and recover from any catastrophic event, whether manmade or naturally occurring' (White House 2011: 8). Counter-terrorism strategy emphasises continuity, knowing that terrorism will be defeated and that people will go about their lives as they have always done, with resolve and resilience (White House 2011: 19). There is, thus, very much a human element to resilience here. It is as much about mental resolve and psychological capacity as it is about physical protection or material capabilities with strong emphasis on the United States as a nation and Americans as a people.

Resilience in the National Security Strategy of the United Kingdom

It is easy to see why the notion of resilience has become popular in UK security discourse and this section will explore some of the main arguments presented in favour of a resilience-building approach. However, it should also be noted that the idea of resilience is much more prominent in areas of civil protection, counter-terrorism and community response and does not offer much to those more traditional areas concern as might be found in defence review strategies. Nevertheless, promoting resilience does fit strongly with the overall framing of the security and even military discussions of a changing world. Thus, it is right to begin with the significance of 9/11, the emergence of post-Cold

War security challenges and the prevailing view of global uncertainty and continuing change. However, it will be argued that the most distinctive feature of the UK approach to resilience is that it operates in a less formal way by focusing on individual and community resilience.

The 2015 *NSS* talks of a rapidly changing, globalised world where overseas events increasingly affect what happens at home. It talks of the need for new policies and capabilities, new allies and partners, in order to tackle immediate challenges (Cabinet Office 2015: 10). The security discourse incorporates systemic changes including the increasing complexity of the system itself as well as the constant pressure of external shocks and threats. In a post-9/11 world, resilience fits with the idea of responding to global terror threats as well as economic shocks, natural disasters, flu pandemics and ecological concerns. While this might affect how military protection is understood, this section, in keeping with the focus on resilience, looks at how there has been a significant shift in the way civil protection is understood. Bruce Mann, former Director of Civil Contingencies at the UK Cabinet Office presents the view that the Cold War approach to security was managed in a top–down, exclusive way by central government and concerned itself with a single, monolithic threat. The new approach involves a broad range of organisations building preparedness against a range of external threats and security risks. This model is based on the notion that we live in a modern network society with greater connectedness and interdependency, and hence also greater vulnerability (Mann 2007). Resilience fits easily into political vocabulary. It is consistent with new ideas about forms of governance, network forms of organisation, individual responsibility and ways of dealing with risk. It therefore sits at the intersection of global security challenges and the notion that societies are fundamentally changing. *Resilient Nation,* a pamphlet from the think-tank Demos that has influenced government thinking on resilience, argues that societies are more networked than ever before and that resilience ought to be rooted in communities more than in formal institutions and organisations. The latter should mainly act to encourage individuals and communities to play a more active role since resilience is ultimately about realising the potential communities have and taking time to support and influence their actions (Edwards 2009: 82).

Resilience features prominently in the past three UK *National Security Strategies* (NSS). Its importance is premised on this view that the world has fundamentally changed and that new strategies are required to deal with an increasing range of threats and risks. The clear divisions of the Cold War have given way to a complex array of new dangers coming from multiple sources – from natural disasters to cyber-attacks (Cabinet Office 2015: 15). The 2015 NSS frames its strategy in relation to three particular global challenges. The first is the increasing threat posed by terrorism, extremism and instability most notably from ISIL, but with an emphasis on domestic extremism as well as international instabilities. Russia is singled out for the rise of state-based, geostrategic threats while technological developments and cyber threats are the third cause for concern (Cabinet Office 2015: 12). In summary, the world is said to be changing 'rapidly and funda-mentally' with 'long-term shifts in the balance of global economic and military power', more competition among states and the rise of powerful non-state actors, all of which means the increasing likeli-hood of unexpected developments (2015: 15).

The United Kingdom, it is claimed, has a unique global influence. This extends across foreign policy, defence and security, development strategy, the business world and academia, linking people to culture and a powerful set of ideas and values (2015: 47). Britain also has a unique position in its openness to global forces. Its connectedness to global networks is seen as presenting great opportunities (usually seen in financial terms), but also multiple vulnerabilities. The 2010 NSS notes the changing nature of risk and the need for a hard-headed reap-praisal of foreign policy and security objectives in order to combat new risks in a fast-changing world (Cabinet Office 2010a: 9). Taking advantage of Britain's global position requires a 'whole of govern-ment' approach, with security strategy going beyond military effects to place more emphasis on 'domestic resilience and a stable global environment' (Cabinet Office 2010a: 10).

If networks expose us to vulnerabilities, they also form the basis of our resilience. Terrorist attacks can be withstood through use of com-munity network structures. The 2010 NSS talks of how our networked world connects states, interest groups and individuals, helping to spread our values, but also those of others (Cabinet Office 2010a: 16). It talks of the importance of: ensuring a secure and resilient United Kingdom – protecting our people, economy, infrastructure, territory and way of life from all major risks that can affect us directly – requiring both direct protection against real and present threats such as terrorism and cyber-attack, resilience in the face of natural and man-made emergencies and crime, and deterrence against less likely threats such as a military attack by another state (Cabinet Office 2010a: 22). UK resilience is defined as being prepared for all kinds of emergencies, being able to recover from shocks and to maintain essential services (Cabinet Office 2010a: 33). The 2008 NSS likewise talks of the need to improve our understanding of the changing nature of threats and risks faced and how we should respond to them. In particular, it emphasises the importance of broader partnerships. It calls for a coalition of public, private and third sectors, between owners or operators of critical sites and essential services; with businesses, with local authorities and communities, and ultimately with individuals, 'where changing people's behaviour is the best way to mitigate risk' (Cabinet Office 2008: 8). By 2015 the NSS is able to proclaim that the United Kingdom has a 'strong, diverse and resilient society' with strengthened domestic resilience founded on greater powers for local communities, greater investment in infrastructure and effective devolution of powers (2015: 13).

What is noticeable from NSS documents as well as the 2010 *Strategic Defence Review* is the clear separation of conventional military issues from risk and resilience discourse. The military forces so contribute to the resilience strategy in a limited way. There is mention of how they provide specialist capabilities, support civil authorities when capability or capacity is stretched, supporting response to natural disasters in particular. Then there is military resilience which is how the military itself is able to withstand and recover from extraordinary events (Ministry of Defence 2007: 2–36). However, documents such as the defence review of 2010 cover military matters in a more traditional way with resilience only appearing when civil emergencies are discussed. Then the discussion develops in a radically different direction, covering such things as terrorism, cyber-crime and energy security. Resilience emerges most strongly in the section on civil emergencies with an emphasis on building community resilience, promotion of small enterprises and the importance of public–private cooperation. It is argued that the introduction of a new strategic national framework and other public information products will empower communities and local practitioners to work more effectively together (Cabinet Office 2010b: 49). The incorporated defence review in the 2015 NSS also concentrates on geostrategic matters such as Russian assertiveness and the need for international standards of cooperation. There is strong emphasis on traditional defence objectives – promoting the British armed forces as the strongest in Europe and capable of projecting power globally (2015: 24). There is then the same kind of switch to an entirely different discourse when talking about cyber-threats, flooding and energy security. It is emphasised that response to a recovery from an emergency should first and foremost be carried out at a local level, involving local government, businesses, voluntary groups and the local community (Cabinet Office 2015: 45). The government's role is to act as a facilitator for these local organisations – providing advice, support and infrastructure 'to enable them to fulfil their statutory responsibilities' (Cabinet Office 2015: 45).

The most distinctive aspect of the approach to resilience being developed in UK security discourse is the strong focus on the role of the community. Indeed, as will be argued later, this might be said to be a strong case of Anglo-Saxon governmentality with the UK's *Strategic National Framework on Community Resilience* placing great emphasis on liberal self-governance whereby individuals and local groups learn to help themselves (Cabinet Office 2011a: 4). It promotes the idea of people 'taking responsibility for their own resilience and recovery', suggesting they might challenge local decision-makers to ensure that adequate provisions and preparations are made (Cabinet Office 2010b: 7). Governance from a distance works by claiming to encourage rather than compel people, emphasising the benefits of being better prepared both as individuals and as members of a community (Cabinet Office 2010b: 5). The facilitative role of government is clearly evident in the framework statement which seeks to provide a set of guiding principles, 'inviting' individuals, communities and practitioners to 'engage' in community resilience, explaining the desired outcomes, facilitating dialogue with relevant partners, sharing good practice, seeking views, ideas and support for further development of this work (Cabinet Office 2010b: 9). In short: 'the Government role is to support, empower and facilitate; ownership should always be retained by communities who have chosen to get involved in this work' (Cabinet Office 2010b: 14).

Further evidence of this strategy can be found in the government pamphlet *Preparing for Emergencies: Guide for Communities*. The aim is to make communities better equipped and more aware of their vulnerabilities and the risks they face. The aim is to motivate people to 'personally take action to prepare for the consequences of emergencies' (Cabinet Office 2016a: 5), to get them to work in partnership with local organisations and to use existing skills, knowledge and resources in response to possible challenges. There is a certain amount of pragmatism to this approach. Rather than trying to create something new, the aim is to draw on existing resources and relationships:

Community resilience is not about creating or identifying a new community or network; it is about considering what already exists around you, what you already do, who you already talk to or work with; and thinking about how you could work together before, during and after an incident or emergency. (Cabinet Office 2016a: 9)

We can get an idea of the implementation of resilience measures in practice by looking at the website of the UK Civil Contingencies Secretariat (CCS) which was established in 2001 to promote resilient communities and partnerships of different practitioners across the public, private, business and voluntary sectors. A 'generic' level of capability is provided through government departments and agencies. Business continuity management (BCM) is enforced through legislation that requires crisis management capability of those institutions providing important services such as health services, food and water, transport, utilities and financial services. The Business Advisory Group on Civil Protection was established in 2006 as a forum where the government and business representatives meet to discuss civil protection issues. This includes representatives of the British Bankers Association, the British Retail Consortium, the Institute of Directors and the Federation of Small Business. The Business Advisory Group discusses the government's view of current risks and threats. Finally, there has been a re-launched Preparing for Emergencies website providing information and resources to businesses and others engaged in continuity management. All this is strongly enhanced by the 2004 Civil Contingencies Act which makes local authorities and businesses responsible for drawing up contingency plans. The Act works through newly created Regional Resilience Teams along with Regional Resilience Forums and Regional Civil Contingencies Committees. Among other things these bodies are responsible for drawing up regional risk maps, co-ordination plans, information sharing and training exercises. The 2008 NSS proudly notes how 'the Government has mounted a sustained effort to improve the resilience of the United Kingdom to all types of risks', noting how the Civil Contingencies Act sets out the responsibilities of front-line responders to assess local risks, keep community risk registers, prepare plans, inform the public and promote business continuity (Cabinet Office 2008: 41). As we will go on to argue in relation to governmentality, this is all very much about the governance of communities and individuals and about distributing a series of duties and responsibilities.

UK Counter-Terrorism Discourse

The UK's main counter-terrorism strategy, introduced in 2003 and subsequently revised, is called CONTEST and comprises four elements Prevent, Pursue, Protect and Prepare. Prevent is aimed at countering radicalism and stopping support for terrorism; Pursue is aimed at the detection and prosecution of terrorists; Protect seeks to stop attacks and safeguard infrastructure; while Prepare aims to mitigate the effects of attacks should they occur. The Prevent element of this strategy is particularly important and reinforces the arguments about communities and community resilience that were discussed in the previous section.

The UK government's counter-terrorism strategy uses very similar arguments to the ones just discussed, but in addition, takes a very strong normative stance which – as we already found in US approaches – places great emphasis on shared values as well as responsibilities. As with its American equivalents, the main CONTEST document frequently refers to 'community', 'partnership' and 'shared values', giving a sense of cohesion existing among decent, law-abiding people. While solidifying the notion of who we are, the framing also creates a sense of underlying threat and discord. While emphasising cohesion, it also emphasises increasing social and global complexity with multiple agents and actors and a myriad of duties and responsibilities. While the discourse repeatedly uses the terms 'our' and 'we' to emphasise inclusion, it also plays up the idea of risks, vulnerabilities and increasing uncertainty. It is recognised that 'in all these areas our *Protect* work is becoming more complex' (Home Office 2011: 13), that global interconnectedness means we depend upon security measures in third countries, but at the same time we are reassured by the fact that our own government is carrying out an annual National Risk Assessment to deal with the vulnerabilities we face. This also justifies the Prepare strategy which is more disciplinary in its use of monitoring, surveillance and normative assumptions in relation to acceptable behaviour.

To justify the normative stance as well as the more disciplinary aspects of government strategy the counter-terrorism discourse makes frequent reference to radicalisation. However, this is referred to in a bland and apolitical way as the process by which people become terrorists (Home Office 2011: 36). It is not made clear why radicalisation is taking place, indeed the document makes a virtue out of the fact that it will not jump to any conclusions: 'The grievances upon which propagandists can draw may be real or perceived, although clearly none of them justify terrorism' (Home Office 2011: 36). While presenting this as a positive thing, it suggests an unwillingness to tackle underlying causes. The CONTEXT document also uses extremism to refer to groups, individuals, ideas and material and explicit use of the terms 'Islam' and 'Muslims' clearly identifies where the main threat is coming from. The Prevent strategy, it is argued, must be clear in its purpose and methods, working to meet the small number of people who might be vulnerable to radicalisation (Home Office 2011: 60). The aim of government strategy is to focus on community cohesion, address community grievances, identify vulnerable individuals and engage in resilience building through education, welfare and community organisations.

The Prepare aspect of CONTEST works 'to mitigate the impact of a terrorist attack where that attack cannot be stopped' (Home Office 2011: 13). It includes work to bring a terrorist attack to an end while increasing our resilience in order to deal with its aftermath. The main way that resilience is understood in relation to Protect is in relation to the resilience of infrastructure. As we shall see as we go through more examples, countries most often approach resilience in relation to vital infrastructure and place emphasis on what is classified here as Protect. The UK approach to resilience goes beyond this in placing greater emphasis on Prevent, understood as resilience-building within communities. It should be noted, for example, that France has been criticised for lacking a comparable Prevent programme directed against radicalism within communities (Hecker 2015).

The UK approach focuses on communities in two ways. It targets those areas perceived to be vulnerable to radicalisation and it also calls on communities to develop their resilience against possible attacks. The former is focused on shared values and seeks greater community cohesion. It calls for greater awareness and vigilance within vulnerable communities, particularly towards people who might be showing signs of radicalisation. As part of this approach the UK government has published a Counter-Extremism Strategy which argues the need to 'review, understand and address the reasons why some people living here do not identify with our country and our values (Home Office 2015: 17). As part of strategy a new Cohesive Communities Programme will help those communities who are 'most at risk of isolation'. However, there are significant limits to this approach despite the emphasis on community cohesion, with many considering the primary aim of Prevent to be surveillance and concern with recruitment. Three-quarters of the Prevent budget is spent on policing functions and tracking people (Youngs 2010: 152).

The second focus is more generic and relates to the kind of issues outlined in the *NSS*. It requires developing resilience within communities through developing consciousness of the risks and threats they might face while promoting preparedness, willingness to learn and adaptive capabilities. The government presents its main role as a coordinating one, helping to inform the public of the risks they face, implementing measures to support business continuity, helping businesses prepare for disruption and enhancing cooperation between public and private sector providers of national infrastructure (Home Office 2015: 94). We might consider this part of a broader shift to 'governance from a distance' that works by encouraging partnerships and local ownership. The CONTEST document talks of a generic approach to resilience capabilities that makes best use of resources while avoiding duplication (Home Office 2011: 93). Devolving powers to local actors, Prevent is presented as:

primarily a local strategy and while the Home Office will retain overall responsibility for the strategy, it will largely be implemented in prisons, colleges, and universities by our partners in the Devolved Administrations, local authorities, the police and community organisations. This local work will be coordinated by a network of local managers, within local authorities and docked with existing safeguarding and crime reduction partnerships. (Home Office 2011: 112)

The reality is that that these partners have been forced into a certain way of acting. The 2004 UK Civil Contingencies Act compels them to make risk assessments, draw up contingency plans and run training exercises. It forces them to participate in Regional Resilience Forums and Regional Civil Contingencies Committees. More specifically, the UK government has introduced a statutory Prevent duty requiring all local authorities, schools, universities and colleges, National Health Service bodies, the police, probation services and prisons to be clear on taking action to prevent people being drawn into terrorism (Home Office 2015: 17). This represents devolution of sorts, but is clearly more of a devolution of responsibility rather than power, backed up with hierarchical state authority should it be required. As to the normative element of the counter-terrorism approach, this also contains an element of devolution backed up by the more coercive notion that we must all share certain core values:

> Government cannot do this alone. At the centre of this strategy is the same open, inclusive and pluralistic proposition that is at the centre of our national values. We will work in partnership, with every person, every organisation, from every walk of life, who understands the benefits of our shared values and wants to stand up for them, to defeat extremism. (Home Office 2015: 16)

In the concluding section we will argue that this constitutes a form of governmentality that works by shifting the state's responsibilities on to individuals, communities and local actors and promoting the use of the private sector, while maintaining hierarchical state command. As a form of governmentality, it works directly on people by forcing us to face up to dangers and threats, but presenting this as a form of support with the government informing us how we should help ourselves, become familiar with possible threats and learn to adapt our behaviour to respond to terrorist threats and other risks and challenges.

Security Discourse in Germany and France

While a lengthy analysis of German security strategy and counter-terrorism policy would make for a worthwhile project, the point to note for this chapter is that resilience is mentioned for the first time in the White Paper of 2016. This section looks briefly at some of the main arguments to emerge before turning to French discussion of resilience. Here we will examine the emergence of resilience in French defence and security strategy, with a brief discussion of French counter-terrorism.

The German approach to security, like the others discussed here, emphasises the need for a comprehensive and coordinated policy and argues that this can only be ensured if all German national institutions take a 'whole-of government', long-term approach to their responsibilities and capabilities (Federal Ministry of Defence 2011: 5). What is distinctive in the German approach, understandable given its history, strategic location and the expectations flowing from these, is the emphasis placed on political and diplomatic initiatives alongside economic, social and military measures. German security strategy is more humanitarian in orientation, its foreign policy being based on civilian missions which places it more in line with EU approaches. It is noticeable there is none of the 'our values' rhetoric or 'resilience of the nation' characteristic of US, British and French national security discourse and there is a far more reasoned and conciliatory attitude towards Russia and other nations. Indeed, the only occurrence of the word 'resilient' in the 2011 strategy is in relation to a partnership with Russia. We might also note that some of the arguments for a more flexible and adaptable security strategy are also consistent with the resilience thinking discussed in the sections above and that German security strategy, like its British, American and French counterparts, justifies this in relation to 'constantly changing challenges to security in a globalised world' with political, societal, economic and, technological conditions changing at a rapid pace (Federal Ministry of Defence 2006: 73).

This argument continues in the 2016 White Paper. German security strategy is framed in the following way. The country is highly interconnected, but also vulnerable to the spread of risks including cyber-attacks, terrorism and violent extremism. Germany's economic, political and military significance gives it more opportunities to exert influence but also creates more vulnerability and an increased responsibility to help shape the global order. National identity and the way security is understood is a product of history and is enshrined in the constitution. German identity is also regarded as inseparably connected with European identity with Germany considered to have a major responsibility for the European project. This project is now under serious pressure due to the challenges of the financial crisis, refugee crisis and external borders instability as well as Member States placing more emphasis on their own national interests (Federal Ministry of Defence 2016: 33).

Domestically, it is noted how Germany's strong economy benefits from a stable society, high-quality infrastructure and a highly skilled workforce. The strategy speaks positively of the impact of immigration and multi-culturalism as well as the complex mix of bilateral, transatlantic and multi-lateral ties and strong network of institutional structures that provide both legitimacy and effectiveness (Federal Ministry of Defence 2016: 22). However, changes in global circumstances enhance the need for a whole-of-government approach to security. This means strengthening the resilience and robustness of the country to deal with current and future threats with greater cooperation between the government bodies, private operators of infrastructure and citizens (Federal Ministry of Defence 2016: 48). This leads to an understanding whereby:

the objective of resilience is to improve the ability of both state and society to withstand and adapt to disruptions, such as those caused by environmental disasters, severe system failures, and targeted attacks. The objective is to enable the state, the economy and society to absorb adverse events while continuing to function. Overall resilience can be strengthened by continuously building up resilience in the areas mentioned above. (Federal Ministry of Defence 2016: 49)

This tends towards a definition of resilience as robustness rather than adaptation, albeit one that is premised on the recognition of changing circumstances. It notes that while absolute security is unattainable, a comprehensive security policy can significantly reduce risks. This is conceived of as a 'resolute approach' based on a 'whole-of-society-endeavour' and carried out in a 'whole-of-government manner' (Federal Ministry of Defence 2016: 59). The spectrum of tasks includes national and collective defence, civil protection and disaster control with 'whole-of-society resilience' built around a common understanding of risks among the government, industry, the scientific community and society (Federal Ministry of Defence 2016: 59). There needs to be continuous identification of areas requiring protection, further development of civil defence planning, harmonisation of crisis management procedures, regular exchange of information and expertise and the institutionalising of a 'whole-of-society discussion on future security requirements' (Federal Ministry of Defence 2016: 59).

We can say that there is something of a transformative notion of resilience, but always with a return to the importance of state and society which is clearly distinctive from the more devolved and individualistic Anglo-Saxon approaches. A transformative approach recognises the need 'to be prepared to continuously and flexibly refine existing structures, infrastructure and processes' while recognising 'the limits of security and acceptable levels of risk for the state, the economy and society' (Federal Ministry of Defence 2016: 60). Again, it is emphasised that 'building long-term resilience in our open and democratic system is therefore a whole-of-society task' and that 'society's ability to protect and help itself in the event of a crisis complements public and commercial measures to prevent and manage crises' (Federal Ministry of Defence 2016: 60).

Globally, we have seen that German security strategy is framed by the discourse of new, transnational challenges. States and societies are ever more interdependent so that resilience-building is interconnected and multi-layered. Enhancing resilience at the international level will benefit security at the national level (Federal Ministry of Defence 2016: 60). The framing of these security challenges requires 'greater agility and flexibility in dealing with the known and the unforeseeable' (Federal Ministry of Defence 2016: 56).

Despite this terminology, this still relates to a fairly standard global agenda – strengthening good governance and human rights and using foreign and development policy to support the establishment of viable and legitimate states and social structures (Federal Ministry of Defence 2016: 62). A European security strategy should place more emphasis on human security to 'reaffirm that a comprehensive understanding of security, comprising not only political and military but also human, economic and environmental dimensions' (Federal Ministry of Defence 2016: 78). This 'comprehensive and sustained approach' should prioritise longer-term prevention and stabilisation measures, including civil society and cultural factors and ensuring that local and regional actors 'are enabled to assume responsibility for themselves' (Federal Ministry of Defence 2016: 50).

2008 French White Papers on defence and national security also set out how the world has changed profoundly as a result of globalisation, information exchange and increased trade (Présidence de la République 2008c: 5). They note the emergence of various new risks and vulnerabilities that are said to threaten the French population and territory. These are numerous and include terrorism, cyber threats, organised crime, pandemics and technological risks. The development of networks and circulation of people, goods, capital and information are said to make national borders less relevant. Although these are seen as producing greater vulnerability in making the spread of threats and crises more likely, they are also seen as an asset that allows the construction of joint responses with allies and partners to the common problems we face today (Présidence de la République 2013: 11). France's position in the world is actually presented in a fairly positive light insofar as it no longer faces direct conventional threats – thanks largely, it seems, to the European Union (Présidence de la République 2008c: 13). This is in stark contrast to the UK NSS which contains very little positive promotion of the EU. The French white papers, by contrast, make frequent reference to the common risks faced by all members of the EU and how this shared concern has led to the development of common instruments to confront risks (to be discussed in the next section).

The 2008 White Paper is notable as the first attempt to introduce the term resilience into French security discourse, defining it as 'the determination and the capacity of a country, a society and a government to withstand the consequences of a major aggression or disaster, and then rapidly to restore their capacity to function normally or at least in a socially acceptable manner. This concerns not only government, but the whole of civil society and all actors in the economy' (Présidence de la République 2008c: 59–60).

There are a few other arguments that, by now, are familiar to us. The White Papers introduce five strategic functions: knowledge and anticipation, prevention, deterrence, protection and intervention. In particular, the discussion of knowledge and anticipation raises familiar issues of uncertainty and instability and the difficulties of trying to know the risks we face (Présidence de la République 2008c: 5, 2013: 125). There is strong affirmation of the relevance of the concept of national security as a way of responding to changes arguing the need to go beyond mere protection of the territory and the population against external aggression from states by dealing with 'all the risks and threats, direct or indirect, likely to have an impact on the life of the nation' (Présidence de la République 2013: 125).

The arguments for protection and prevention suggest the need for a new approach to security. It is argued that guaranteeing the resilience of the Nation and the nature of the risks faced requires more responsive and flexible methods of intervention. Very different contexts and rapid changes in the intensity of threats and risks requires more versatile and interoperable resources (Présidence de la République 2013: 75). Prevention requires the development of anticipatory capacity based on knowledge of the risks and threats faced. The French government launched a national risk assessment approach in 2010 to supplement national security planning and enhance a capacity-based approach to various risks faced across different sectors. All this is presented as constituting a 'new methodology' addressing the need, at a time when 'strategic uncertainty has become a fundamental tenet of our environment', for NSS to embrace 'flexibility and adaptation, transparency and democratic ownership' (Présidence de la République 2013: 300). This argument, aimed at building the resilience of the Nation, sounds similar to the arguments presented in the sections on the United States and United Kingdom, but despite the rhetoric of change, flexibility and adaptation, the French discourse on resilience retains a traditional focus that differs from the more Anglo-Saxon understandings of state-society relationships.

For example, it is argued that protection remains the primary objective of NSS and that this requires the capability for deterrence and intervention (Présidence de la République 2013: 67). This is in contrast to developments in Anglo-Saxon approaches which suggest that full protection is no longer possible and that a shift to a strategy of resilience is necessary in order to deal with increasingly ineffective forms of protection, deterrence and intervention. The French White Paper later argues that primary responsibility for ensuring protection against the risks and threats is provided by civil ministries in coordination with local and regional government and public and private operators (Présidence de la République 2013: 75). This indicates how French conceptions of security strategy remain state-driven as opposed to the more community-driven arguments to be found in US and UK approaches, at least as far as civil protection is concerned. Prevention strategy is likewise state-driven – it is the state that is tasked with identifying the main risks before they become threats and that these analyses and forecasts are then to be shared with other countries, particularly EU partners (Présidence de la République 2013: 76). There is little discussion of how communities or individuals might be encouraged to identify such risks. When resilience is introduced as a key idea, it is introduced not as an alternative to state strategy, but in order to organise cooperation between central government and local governments and between the state and private enterprises in strategic sectors (Présidence de la République 2013: 60). It is also the case that resilience is understood in terms of restoring the normal functioning of the country (Présidence de la République 2013: 75). This is in contrast to contemporary views in the Anglo-Saxon literature that suggest that crises should be seen as opportunities not to return to how things were, but to reorganise how we operate.

Some of the rhetoric in the White Paper has an Anglo-Saxon tone, but delivers a conflicting message. For example, 'The defence and national security strategy must provide greater organisational efficiency and consistency in mobilising all stakeholders to bolster the resilience of the Nation' (Présidence de la République 2013: 11). While sounding different, with its use of words like stakeholder, the passage actually reinforces a traditional message. The focus is not on building resilient communities or individuals, but on the resilience of the nation, something that runs deep in French political culture. Indeed, when resilience is mentioned in the latest White Paper, it is nearly always in relation to the resilience of the nation. Indeed, 'there can be no effective defence and security without the support of the nation, which legitimises efforts in this field and guarantees common resilience' (Présidence de la République 2013: 22).

[T]he population's support for the action of the armed forces, together with the capacity for resilience in the event of a crisis depend largely on the bond between these forces and French society. It is therefore of vital importance to maintain and develop, among our citizens, a defence and security mindset, which is the expression of a collective will based on the cohesion of the nation. (Présidence de la République 2013: 115)

In keeping with French republicanism, these words emphasise such values as universalism, solidarity and national cohesion. There is certainly some sense of trying to influence the way that citizens think about the world and their responsibilities, but this is a far cry from the individualism of Anglo-Saxon approaches. Resilience, as it is emerging in French security discourse – and it should be said that this is the one area of French policy-making where resilience has made headway – is still very much subordinate to distinct cultural and political conceptions of nation and citizen that are at odds with the more neo-liberal, individualist conceptions that dominate Anglo-Saxon discourse.

Arguments about national cohesion inevitably link with debates around counter-terrorism and the perceived failings of the French integration model. In light of the terrorist attacks in France, perhaps the most significant criticism has been the absence of counter-radicalisation measures such as might be found in the UK approach. For all its faults, the UK approach to counter-terrorism is regarded as showing greater sensitivity than the French approach with regard to different ethnic and religious minority groups (Foley 2013: 277). Thus far, there have been few attempts to work within communities with more moderate elements, or those, such as imams, in a position of influence (Hecker 2015). And what is most significant for this study, is that there is no discussion of resilience and the role is might play within communities, both to make them more resilience in the face of threats, or to deal with counter-radicalisation and community cohesion. As we go on to examine, this is quite different from the approaches, not only of the UK and US, but also that of the EU.

The EU's Global Security Strategy

Resilience is now a big deal in EU security strategy. In 2016 the *EU Global Strategy for Foreign and Security Policy* was launched by Federica Mogherini, High Representative for Foreign Affairs and Security Policy and Vice President of the European Commission. This document, written by Nathalie Tocci, mentions resilience forty-one times and clearly this idea is going to be a prominent part of future strategy both in relation to the neighbourhood and the wider world. However, the introduction of resilience into EU security discourse is not necessarily such a radical departure from previous strategy. The 2016 strategy talks of 'a more difficult, more connected, contested and complex world' (European Union Global Strategy 2016: 15), but such a framework was outlined as far back as 2003. This section briefly introduces the earlier strategy documents in order to provide some context for developments.

The European Security Strategy, launched in 2003 and subtitled 'A Secure Europe in a Better World' is now somewhat dated, but is a crucial document in the evolution of EU policy and thinking and constitutes the first attempt to set out a common security perspective. It also goes about framing security questions in the now familiar way by emphasising changes in the global context, post-Cold War. This environment is presented as one of increasing interconnectedness, open borders and interdependence which of course matches with the self-image of the EU. This brings many advantages including economic development, technological progress, freedom and democracy, but also creates greater European dependency and vulnerability (European Council 2003: 2). Globalisation makes threats more complex and interconnected, the main arteries of our society such as information systems and energy supplies are said to be more vulnerable while differentials of power and differences in values are more exposed than before (European Council 2008a: 1). The European Security Strategy and its 2008 Review document are keen to emphasise the idea of new threats. Large-scale aggression against Member States is unlikely and traditional concepts of self-defence need rethinking. New threats are seen as more diverse, more dynamic, less visible and less predictable (European Council 2003: 3). These new threats include terrorism, regional conflicts, state failure, bad governance and organised crime. The first line of defence for many of these threats will be further afield, requiring the EU to develop and better coordinate its overseas strategy. Terrorist networks, organised crime and the effects of state failure will spread if not tackled and requires the EU and the Member States to develop strategies based on prevention and pre-emption (European Council 2003: 7).

The EU's emphasis of state failure and bad governance is striking. In the European Security Strategy it is noted that:

The quality of international society depends on the quality of the governments that are its foundation. The best protection for our security is a world of well-governed democratic states. Spreading good governance, supporting social and political reform, dealing with corruption and abuse of power, establishing the rule of law and protecting human rights are the best means of strengthening the international order. (European Council 2003: 10)

Similar arguments can be found in the National Security Strategies of the United States, United Kingdom, Germany and France. The French

White papers discussed above are particularly keen to use the failed and fragile states argument in order to justify intervention. However, the EU's approach should be understood in the context of promoting the EU's 'normative power' and its efforts to appear as a 'global actor' with a coherent and coordinated projection of its interests and values. This 'distinctive European approach to foreign and security policy' (European Council 2008a: 2) will be covered in more detail in Chapter 4 when looking at the role resilience-building plays in humanitarian and development policy.

The 2016 Global Strategy does also develop some of these humanitarian themes, but it is more strategically concerned with Europe's closer neighbourhood where building resilient states and societies is now declared a strategic priority across the EU's east and south (European Union Global Strategy 2016: 25). Admittedly this area is quite broad – from Central Asia down to Central Africa – and therefore contains many of the regions where the EU is carrying our humanitarian and development work. Indeed, all elements of this strategy are brought together in the following statement:

It is in the interests of our citizens to invest in the resilience of states and societies to the east stretching into Central Asia, and to the south down to Central Africa. Under the current EU enlargement policy, a credible accession process grounded in strict and fair conditionality is vital to enhance the resilience of countries in the Western Balkans and of Turkey. Under the European Neighbourhood Policy (ENP), many people wish to build closer relations with the Union: our enduring power of attraction can spur transformation in these countries. But resilience is also a priority in other countries within and beyond the ENP. The EU will support different paths to resilience, targeting the most acute cases of governmental, economic, societal and climate/energy fragility, as well as develop more effective migration policies for Europe and its partners. (European Union Global Strategy 2016: 9)

As with previous strategy, emphasis is placed on state fragility. However, the EU approach is more explicit now in claiming that building resilient societies is the best way of dealing with this problem.

The EU's Global Security Strategy is therefore quite clear that promotion of the EU's strategic interests is the main reason for the uptake of resilience. Dealing with fragility beyond the EU's borders is necessary when this threatens its vital interests. Resilience, understood somewhat conservatively as 'the ability of states and societies to reform, thus withstanding and recovering from internal and external crises' (European Union Global Strategy 2016: 23) is said to be of benefit to everyone, but particularly the EU. Outlining what this means, the strategy suggests that:

A resilient state is a secure state, and security is key for prosperity and democracy. But the reverse holds true as well. To ensure sustainable security, it is not only state institutions that we will support. Echoing the Sustainable Development Goals, resilience is a broader concept, encompassing all individuals and the whole of society. A resilient society featuring democracy, trust in institutions, and sustainable development lies at the heart of a resilient state. (European Union Global Strategy 2016: 23–4)

This statement could be interpreted in different ways and certainly gives some support to previous strategies of democracy promotion and institution building. However, a number of scholars see the new strategy as placing greater emphasis on a pragmatic approach that is prepared to 'lower the level of ambition' on democracy promotion and human rights (Biscop 2016). Ana Juncos notes how this more pragmatic approach fits with existing understandings of global governance that place greater emphasis on local practices, capacity-building, flexibility and local ownership (Juncos 2017: 2).

However, it is fair to say that the EU's new Global Strategy raises more questions than it answers and that it is torn between the more pragmatic approach and continuing a commitment to more universal values, from which the EU derives much legitimacy. Continued support for universal values such as peace and security, prosperity, democracy and a rules-based international order (European Union Global Strategy 2016: 13) is somewhat at odds with the declaration of 'principled pragmatism' as a new approach for a more complex world (European Union Global Strategy 2016: 8). It has to be seen how this tension resolves itself. It could be that principled pragmatism just means looking after Europe's interests. This could explain why the policy towards Europe's neighbours to the South and East is to strengthen state–society resilience (European Union Global Strategy 2016: 23). However, if resilience is now understood as promoting Europe's strategic interests through strengthening state–society relations, then we are in fact a long way away from the Anglo-Saxon understanding of resilience with its focus on individuals, communities, pragmatism and local solutions.

European Union Counter-Terrorism

The main EU counter-terrorism strategy dates back to 2005 and the period following 9/11 and the Iraq invasion. It is therefore in serious need of updating, although there have been significant supplementary measures to counter radicalism. Aspects of the EU approach to counter-terrorism are remarkably similar to the UK approach and the main strategy document must have been influenced by then recently launched CONTEST strategy.

Indeed, the structure of the EU's counter-terrorism strategy follows the UK approach in close fashion. It too is divided into four sections – Prevent, Protect, Pursue and Respond. The idea of Prevent is to stop people turning to terrorism and to tackle the root causes of radicalisation and support for terrorism. As with the prevailing view of the EU Commission as facilitator, the strategy argues that the main responsibility in combatting radicalism lies with Member States but that the Commission can play a role in coordinating national strategies and helping share information and good practice (European Council 2005). The key challenges for an EU counter-terrorism strategy are thus to help foster common policies, promote best practice and shared knowledge, better communicate EU policies, promote good governance, democracy, education and economic prosperity to deal with underlying causes, develop inter-cultural dialogue, examine environments for recruitment, improve the collection and use of data, improve community policing and monitoring of travel and disrupt those seeking to radicalise others (European Council 2005: 7–8).

The Protect approach seeks to strengthen the resilience of those key targets that are vulnerable to attack and to reduce the impact that such an attack might have. Again, Member States are seen as having primary responsibility, but it is necessary to recognise the increasing interdependence of border security, transport and infrastructure. Protect measures represent a form of governing people, more of the character of biopolitics, as Michel Foucault described it. This includes improving the technology for capturing passenger data, biometric travel documents and visa information, enhanced airport security, methodologies for protecting crowded places, effective border management (through Frontex) and common standards on aviation, maritime and port security (European Council 2005: 11). The EU's task here is to improve the resilience of cross-border infrastructure and facilitate cooperation across Member States.

The Pursue element involves tracking terrorists across borders, breaking up their networks, impeding their operations and bringing them to justice. To do this the EU will work to develop collective capabilities and support Europol, Eurojust, Frontex and other EU bodies as well as enhancing the capabilities of third countries. Again, the Commission offers a form of governance from a distance by promoting peer review of national arrangements and the mutual recognition of judicial decisions (European Council 2005: 15).

Finally, should an attack occur, Respond requires effective management of the situation and minimising the effects of terrorist action. The Response strategy is about improving capabilities for response and better coordinating in the aftermath of an attack. Member States again play the lead role but with EU back-up including the use of the EU's Civil Protection Mechanism (discussed in the next chapter). Planning such a response requires anticipatory action and a risk-based assessment of the events most likely to occur (European Council 2005: 16).

The EU has put in place various trans-border measures to deal with security threats. This covers border security, biometric passports, cyber security and protection of information systems and a legislative framework for transport security (European Council 2005: 6). The EU's Civil Protection Mechanism draws on Member States' capabilities to try and coordinate a response to any significant crisis including terrorist attacks and there are other coordination systems such as ARGUS. Peer review is used to evaluate response to various incidents and to make recommendations for improvement (EU Counter-terrorism policy main Achievements and future challenges European Commission 2010: 9).

Nevertheless, the EU suffers the clear disadvantage of being a transnational body. The attempt to create openness across the EU, the free movement of people and the interlinking of internal and external security aspects creates new security concerns and risk, and also conflicts with the continued significance of national policing and security measures. While emphasis is placed on the role of Member States, coordinating their activities is a far from easy task. Indeed, critics of the EU's strategy describe it as unwieldy and unable to achieve effective police and judicial cooperation (Keohane 2006: 64). Daniel Keohane writes that the paradox is that Member States increasingly recognise the need for greater cooperation against trans-border terrorism, yet national intelligence agencies are reluctant to share information and governments are fearful of undermining their own national security policies or threatening their own sovereign practices (Keohane 2006: 66).

It is not a surprise, therefore that 'softer', values-driven options are prominent in EU approaches. In particular, the EU has been strongly influenced by UK policies on counter-radicalisation and it is in this area that ideas of resilience and resilient communities are implicit. The EU's counter-radicalisation strategy of 2005 was adopted under the UK's presidency and is largely based on the Prevent strand of the UK's CONTEST strategy. Like the UK approach, however, the counter-radicalisation strategy has drawn criticism for creating a climate of suspicion towards Muslim communities in Europe, notably from the former head of MI5, Baroness Manningham Buller (Bigo et al. 2015: 11).

Later assessments of EU counter-terrorism policy revisit issues of radicalisation and recruitment by trying to promote democracy and mainstream views (European Commission 2010c: 4). Objectives to counter-radicalism include the establishment of a European knowledge hub on violent extremism, training of front line workers so they can recognise signs of radicalism and raising awareness of groups at risk. The EU can also use things like its Erasmus programme to help build resilience to extremist views among young people (European Commission 2010c: 10) and the EU will promote the best practices among Member States in such areas as education, vocational training, job opportunities and integration. In all this the idea of resilience is implicit rather than explicit. Where it is used explicitly it refers to resilience against extremist views (European Commission 2014). However, in following the UK approach, the EU stance on counter-terrorism, and counter-radicalism in particular, is clearly open to the idea of building resilience among communities, albeit, with all the problems this might pose.

Analysis: National Security, Counter-Terrorism and Governmentality

Security is almost impossible to define, or to restrict to simple arguments. However, our investigation of resilience begins with this chapter on national security, homeland security and counter-terrorism because these areas, in a sense, form the global picture and because strategies in these areas present a particular worldview and frame the way we see contemporary issues and their wider environment. In this section, we develop an account of the relationship between resilience and forms of governance as seen through the Foucauldian lens of governmentality. We might do this critically, however, insofar as some of these technologies and techniques of governance actually work to reinforce the things they claim to replace. So national and homeland security governance appears to operate from a distance, yet also reinforces aspects of the strong state and hierarchical governance. It might appear to switch focus to the micro level of self-management, yet this is an important means by which the macro power of the state is reproduced. This new governance is more neo-liberal in character and works through an appeal to individuals to be responsible and self-managing, innovative and risk-aware. Neo-liberal governmentality devolves responsibility and management of crises to the community and individual, while ensuring disciplinary power is maintained through use of indicators and monitoring techniques.

To start with worldview (to deliberately borrow a Gramscian term) is to start with the 'bigger picture' and to examine how approaches to resilience start by framing the world in a particular way and that these arguments about the changing nature of the world help justify particular approaches to governance. This is the most consistent feature across the different varieties of resilience examined here and similar global framings can be found in all the main policy documents on national (and EU) security. This chapter began with the US approach to national security because the United States is the world's dominant power and therefore how it sees the world and presents its strategy is of great consequence for everyone else. A decade on from 9/11, homeland security is said to have entered a new era defined by long-term changes in the security environment combined with critical advances in security capabilities. Global changes and such things as rapid technological change, energy instability, population challenges and economic volatility impact on how we live, work, communicate, travel and have access to knowledge (United States Government 2015: 13). Elsewhere we find the 2013 French White Paper on Defence and National Security stating that France faces a highly unpredictable range of challenges, surprises and strategic shifts with major, unpredictable consequences and a more numerous and diverse range of risks (Présidence de la République 2013: 10). The UK's NSS talks of unexpected developments in a rapidly changing world where the UK's interests are more complex and diverse (Cabinet Office 2015: 15). The EU, perhaps reflecting its own character, places emphasis on increasing inter-connectedness and diversity of flows (European Council 2003: 2), connectedness and complexity (European Union Global Strategy 2016: 8). This common emphasis on increasing complexity and uncertainty, constant shifts and surprises, acts as a powerful framing device that works in a number of ways – perhaps to justify US retrenchment or the EU's focus on 'soft power' – but also to justify a certain form of governance that recognises the world as a complex system requiring the kind of pragmatic and adaptive behaviour promoted by resilience thinking. Even where this does not impact directly on defence and security policy, the framing acts as a justification for a resilience approach across various other areas.

Discourse theorists might look at the way resilience is presented in this macro-picture and claim it is doing two things – shaping our view of what the world is like and the possibilities and restraints it presents, and shaping our subjectivity, expectations and behaviour in relation to this. By presenting the world as difficult to control or predict, we have to fall back upon ourselves and our own values. For example, Sabine Selchow's discursive examination of the way resilience is presented in the US NSS argues that it is presented in very generic terms, making it difficult to dispute or question. Resilience acquires abstract qualities, standing as a signifier for global values that gives it a natural quality. At the same time, these global values, like tolerance and openness, are 'our' values, or perhaps even something uniquely American (Selchow 2016: 12). As we have seen, there is a very strong element of identity-forming here, particularly in reference to the American nation and US leadership of the global community.

Domestically, however, the resilience approach works to focus attention on the role of individuals and the community. This section develops the argument that governmentality works by taking population as its main concern and that resilience, understood through this lens, prioritises governance through individuals and the community. The Anglo-Saxon approach of the US and UK makes this focus on community particularly prominent and we will focus here mostly on the arguments by resilience advocates in the UK. Combined with the argument that the global picture is increasingly complex, uncertain and uncontrollable, the argument for resilient individuals and communities seeks to shift governance away from large-scale intervention towards the management of populations through self-direction and responsibilisation. This is clearly summed up in *Resilient Nation*, a pamphlet from the British think-tank *Demos* that has had a big impact on the UK's Cabinet Office. Noting the difference in interpreting resilience as discussed in the previous chapter, the author, Charlie Edwards, argues:

[W]e need to rethink the concept of resilience in a way that resists the temptation to think only in terms of the ability of an individual or society to 'bounce back' but suggests a greater focus on learning and adaptation. In a new definition of this concept, responsibility for resilience must rest on individuals not only on institutions. *Resilient Nation* raises some profound challenges and issues around the role of individuals and communities in the UK, and the relationship between the state and citizens. (Edwards 2009: 10)

Governmentality works by promoting the belief that the environment is changing rapidly, with disasters becoming more frequent and intense and that consequently more responsibility falls upon individuals and communities to mitigate and prepare for events (Edwards 2009: 15). In an increasingly uncertain world, large-scale state protection no longer works, it is claimed. Indeed, 'there is no longer any identifiable body which has the capacity to respond to the full gamut of risk' (Edwards 2009: 48). This remarkable claim, which at first might seem to invalidate the whole idea of NSS, in fact works to justify a neo-liberal form of governance, where resilience invokes a positive picture of innovative behaviour and risk taking. This is clearly evident in the following passage from the *Demos* pamphlet:

[A]s humans we have the capacity to learn and adapt. Just as humans change their habits continuously, especially after emergencies, other communities – like the business community – constantly reorganise themselves, especially after a major shock like the credit crunch and/or when the profit margin is at stake. And this goes for society as well: we adapt our lifestyles, change our habits and learn from people around us. In short, we need to find a new definition of resilience that suits our complex lives and reflects our collective response to risk. (Edwards 2009: 17)

Promoting the idea of 'human' qualities gives a positive view of our resourcefulness and capability while conversely taking neo-liberal conditions for granted as a natural way of life. We find ourselves in a world of individualised decision-making and just-in-time lifestyles and a highly developed consumerist society, the consequences of which we need to think through. We draw on the strength of our resourceful character, while gaining from the complex networks in which we are engaged to compensate for the 'brittle world' in which we find ourselves, with its increasing expose to shocks, disruptions and stresses (Edwards 2009: 32, 48). The community is understood in terms of a dense network based on voluntary organisations, businesses, local authorities, regional government, local leaders, faith groups and other community bodies. This links very much with past discussions in the United Kingdom and United States about the importance of social capital and with more specific political discourses today such as David Cameron's message about 'big society'. Such approaches define society in terms of families, neighbourhoods, networks and communities which form the fabric of our everyday lives (Cabinet Office 2010d). The power of the argument is that more control is being given to local people with emphasis on their everyday needs. There is a belief that devolving responsibility is a common sense or pragmatic approach to the everyday problems people face and that 'individuals, community and voluntary sector groups and local businesses are better placed than government to understand and respond to the needs of the local community' (Cabinet Office 2010b: 49). Charlie Edwards conceptualises this as a laissez faire, devolved and pragmatic form of governance:

[C]ommunity resilience requires an altogether more nuanced and subtle approach that is premised on institutions and organisations letting go, creating the necessary framework for action, rather than developing specific plans and allowing community resilience to emerge and develop in local areas over time. And although central government often requires a uniformity of approach, seen from above, community resilience resembles a patchwork of ideas, action and exercises. No single plan exists, never should and hopefully never will. The role of central government in community resilience will always be limited. It will not be the main protagonist, a supporting actor or an extra – rather its role will be played out behind the scenes by a supporting cast of players who ensure the system is operating to the best of its ability. (Edwards 2009: 80)

UK policy documents reflect this approach, promoting the view that the government's role is that of facilitator, helping local people and organisations though providing advice, support and infrastructure in order for them to assess risk, plan and communicate. Policy documents talk of embedding work already underway and sharing experiences and learning from exercises and real events. However, while this works from a distance, the government maintains discipline through dual processes of moral responsibiliastion and legislative regulation and monitoring. Responsibilisation of populations is a core feature of governance as governmentality and works by seeking to embed a set of informal norms and values that shape people's conduct and self-understanding. Like the big society argument, it seeks to promote community self-organisation, and does so through the 'letting go' approach quoted above. According to the *Strategic National Framework on Community Resilience*

People in resilient communities use their existing skills, knowledge and resources to prepare for, and deal with, the consequences of emergencies or major incidents.

They adapt their everyday skills and use them in extraordinary circumstances.

People in resilient communities are aware of the risks that may affect them. They understand the links between risks assessed at a national level and those that exist in their local area, and how this might make them vulnerable. This helps them to take action to prepare for the consequences of emergencies.

The resilient community has a champion, someone who communicates the benefits of community resilience to the wider community. Community resilience champions use their skills and enthusiasm to motivate and encourage others to get involved and stay involved and are recognised as trusted figures by the community.

Resilient communities work in partnership with the emergency services, their local authority and other relevant organisations before, during and after an emergency. These relationships ensure that community resilience activities complement the work of the emergency services and can be undertaken safely.

Resilient communities consist of resilient individuals who have taken steps to make their homes and families more resilient. Resilient individuals are aware of their skills, experience and resources and how to deploy these to best effect during an emergency.

Members of resilient communities are actively involved in influencing and making decisions affecting them. They take an interest in their environment and act in the interest of the community to protect assets and facilities. (Cabinet Office 2010b: 15)

This gives the UK approach to resilience a distinctive character, somewhat similar to the US approach to community, but with a more developed sense of responsibilities and pragmatic initiatives. However, from a governmentality perspective there are significant issues concerning how genuine this community engagement really is. Critics like Dan Bulley argue that this process is really about shaping community behaviour and promoting certain identities. Hence devolving responsibility to different community 'champions', organisations and other actors is less about empowerment and more about forming subjects – 'placing them in a hierarchy, drilling (and scaring) them into more manageable, directable (and resilient) individuals and communities' (Bulley 2013: 273).

Problems of community engagement and responsibilsation are particularly visible in British counter-terrorism strategy. The UK approach to resilience and counter-terrorism clearly takes a values-based stance. However, this creates a tendency to treat the Muslim community in a broad, mono-cultural way. British Muslims are forced into subject positions of either moderate or extremist which bears very little relation to the actual values and identities of the communities themselves and does not treat Muslims as citizens with their own ideas (for a range of views on this see Kundnani 2009: 35–41). The clumsier these efforts are at social engineering, the less likely it is that the strategy will identify the real underlying issues. While the aim of resilience-building is social cohesion, the effect of the counter-radicalism strategy is often to cause mistrust and suspicion. Most local community workers see it as an exercise in intelligence gathering. Kudnami says there is strong evidence that the Prevent programme has been used to establish the most elaborate system of surveillance that, among other things, embeds police officers within the delivery of local services and identifies areas where intervention should take place (Kundnani 2009: 6, 8). Strong pressure is put on community organisations to accommodate to police needs, while there is little movement in the other direction. Prevent claims to be about community cohesion, but is felt by some as simply a way for the authorities to gather data (Richards 2012: 149). The EU's counter-terrorism strategy is based on the UK Prevent programme but likewise priorities law enforcement and surveillance, extending the remit of Europol, employing more security technology, developing biometric identifiers and giving a central role to private security companies (Youngs 2010: 40). The consequence is that community intervention appears as heavy-handed and top–down. A review of the UK policy in 2011 looked at the tensions between community cohesion work and police counter-terrorism activity, and the possible stigmatisation of the Muslim community. But Prime Minister Cameron's response has been to question state multiculturalism and assert the need for a more 'muscular liberalism' in dealing with radical and divisive ideology (Richards 2012: 150–2).

Such an intervention into Further and Higher Education is presented as a reasonable managing of the public interest. In the university sector, while it claimed that the government 'has no wish to limit or otherwise interfere with this free flow of ideas', academics have 'a clear and unambiguous role to play in helping to safeguard vulnerable young people from radicalisation and recruitment by terrorist organisations' (Home Office 2011: 67). The governmentality aspect of this works by emphasising the notion that the free exchange of ideas is not only a right but a responsibility. While any reasonable government would wish to preserve civil liberties, universities and colleges must realise that they have a duty to prevent certain ideas (never defined) from being circulated or face the consequences. It is not at all clear what the legal, never mind the moral obligation to staff and students actually is, but the overwhelming sense is one of a normative agenda that works by getting people to regulate their conduct in a particular way.

As an exercise in governmentality, this approach is presented as if it was devolving responsibility to local institutions and groups who can make their own decisions about what is good practice. But is in a reality a top–down approach whereby government tells people what to do and forces them to agree to a particular agenda and way of seeing things. In the words of the document: 'The department of Business, Innovation and Skills will lead the delivery of *Prevent* in these sectors by helping universities and colleges better understand the risk of radicalisation on and off campus' while later this is even presented as something enabling: 'We will fund the National Union of Students (NUS) to undertake a programme of work to ensure that their sabbatical officers and full time staff are fully trained and equipped to manage their responsibilities'. Then finally, 'As with schools, we look to universities and colleges of further education to develop constructive dialogue with local *Prevent* groups and community organisations' (Home Office 2011: 67).

The top–down nature of the intervention is also manifested in the strong use of indicators and performance measurement. The progress of CONTEST will be measured against a set of performance indicators, complemented by deeper evaluation of specific programmes and supported by wider research and 'horizon scanning' which will help in keeping ahead of new or changing threats and vulnerabilities (Home Office 2011: 15). Governmentality combines a concern with monitoring population with a reflection on its own methods and techniques of intervention which are also subject to monitoring and measurement in related to certain purported aims of proportionality and effectiveness:

[W]e are also determined to have a strategy that is not only more effective but also more proportionate, that is better focused and more precise, which uses powers selectively, carefully and in a way that is as sparing as possible. These themes and this language also runs through this strategy – in *Pursue*, *Prevent* and in *Protect* and *Prepare* – and are reflected in its founding principles. (Home Office 2011: 15)

Turning to France and contrasting the influence of resilience in UK policy-making with the slower uptake in France, we find the beginnings of a debate but also underlying reservations. So far, the term has not entered into widespread use. Indeed, it is absent from counter-terrorism policy, particularly since counter-terrorism in France has yet to really develop the counter-radicalism approach found in the United Kingdom. Instead, we find a tentative uptake of resilience in defence and national security policy. As well as a tentative engagement, we also find a somewhat wary response to the introduction of this idea, particularly given its Anglo-Saxon origins. This is noted in a number of telling responses following the first mention of resilience in the 2008 White Paper. Cornier et al. note that while widely accepted in some countries, resilience is new to France and remains a vague idea rather than a strong concept. This is contrasted with the situation in the United Kingdom where resilience is seen as an important aspect of deterrence, not only helping to prevent terrorist attacks, but also to minimise the consequences. Hence the authors argue that France must develop its own understanding of resilience and build the tools and procedures necessary to make it work, not just in theory, but also in practice (Cormier et al. 2010). Comments on the website of the French War School also recognise that resilience can become a significant new concept in the French political vocabulary, but it is necessary to understand the term's strong cultural connotations. In Anglo-Saxon culture it is strongly linked to a sense of community, something said to be missing from French understandings of the term. Given new threats and vulnerabilities, especially in the fields of information and communication, there is a need to go beyond previous understandings of deterrence (Bourgerie 2009). Of particular importance is the ability to inform and mobilise the population. Similar points are made in one of the few French books on resilience, with the suggestion that much confusion has resulted from the introduction of this very British idea into the French White Paper and strategic studies (Henretin 2010: 11).

An article by Francart (2010), originally published in *Revue Défense Nationale* notes how the British understanding of resilience sees crisis management requiring the involvement of more people in a wider range of activities. In particular, the British are seen as having recognised the need to involve civil society. In sum, the response in France has been to recognise that the British approach places a stronger emphasis on the role of civil society, communities and individuals. This puts the UK approach much closer to governmentality compared to French strategy which has yet to realise the implications resilience has for governance. It remains a term used in the context of national security concerns rather than something that shifts focus to the governance and responsibilisation of populations or communities. The fact that resilience has emerged in French security discourse and that this particular aspect of resilience is being recognised in various responses to the White Papers does however suggest that the governance aspect of resilience may well develop in the future.

Finally, the German uptake of resilience can be contrasted with the Anglo-Saxon approach insofar as it lacks the emphasis on individual and community resilience and instead argues for a 'whole of society' approach. The state is seen to have responsibilities in relation to society as a whole with building resilience a 'whole of society' task (Federal Ministry of Defence 2016: 60). We might later tease out this issue insofar as resilience promises a more societal focus, but in fact societal resilience means different things in the United Kingdom and Germany. In the UK, where the term is widely used, the actual needs of society are downplayed in favour of a focus on certain elements – in particular targeting the community and the individual. German resilience discourse, by contrast, makes little mention of societal resilience, but places much more emphasis on the importance of society as a whole with the state–society relationship seen as fundamental to future national security. This suggests that while resilience is making slow inroads into German national security and civil protection discourse, the full Anglo-Saxon connotations of this are yet to be felt with less of the arguments for individualised responsibility in evidence. While the Anglo-Saxon approach to resilience seeks to responsibilise individuals and communities, the German understandings continue to give the state the central role and to see society in a more traditional sense as a collective entity in need of legal and governmental support and protection.

Conclusion

All security strategies share a similar starting point. This is the global context and the perception that the world is increasingly complex, uncertain and unpredictable. Different emphasis develops depending on a particularly country's perceived place in the world, social and historical identity and strategic interests. Resilience emerges in relation to perceived new challenges, while it also serves a more organisational function in stressing the need for a more coherent and coordinated set of security and counter-terrorism practices. The global situation is described as 'fluid' (United States Government 2010: 9) meaning more challenges, but also certain opportunities.

In this particular field of national or homeland security, we find an uneven emergence of the idea of resilience. It clearly plays a very prominent role in Anglo-Saxon thinking, probably more so in the United Kingdom than the United States due to the strong emphasis on community resilience. French commentators note how the civil society or community aspect of resilience is largely missing, something that is also the case in Germany where the emphasis falls on the needs and efforts of the whole of society.

Yet it is this aspect in particular – the focus on communities, individuals and populations – that gives resilience the character of governmentality as understood throughout this book.

The UK approach, being most focused on the governance of communities and individuals, best represents a form of governmentality that operates from a distance through 'helping people help themselves'. It encourages reflexive behaviour, awareness of what exists, what we do, what is around us (Cabinet Office 2010b: 9). Governance occurs from a distance through facilitation of local groups and seeks to reach right down to individuals who should be able to take responsibility for their own resilience and recovery (Cabinet Office 2010b: 7). The community plays two central roles – downwards as a conduit of information and resources and upwards by providing feedback and experiences from individuals and neighbourhoods (Edwards 2009: 19). The Anglo-Saxon approach places emphasis on initiative and ingenuity, particularly of the people, the private sector and engaged communities (United States Government 2010: 16).

By contrast, Germany advocates a 'whole of government' approach that emphasises the importance of the state and a 'whole of society' focus on society as a whole rather than on particular communities. There is also more emphasis on protection and 'robustness' rather than flexible adaptation. In France too, the emphasis remains on protection, with the state, not society, responsible for the identification of key risks and responsibilities. The French notion of the 'resilience of the Nation' is one that is top–down and centralised. It emphasises solidarity and national cohesion and makes no mention of community resilience, giving little encouragement for communities to be reflexive or help identify risks.

However, the Anglo-Saxon approach is not such a soft, or distant, form of power as it first seems. We saw how there are concerns about the coercive nature of much government legislation, particularly in relation to counter-terrorism. In the field of national security and counter-terrorism this is perhaps not so surprising, although it does raise issues about the nature of the 'strong state' and whether governmentality really is something that operates at arm's length. This also coincides with debates about neo-liberal governance and the desire to force through a strong agenda of embedding norms of neo-liberal conduct. These are presented in positive terms, invoking 'human' qualities such as resourcefulness and adaptability. However, we are also told we have little choice but to accept the need to behave in such a way and to use such qualities in order to chart our way through an increasingly complex and 'brittle' world. This is reinforced by strengthened powers of compulsion – seen in UK legislation on counter-terrorism, and increasing use of surveillance and policing powers across all cases examined. It may be governmentality, but it has a strongly disciplinary character reflecting a more hierarchical relationship between state and society.

Thus, governmentality can be seen to be reinforced in two ways in this policy field. First, discursively through a strong normative agenda. This is seen in the United Kingdom and United States with their whole of nation, 'our values' arguments and in the United States the argument that resilience is 'the shared responsibility of the entire nation' (FEMA 2015: 2). The French discourse also links the resilience of the Nation to the reassertion of national values and identities. In the Anglo-Saxon approach this is then combined with more everyday micro-features that reinforce norms of conduct at the behavioural level, particular through the promotion of such neo-liberal qualities as reflexivity, awareness, resourcefulness and innovativeness. To summarise the UK approach: 'We will expand and deepen the Government's partnership with the private and voluntary sectors, and with communities and individuals, as it is on these relationships that the resilience of the UK ultimately rests' (Cabinet Office 2016b). These issues are crucial from a governmentality perspective and will be further examined in relation to disaster preparedness and infrastructure protection (see Chapter 3).

3 | Disasters, Emergencies and Infrastructure Protection

This chapter covers a number of connected areas that can be treated together. In the broadest sense, we are concerned here with disasters, emergencies and risks that occur within the countries covered in our analysis. In contrast to Chapter 2, the nature of these threats and disasters tend to be of a natural character although they may be exacerbated by human action. In contrast to Chapter 4, these are matters within a given territory, of a domestic or trans-border character rather than international interventions seeking to provide assistance to poorer states. Chapter 3 examines a range of strategy documents and policy papers to get a feel for the types of issues and actions being discussed by policy makers as well as considering what reasons, strategies or motives lie behind these approaches and whether different countries and organisations have different approaches or motivations.

The baseline is provided by the UK case which, while addressing technical issues like infrastructure provision, maintains the focus on individual and community resilience. The US approach is found to have a similar emphasis in contrast to France and Germany where discussion of resilience is emerging, but where the idea of community resilience is largely absent. The chapter also gives extensive coverage to EU discussions of resilience since this is a significant area of developing debate across Europe.

The UK Approach to Critical Infrastructure Protection and Emergency Preparedness

This time we start the chapter with the UK approach to resilience, drawing on the vast amount of material available on UK government websites. The focus of this chapter is not on specific areas such as climate change, flooding or telecommunications policy, but on critical infrastructure protection (CIP) and emergency response in a more general sense. In the UK's case, and following on from the findings of Chapter 2, the intention is to link these to community resilience. The UK sections will proceed by setting out the British government's approach to infrastructure protection and emergency response, to examine key ideas like preparedness, and to move to the promotion of community resilience in dealing with some of the issues raised.

The UK government defines critical infrastructure as 'those facilities, systems, sites and networks necessary for the functioning of the country and the delivery of the essential services upon which daily life in the UK depends' (Cabinet Office 2010c: 8). It also talks of Critical National Infrastructure (CNI) as: 'Those infrastructure assets (physical or electronic) that are vital to the continued delivery and integrity of the essential services upon which the UK relies, the loss or compromise of which would lead to severe economic or social consequences or to loss of life' (Cabinet Office 2010c: 8). CNI covers nine areas – energy, food, water, transportation, communications, emergency services, health care, financial services and government.

In response to flooding in 2007 and the subsequent Pitt Report, the UK government set about establishing a cross-sector programme to improve critical infrastructure resilience in the face of natural hazards. In particular, the government launched the Critical Infrastructure Resilience Programme aimed at encouraging a better co-ordinated and more systematic approach to critical infrastructure and essential services. This would clarify the roles of the government, public sector bodies and private service providers and businesses. Relevant government departments would work with the private sector infrastructure operators to build resilience into critical infrastructure assets and to encourage business continuity (Cabinet Office 2010c: 5–6).

The Pitt Recommendations were agreed as necessary for guaranteeing a minimum interim standard of protection from flooding for CNI across all sectors with further consideration of matters of cost, practicality, scale of activity and impact on owners. Considerations require taking into account probability of occurrences, severity, vulnerability and impact. Focusing on the promotion of resilience, this is defined in the Pitt Report as 'the ability of a system or organisation to withstand and recover from adversity', but suggests that the importance of protection must be balanced against the need to reduce the impacts of failure. In other words, this should not be protection at all costs. The UK government's response stresses the need to balance investment in CIP with the needs of emergency response and recovery capabilities. It stresses interdependencies within and between sectors 'in an increasingly networked society' (Cabinet Office 2010c: 7). The government's role is to build resilience into infrastructure provision and to ensure continuity of supply through such things as better designed assets, building additional network connections, providing backup facilities to ensure continuity, moving key components out of harm's way, better sharing of information on infrastructure network performance and standards as well as enhancing skills and capabilities to respond to emergencies (Cabinet Office 2010c: 7).

The Cabinet Office is responsible for developing a cross-sector resilience-building programme and for coordinating this across different government departments and the public and private sectors. Flooding is the first natural hazard to be considered by these plans based on its place as the highest identified risk in the government's National Risk Register (NRR). Other natural hazards will be considered as the approach develops. Despite the focus on natural hazards, the programme will also seek to work with those dealing with other national security threats, particularly the CONTEST counter-terrorism strategy that was discussed in Chapter 2. A wider strategic framework – CNI Protection in the UK: Framework and Guidance – seeks to provide the common basis for all those involved in national infrastructure protection ranging from natural hazards to counter-terrorism. Shared procedures will be developed where possible in order to provide a coherent approach to resilience across all sectors. The Critical Infrastructure Resilience Programme will also coordinate its activities with the Adapting to Climate Change Programme to meet the longer-term obligations of the Climate Change Act, and will work with Infrastructure UK to enable long-term planning and investment in infrastructure and delivery.

The Critical Infrastructure Resilience Programme can be seen as an example of the UK government promoting better communication, cohesion and planning across different sectors of government, society and infrastructure. It aims to reduce the most substantial risks, assess vulnerability and minimise disruption while providing a shared framework for cross-sector activity. It seeks to enhance collective capacity to absorb shock and respond quickly and to improve engagement and information-sharing to ensure effective emergency response (Cabinet Office 2010c: 9). It argues for a 'joined-up' approach involving other government programmes including protection against terrorist attacks and climate change. The emphasis on cohesion is also evident in the focus on the government's relationship with the infrastructure owners and the relevant regulator. Voluntary cooperation is the preferred means of achieving shared aims, but stricter legislative powers will be employed if necessary. Governance from a distance will also be supported by monitoring techniques including setting standards and timeframes, developing a programme of measures for achieving the defined level of ambition, mechanisms for reporting progress on the implementation of the programme and a process for benchmarking business continuity plans (Cabinet Office 2010c: 7).

Alongside the Critical Infrastructure Resilience Programme, we find the National Resilience Capabilities Programme (NRCP). This broader programme covers most types of civil emergency including accidents, natural hazards and human-made threats. As the name suggests, the aim is to build capability to deal with such emergencies with the main focus on response. This means ensuring such things as proper training, right equipment and supplies, clear plans and so on. As with other UK approaches to resilience, there is a strong emphasis on monitoring and information-gathering which will be fed back into government understanding of the UK's ability to respond to civil emergencies. The programme consists of capability 'workstreams' dealing with central, regional and local response capabilities in areas of essential services such as food, water, fuel, transport, health and financial services. The programme tests for resilience in these areas based around a series of exercises and training, while identifying what central government might do to increase resilience capabilities.

The Programme concentrates on building public awareness. A well-informed public, it is argued, is better able to respond to emergencies and minimise the impact these have on the community. Informing the public is also important in building trust. In many cases it will be the government that will first provide warnings and information for the public, but the NRCP is designed to responsibilise other organisations and local actors who must help raise awareness about risks and emergencies, establish procedures for dealing with emergencies should they occur and undertake risk assessment. The latter aspect is supported by the NRR, first published by the government in 2008 in response to the National Security Strategy. This helps to provide advice on how people and businesses can prepare for civil emergencies while the NRCP aims to ensure that organisations have in place the necessary arrangements to inform, advice and warn the public.

In these programmes and practices, we see certain strong features of the UK's resilience approach. These can be said to entail a coordinated approach that strives to provide an effective and cohesive response, an emphasis on communicating with the public, responsiblisation of local actors and organisations, the policy of subsidiarity whereby response should be coordinated at the lowest level where possible, and an emphasis on preparedness. In its guidelines on emergency response and recovery, the UK Cabinet Office talks of how 'all organisations and individuals that might have a role to play in emergency response and recovery should be properly prepared and be clear about their roles and responsibilities' (Cabinet Office 2013a). This is consistent with our arguments for governmentality, indicating how government policy is devolving responsibilities and engaging a range of actors at different levels. Subsidiarity seeks to do this at the lowest appropriate level, supported by government coordination where necessary. The government's role is to ensure that there is clarity of purpose and that supporting objectives are agreed, understood and sustained by all involved. In the rest of this section we will set out in more detail how the role of government in securing integration, effective coordination, cooperation and continuity is to be achieved. Having set out the role of government and the process by which other actors are responsibilised (and governmentalised), the next section will concentrate on setting out the UK government's attempts to build community resilience in this particular area of policy-making.

For all the talk of community resilience, it is absolutely the case that central government continues to play the dominant role as we saw in Chapter 2. The Home Office is the lead department for terrorist-related emergencies while other government departments will offer support for the wider impacts. The Cabinet Office works to clarify responsibilities. If these are unclear, it will advise on the lead government department. The responsibilities of the Cabinet Office itself include working with local and regional partners in emergency planning and government coordination, maintaining continuity of central government, ensuring a Lead Government Department is in place and providing staff to run crisis facilities (Cabinet Office 2013b: 19–20). In turn, Lead government Departments must maintain a state of readiness for responding to emergencies, planning, training and exercising and engaging in other preparatory work, while identifying other departments and agencies whose assistance might be needed. They should identify the capabilities of local responders and maintain awareness of the risks, threats and vulnerabilities within each field of responsibility.

Within the Cabinet Office is the Civil Contingencies Secretariat (CCS). This takes the lead initially, before the responsible Lead Government Department takes over. The Cabinet Office will then continue to provide support to Lead Government Departments during the planning, response and recovery phases. It promotes resilience-building through engaging key players and promoting the aims of anticipation, assessment, preparation, prevention, response and recovery as part of an integrated response to emergencies (Cabinet Office 2004a: 12). Anticipation and assessment requires the conducting of risk assessments covering both long-term and shorter-term challenges (horizon scanning). As a result of the assessment of the risks, prevention measures are adopted including strategies for reduction or redistribution of risk. Preparedness plans require flexibility towards risk and unforeseen events, identifying key personnel, assets and arrangements (Cabinet Office 2004a: 9). Following response, the recovery phase is rooted in the community and requires interaction among a variety of government departments and local agencies. Throughout this, the CSS plays a key role in the gathering of information including identifying risks based on stakeholder and local knowledge, identifying assets, resource requirements and procedures, identifying relevant legislation and regulations and promoting best practice and learning lessons from previous incidents. The CSS is responsible for the NRCP (Cabinet Office 2004a: 21).

Moving to other responders, the government classifies these as Category 1 organisations that form the core response to most emergencies and Category 2 organisations who are 'cooperating bodies'. Category 1 organisations include the emergency services, local authorities and National Health Service bodies and are subject to the full set of civil protection duties. Their requirements are to:

1. assess the risk of emergencies occurring and use this to inform contingency planning
2. put in place emergency plans
3. put in place BCM arrangements

4. put in place arrangements to make information available to the public about civil protection matters and maintain arrangements to warn, inform and advise the public in the event of an emergency
5. share information with other local responders to enhance coordination
6. cooperate with other local responders to enhance coordination and efficiency
7. provide advice and assistance to businesses and voluntary organisations about BCM (Cabinet Office 2013c).

Category 2 organisations include the Health and Safety Executive and transport and utility companies. These play a lesser role in planning work, but have a (lesser) set of duties requiring cooperating and sharing relevant information with other Category 1 and 2 responders. Together, Category 1 and 2 organisations are required to form Local Resilience Forums to facilitate coordination and cooperation between responders at the local level. These, in turn, correspond to Local Resilience Areas based on the police area in which the responder's functions are exercisable. These provisions are actually strongly enforced through the 2004 Civil Contingencies Act which places duties on local authorities and others to ensure they provide advice, assistance and measures to relating to BCM.

The UK's approach to emergency planning requires these organisations to take into account the needs of different groups – victims, the vulnerable and responder personnel. Planning should aim at minimising the effects of an emergency and ensuring long-term recovery (with government information provided in the National Recovery Guidance). Planning for the response phase requires crisis management to prevent or avert an emergency and address immediate effects while impact management deals with wider consequences. The government promotes the development of sub-national resilience capability based on a partnership with local responders and other organisations to ensure effective and coordinated planning and response. Subsidiarity places emphasis on local decision-making, backed by government support where necessary. Plans for the recovery phase should deal with 'rebuilding, restoring and rehabilitating the community following an emergency' (Cabinet Office 2013b: 10). This phase is long-term and seeks to support affected communities in the reconstruction of physical infrastructure 'and restoration of emotional, social, economic and physical well-being' (Cabinet Office 2013b: 6–8). At this point we have arrived at UK government promotion of community resilience and the next section will look at the government approach to building this and business continuity.

Building Community Resilience and Business Continuity

The *Strategic National Framework on Community Resilience* has already been discussed in Chapter 2. It defines community resilience as: 'Communities and individuals harnessing local resources and expertise to help themselves in an emergency, in a way that complements the response of the emergency services (Cabinet Office 2011a: 11). The emphasis placed on getting people to help themselves is key to this strategy and indicates why this might be seen as a form of governmentality that encourages individual initiative and enterprising behaviour. The role of government, it seems, is to encourage people to take their own initiative. Indeed, it is argued that in many areas people are already taking responsibility for their own resilience and recovery, working with decision makers to determine the allocation of resources, making preparations and determining the recovery process (Cabinet Office 2011a: 7). As well as community resilience, there is a description of the resilient individual who is able to hold an informed understanding of the risks they face and their likely impacts. Resilient individuals need to be able to assess their vulnerability to risks, using this as motivation to act and be prepared (Cabinet Office 2011a: 11). The Pitt Report also argues the case for building community resilience, recommending that the government 'establish a programme to support and encourage individuals and communities to be better prepared and more self-reliant during emergencies, allowing the authorities to focus on those areas and people in greatest need (Cabinet Office 2011a: 8).

To this end, the UK government is supporting a Community Resilience Programme that provides information in order to encourage communities and individuals to think about their vulnerabilities and the infrastructure they rely on as well as the risks they face. People are told to consider this information and prepare themselves to be able to deal with the potential consequences of an emergency (Cabinet Office 2011a: 8). The stated aims of the Community Resilience Programme include increasing individual, family and community resilience,

engaging existing approaches and successful initiatives, raising awareness of risk and local response capability, removing barriers that might
inhibit or prevent participation in community resilience, encouraging dialogue between the community and relevant practitioners and
providing tools to allow communities and individuals to address the
wider community on the benefits of emergency preparedness (Cabinet
Office 2011a: 5).

Guidance produced by the Cabinet Office captures most of the main
themes present in the Anglo-Saxon approach to resilience and its relationship to society and business. The emphasis is on providing civil
protection so people can go about their business freely and with confidence while the wider UK society – public and private sectors, community and business – are engaged in resilience-building measures within
their particular sectors. Advice is set out in various guides including
Resilience in Society: Infrastructure, Communities and Businesses.
Here it is argued that in order for communities to 'help themselves',
people should ask themselves what they can do. They are asked the
following three questions:

1. Are you aware of the risks you and your community might face,
   e.g., flooding?
2. How can you help yourself and those around you during an
   emergency?
3. What can you do to get involved in emergency planning in your
   community? (Cabinet Office 2014)

Communities will be better prepared if everyone uses their local knowledge and thinks about the potential impact particular emergencies like
flooding or heatwaves could have on them, their family and their community. These arguments are repeated in guidelines to accompany the
Civil Contingencies Act. Individuals and communities are better able to
cope with emergencies if they have spent time planning and preparing
and are aware of the resources, skills and expertise they possess. They
will know their geographical area and the needs of members of their
community and provide a link to existing local networks that response
agencies can use (Cabinet Office 2004b: 46). The guidance promotes
dialogue between the community, emergency practitioners and local
authorities. Response agencies should take advantage of the community's skills, resources, local knowledge and enthusiasm. Community
resilience is rooted in the notion of the everyday, based on the belief

that everyday working practices and day-to-day functioning are the best foundations for developing effective plans (Cabinet Office 2004b: 23). Local authorities are understood in relation to the community they represent and their role in emergency response is seen as reflecting this (Cabinet Office 2004b: 33). Public health, in particular, is seen as important among a wide range of functions that local authorities carry out. The other important partner is the voluntary sector which can provide a diverse range of operational and support skills including psycho-social support (for example, from faith groups), medial, clothing and feeding arrangements, information services, fundraising and equipment. Across all these bodies it is important to coordinate activities in such a way as to raise awareness and understanding, enhance capabilities and motivate and sustain self-resilience (Cabinet Office 2004b: 47).

The role of the community is seen as particularly important in the recovery stage. As the guidance argues:

The management of recovery is best approached from a community development perspective. It is most effective when conducted at the local level with the active participation of the affected community and a strong reliance on local capacities and expertise. Recovery is not just a matter for the statutory agencies – the private sector, the voluntary sector and the wider community will play a crucial role. (Cabinet Office 2004b: 85)

Recovery, defined as rebuilding, restoring and rehabilitating the community is seen as a complex social and developmental process with four interlinked categories of impact that individuals and communities need to consider – humanitarian, economic, infrastructure and environmental. The best results are said to occur when the community can exercise a high degree of 'self-determination'. Regeneration is also a significant theme that resonates with the more dynamic conceptions of resilience. Local communities can seize the opportunity to transform and revitalise their area through new commercial activities, improving skills, raising aspirations and improving the environment. Such transformation is seen as physical, social and economic, but also psychological (Cabinet Office 2004b: 83).

Crises can at times, therefore, been seen as opportunities to regenerate and revitalise the community or area. There are, however, also more mundane interests present in the desire to maintain continuity and 'keep things running'. An important part of the government's 'distant governance' is to ensure good BCM, 'a process that helps manage risks to the smooth running of an organisation or delivery of a service, ensuring continuity of critical functions in the event of a disruption, and effective recovery afterwards' (Cabinet Office 2014). The government role is to ensure that businesses and organisations have a clear understanding of BCM and can identify their key products and services and the threats they face.

Planning and exercising minimises the impact of potential disruption. It also aids in the prompt resumption of service helping to protect market share, reputation and brand. In order to be successful, BCM must be regarded as an integral part of an organisation's normal ongoing management processes. To achieve this top-level buy-in is vital as it disseminates the importance of BCM throughout the organisation. Organisations are encouraged to carry out risk assessments and Business Impact Analysis. The *Keeping the Country Running: Natural Hazards and Infrastructure* guide provides advice on these points as well as outlining standards of resilience. Governance from a distance operates through promoting best practice and information-sharing rather than using additional regulation. As well as good BCM, regulated sectors should consider integrating resilience into annual reports, establishing monitoring and reporting systems for the most vulnerable sites, assessing and monitoring standards of infrastructure resilience, sharing information across sectors, improving resilience business cases and evaluating probability impact (Cabinet Office 2011b: 52).

Resilience is here understood as 'the ability of assets, networks and systems to anticipate, absorb, adapt to and/or rapidly recover from a disruptive event'. A footnote goes on to state that 'in its broader sense, it is more than an ability to bounce back and recover from adversity and extends to the broader adaptive capacity gained from an understanding of the risks and uncertainties in our environment. But for the purpose of this guidance, a narrower definition has been adopted (Cabinet Office 2011b: 14 – footnote 10). This recognises the wider socio-economic implications discussed above, but also accepts the need to concentrate on more technical aspects of infrastructure resilience. These are divided into four elements – resistance, reliability, redundancy and response. Resistance is focused on protection and the prevention of damage or disruption. In line with resilience thinking, the certainty of this and reliability of our knowledge is, however,

questioned. Reliability is about ensuring that infrastructure components are designed in order to operate under a range of conditions.
Again, resilience thinking warns of 'insufficient awareness or preparation for events outside of the range' that might produce significant
wider and more prolonged impacts (Cabinet Office 2011b: 15). The
Redundancy component covers the design and capacity of the network
or system. It includes things like backup installations, spare capacity
and ability to switch to other parts of the network. For example, telecoms resilience works through the ability to re-route communications
traffic. Finally, Response and Recovery concerns planning efforts and
understanding of vulnerabilities as discussed above. In providing a
summary understanding of infrastructure resilience the guidance combines the two elements of design and organisational ability:

[R]esilience of infrastructure is provided through (a) good design of the
network and systems to ensure it has the necessary resistance, reliability
and redundancy (spare capacity), and (b) by establishing good organisational resilience to provide the ability, capacity and capability to respond
and recover from disruptive events. The latter is gained through business
operations and appropriate support for business continuity management.
(Cabinet Office 2011b: 16)

At this point we have moved away from the focus on community
towards more technical solutions to infrastructure problems. It is
worth emphasising, therefore, that even in areas such as telecoms resilience there is some discussion of non-technical solutions, noting that
no one technical solution is going to work all the time. In this particular area, focus can also be placed on the process used in communicating, such as agreed protocols and the better organisation of responders
(Cabinet Office 2013d).

United States Infrastructure Resilience

Presidential Policy Directive 21 (PPD-21) entitled *Critical Infrastructure
Security and Resilience,* was introduced in February 2013 and calls for
an update of the National Infrastructure Protection Plan (NIPP). This
section looks at PPD-21 and the subsequent 2013 NIPP. These place
their emphasis on security and resilience for critical infrastructure
and emphasise changes to infrastructure risks, policies and operating

environments and the increasing need to 'integrate the cyber, physical, and human elements of critical infrastructure in managing risk' (White House 2013: 3). The motivations place strong emphasis on partnership efforts, innovation in managing risk and the need for an 'enterprise approach to risk management' (White House 2013: 1). While this section looks at the NIPP and the Presidential Policy Directive, the following section will emphasise the forceful arguments for building community resilience in the National Plan.

The Presidential Policy Directive on infrastructure security and resilience makes a number of general arguments about the changing nature of security threats and challenges and the increasingly diverse and complex nature of critical infrastructure. This complexity derives from interdependence, multi-level authorities, diverse responsibilities and regulations, varied organisational structures and modes of operating and the mix of physical space and cyber space. Responsibility falls on infrastructure owners and operators to decide on effective strategies to ensure security and resilience. However, this will also require integration into the national preparedness system with its emphasis on prevention, protection, mitigation, response and recovery. PPD-21, therefore, emphasises the importance of coordination and collaboration and shared responsibilities between different levels of government and the public and private owners and operators. The role of Federal government is to promote an integrated and holistic approach that reflects the infrastructure's interconnectedness and interdependency. The strategic imperatives of the Federal Government's approach are:

1. Refine and clarify functional relationships across the Federal Government to advance the national unity of effort to strengthen critical infrastructure security and resilience;
2. Enable effective information exchange by identifying baseline data and systems requirements for the Federal Government and
3. Implement an integration and analysis function to inform planning and operations decisions regarding critical infrastructure (White House 2013).

The rest of the Policy Directive goes on to outline various roles and responsibilities of the Department (and Secretary) of Homeland Security in coordinating the Federal effort and carrying out the responsibilities assigned in the 2002 Homeland Security Act. The Secretary of Homeland Security will evaluate national capabilities, opportunities and challenges, analyse threats and vulnerabilities and identify security and resilience functions necessary for effective public–private coordination. Coordination efforts require the identification of key interdependencies among infrastructure sectors, monitoring the effectiveness of measures taken and providing strategic guidance for promoting a national unity of effort. Additional roles and responsibilities include maintaining national critical infrastructure centres to monitor emerging trends, threats and incidents, provide analysis, expertise, and other technical assistance and exchange of information and intelligence, conduct comprehensive assessments of vulnerabilities, coordinate Federal Government responses to cyber or physical incidents and report annually on the status of national critical infrastructure efforts as required by statute.

PPD-21 prepares the ground for the 2013 NIPP. This defines critical infrastructure as 'systems and assets, whether physical or virtual, so vital to the United States that the incapacity or destruction of such systems and assets would have a debilitating impact on security, national economic security, national public health or safety, or any combination of those matters' (Department of Homeland Security 2013: 7). To protect this infrastructure requires the collective identification of priorities, articulation of clear goals, mitigation of risk, measurement of progress and, crucially, adaptation based on feedback and the changing environment. Managing risk requires an 'integrated approach' across a diversity of actors. The 2013 NIPP is seen as distinctive in elevating security and resilience as the primary aim of infrastructure planning. It updates the risk management framework and aligns with the National Preparedness System in the mission areas of prevention, protection, mitigation, response and recovery. Prevention activities are said to be most associated with addressing threats; protection efforts address vulnerabilities; response and recovery efforts minimize consequences while mitigation transcends the whole threat, vulnerability and consequence spectrum (Department of Homeland Security 2013: 19).

As with other strategies discussed in this chapter, the framing of the approach begins with the argument that we find growing interdependence across critical infrastructure systems and that this is particularly so in relation to information and communications technologies. While offering greater opportunities, it also increases vulnerabilities: 'In an increasingly interconnected world, where critical infrastructure crosses national borders and global supply chains, the potential impacts increase with these interdependencies and the ability of a diverse set of threats to exploit them' (Department of Homeland Security 2013: 8). The United States is also exposed to the effects of extreme weather which compounds the other risks and can have a significant impact on infrastructure operations. The policy and operating environment is also affected by vulnerabilities in the workforce such as a lack of skilled labour and maintenance expertise (Department of Homeland Security 2013: 8).

The NISS approach places such a high emphasis on risk that it might be described as an attempt to govern through risk. Security and resilience, it is argued, are best strengthened through appropriate risk management. Here risk management is taken to be the 'process of identifying, analysing, and communicating risk and accepting, avoiding, transferring, or controlling it to an acceptable level at an acceptable cost' (Department of Homeland Security 2013: 7). Those responsible for critical infrastructure must develop strategies of risk mitigation and other ways to address risk including acceptance, avoidance or transference. Addressing cross-sector dependencies and interdependencies requires information-sharing and planning across the critical infrastructure community.

Therefore, risk management is most effectively achieved through partnerships based on trust, common interest and a shared vision. Risk needs to be identified and managed in a coordinated and comprehensive way across the critical infrastructure community to enable the effective allocation of security and resilience resources. Priorities should be determined jointly by the public and private sector, 'integrating cyber and physical security and resilience efforts into an enterprise approach to risk management' (Department of Homeland Security 2013: 14). Public–private partnerships are seen as central to maintaining security and resilience with the different levels of government and the public and private sectors each bringing unique experiences, capabilities and core competences – the value of which helps bring distinct understanding of various challenges and solutions. Effective partnerships depend upon different attributes including clearly defined purpose and goals, frequent communication, flexibility, adaptability and measurable progress and outcomes to guide shared activities (Department of Homeland Security 2013: 14).

The other element of the NIPP that should be considered is the focus on levels of operation. There is first the recognition that the 'United States benefits from and depends upon a global network of infrastructure that enables the Nation's security and way of life' (Department of Homeland Security 2013: 14). However, the National Plan is more focused on domestic efforts, while recognising the need to work with international partners. At the national level, the plan sets out a series of priorities and goals. These priorities and other risk management activities will be updated regularly. The plan also sets out a continuous cycle of evaluation. This involves the identification of outputs and outcomes associated with national goals and priorities, the collection of performance data to assess progress in achieving these and evaluation of progress towards achievement of the national goals, priorities and vision (Department of Homeland Security 2013: 20). In addition to the National Plan, there will be evaluation of the achievement of the National Preparedness Goal at both the national and community levels and across different sectors, considering their priorities and achievements in collaboration with different critical infrastructure partners (Department of Homeland Security 2013: 4).

The Plan's 'Call to Action' uses the language of empowerment and capacity-building to engage local and regional partners. Most risks and incidents are local in nature, or else have local consequences and it is necessary to develop initiatives on a regional scale in order to complement and operationalise the national effort. Local and regional partnerships are, therefore, seen as an essential part of the national effort and the aim of the Plan is to identify existing partnerships and encourage new ones that can enhance security and resilience. Locally based public, private and non-profit organisations are encouraged to provide their perspective and assessment of risk and mitigation strategies with the state playing the role of facilitator and coordination of planning, resource allocation and evaluation of progress (Department of Homeland Security 2013: 22).

This focus on coordination and facilitation and the empowerment of local actors is a good example of governance from a distance, albeit something that can be combined with decisive state action should the need arise. Another example of governance from a distance is the promotion of Sector Coordinating Councils (SCCs) which are self-organized, self-run and self-governing bodies that enable owners, operators, trade associations, vendors and others to interact across a range of policies, activities and issues. They represent the first point of contact for the Federal Government to engage with each sector's critical infrastructure security and resilience activities. Their various functions include strategic communication and coordination between owners, operators and suppliers and, if necessary, the government; supporting information-sharing; participating in planning efforts related to the revision of the National Plan and Sector-Specific Plans; coordinating exercises and training, public awareness and associated implementation activities (Department of Homeland Security 2013: 35). By contrast, Government Coordinating Councils (GCCs) enable interagency, intergovernmental and cross-jurisdictional coordination within and across sectors. They bring together different representatives from government and each sector. The GCCs and SCCs are important in facilitating public–private coordination across different sectors and constituencies.

Community Resilience in PPD-8

This section looks briefly at Presidential Policy Directive 8, National Preparedness since it is here that we find the strongest link with the more Anglo-Saxon notions of individual and community resilience. PPD-8 aims at an integrated 'all-of-nation' approach to preparedness, producing 'a secure and resilient Nation with the capabilities required across the whole community to prevent, protect against, mitigate, respond to, and recover from the threats and hazards that pose the greatest risk' (White House 2015: iii). The National Plan is aligned with the National Preparedness Goal aimed at coordinating critical infrastructure risk management with national preparedness across different mission areas. PPD-8 is organised around several elements. The National Preparedness Goal states the ends to be achieved, the National Preparedness System describes the means to achieve these, the National Planning Frameworks explain delivery and an annual National Preparedness Report documents the progress being made. Various other guidance documents are aimed at the general public, businesses and non-profit organisations. PPD-8 argues that when everyone comes together the end result is more effective and that 'involving the whole community in PPD-8 activities is what makes this effort unique ... when it comes to national preparedness, all of us have a role to play' (White House 2015). At its core, therefore, is the requirement for everyone to be involved, that 'preparedness is a shared responsibility' and that government departments and agencies must work with the whole community to meet the objectives.

The 2015 National Preparedness Goal aims for a 'secure and resilient nation with the capabilities required across the whole community to prevent, protect against, mitigate, respond to and recover from the threats and hazards that pose the greatest risk'. It emphasises the need for the whole community to work together and argues that individual and community preparedness is fundamental to success. The emphasis on individual and community resilience is clear: 'Each community contributes to the Goal by individually preparing for the risks that are most relevant and urgent for them individually. By empowering individuals and communities with knowledge and skills they can contribute to achieving the National Preparedness Goal' (FEMA 2015: 2).

The National Preparedness System document outlines the approach, resources and tools for achieving the National Preparedness Goal while national planning frameworks focus on each of the mission areas – prevention, protection, mitigation, response and recovery and defines how best to work together to meet the needs of individuals, families, communities and states in relation to these. Federal Interagency Operational Plans cover government activities to deliver on core capabilities in support of state and local plans across the five mission areas. Finally, the National Preparedness Report summarises progress towards the National Preparedness Goal. It provides a detailed analysis of the five mission areas including ranking their core capabilities. Throughout the reports, the government promotes a 'whole community approach' noting that while government 'plays a critical role in coordinating national-level efforts, it is communities and individuals who lead efforts to implement preparedness initiatives throughout the Nation' (Department of Homeland Security 2012: 1). The latest report notes, however, that while individual preparedness is key to community resilience, surveys continue to highlight the difficulties in successfully engaging the pubic (Department of Homeland Security 2016a: ii).

The community is central to mitigation activities and a resilience approach seeks to help community members make informed actions to reduce their risk (Department of Homeland Security 2016a: 17). It is argued that since communities can rarely avoid such risks completely, the Mitigation Framework encourages building community resilience before an occurrence through leadership, collaboration, partnership building, education and skill building (Department of Homeland Security 2016a: 49).

The National Disaster Recovery Framework defines how Federal agencies promote effective recovery and examination of this framework shows the strongest influence of the idea of community resilience. It looks at the ability of a community to recover based on its pre-disaster preparedness, mitigation and capacity building. Hence resilient communities are understood as being those 'with an improved ability to withstand, respond to and recover from disasters', who are able to take timely decisions in response to the impact of disasters and who can engage in successful recovery planning and implementation (Department of Homeland Security 2016b: 5). Within these communities, successful recovery is based on the ability of individuals and families to 'rebound from their losses in a manner that sustains their physical, emotional, social and economic well-being' (Department of Homeland Security 2016b: 5). Individuals, families and households are said to have a key role to play in facilitating both their own recovery and that of the wider community (Department of Homeland Security 2016b: 11). In return, it is important that individuals can draw on community support while local government has primary responsibility for leading and managing community recovery. The Federal Government will act as a partner and facilitator, strengthening its role if this affects national security (Department of Homeland Security 2016b: 6).

All this again illustrates the Anglo-Saxon approach to resilience insofar as it promotes a more distant form of governance through facilitation, encouraging individuals, families and communities to better govern themselves. If this can be seen as a form of governmentality, then there are other elements of the community approach that indicate its more neo-liberal character. As well as devolving responsibility downwards onto individuals and local actors, support for private sector solutions to local problems is a clear government priority. The private sector is seen as a crucial source of resilience through its provision of infrastructure services and other essential commodities and plays a key role in ensuring the 'viability' of a community. Recovery depends on the private sector, working hand-in-hand with the community and other local organisations (Department of Homeland Security 2016b: 14). However, a neo-liberal approach is more than simply the promotion of the private sector. As a form of governance, it installs a sense of enterprise as well as responsibility among individual actors. A more transformative version of resilience is promoted whereby rather than simply returning to a previous condition, recovery offers 'unique opportunities to reduce current and future risk and contribute to a more sustainable community' (Department of Homeland Security 2016b: 8). It is argued that communities 'can capitalize on opportunities' during the rebuilding process, improving their sustainability and 'liveability' goals, promoting future growth, improving economic competitiveness, enhancing the health and safety of the neighbourhood and making smart energy choices (Department of Homeland Security 2016b: 8). Moreover, while resilience involves the ability to withstand and recover, the key issue is the ability of people to prepare for and adapt to changing conditions. The responsibility for this 'begins with the individual and integrates with the larger responsibility of the community' (Department of Homeland Security 2016b: 26).

Critical Infrastructure Protection in France

This section looks at French infrastructure protection which has been undergoing a gradual transition from a strong form of state protection to a greater devolution of powers to the private sector and non-state actors. This has not, however, developed in a uniform manner and significant differences exist across areas of responsibility with the state continuing to play a decisive role in most cases.

Since 2004, civil protection has been subject to greater involvement from non-state actors. Law 2004-811 did two things – first to bring together different crisis management procedures into a unified approach; and second, to give a greater role to municipalities who could now determine their own crisis management procedures at the local level. The law sought both greater coherence under the direction of the state, and greater local responsibility based on empowering municipal actors as well as seeking to promote a stronger understanding of risk culture among institutions, the private sector and civil society.

This started to challenge the traditional notion of civil protection as the sole responsibility of the state with little delegation to municipalities or private actors. For much of the twentieth century the state was, as elsewhere, the main owner and provider of critical infrastructure. Waves of privatisation have changed this situation with the state now required to secure specific obligations of service provision from various private operators. As Léo Bourcart argues (2015: 40), the state has definitely lost a significant part of its crisis intervention capacity as a result of these privatisations and the subsequent law 2015-811. As with the case in other countries, it now seeks to develop a role as coordinator for service provision, rather than direct provider. Civil defence and CIP has gradually shifted away from the idea of strong state protection towards issues like business continuity and preparedness. These developments are justified by the French authorities through the gradual introduction of resilience and the idea that the state must promote preparedness among private actors and the population, rather than trying to do everything itself.

In this context, resilience is introduced as the willingness and ability of a country, a society and its authorities to be able to withstand the consequences of an attack or catastrophe and quickly restore normal functioning, or at least a socially acceptable level of functioning. This concerns not only government, but economic actors and the whole of civil society (Secrétariat général de la défense et de la sécurité nationale 2014a: 9).[1] This statement from the General Secretary for Defence and National Security, giving instructions on vital activities, contains two things of note. Firstly, it supports the view that the French government is pushing for a whole of society approach that recognises that infrastructure is operated privately and that the cooperation of the private sector and civil society is necessary. Secondly, however, it remains wedded to the 'conservative' definition of resilience as restoring normal functioning, rather than the Anglo-Saxon view that crises present opportunities to adapt and reorganise rather than returning to the way that things were previously.

Critical infrastructure protection has, since 2006, been divided into twelve areas of vital importance. The state sector is comprised of civil activities, military activities, judicial activities and space and research. Citizen protection includes health, water management and food. Vital

---

[1] La résilience se définit comme la volonté et la capacité d'un pays, de la société et des pouvoirs publics à résister aux conséquences d'une agression ou d'une catastrophe majeures, puis à rétablir rapidement leur capacité de fonctionner normalement, ou à tout le moins dans un mode socialement acceptable. Elle concerne non seulement les pouvoirs publics, mais encore les acteurs économiques et la société civile tout entière.

areas of the nation's social and economic life are listed as energy, cyber security and electronic communication, transport, finances and industry. Each of these areas is given a coordinating minister.

Each area will identify its production system, critical components and needs for special protection with the government providing overall identification of threats and general vulnerabilities, defining the protection requirements and measures for implementation in line with France's national security alert system – Vigipirate (Secrétariat général de la défense et de la sécurité nationale 2014b). The three levels of protection plans for operators of critical infrastructure are the Plan de sécurité d'opérateur (PSO) for large operators managing several vital infrastructures, the Plan particulier de protection (PPP) based on single operators in specific areas and the plan de protection externe (PPE) for accompanying measures in times of crisis in coordination with civil security forces and other sectors. Within this framework the operators of infrastructure have certain obligations to train their managers and security directors at central and local levels, carry out risk analyses, establish an operator security plan and identify the particular protection plan (PPP). The government, in turn, provides an external protection plan for operational support and will intervene if the operators are unable to cope with the crisis.

The overall legal and regulatory framework for these activities is provided through the Sécurité des Activités d'Importance Vitale (SAIV), the highest level of the system of protection against terrorism and serious risks. This defines security priorities and the procedures for implementation of necessary measures while facilitating relations with and between operators and public authorities and promoting prevention, preparedness and awareness. It is here that the reality of the French system becomes more evident. Rather than devolving significant power down to the twelve areas of vital importance the emphasis is on collective ownership of the defence strategy and the resilience of the nation. A hierarchical distribution of crisis responsibilities is preserved with the state playing the leading role in determining how implementation is to take place (Secrétariat général de la défense et de la sécurité nationale 2014a: 9). Bourcart (2015: 49) is correct, therefore, to suggest that a paradox exists at the heart of the French approach to civil protection. The state declares its intention to devolve powers to civil society and the private sector, but at the same time implements top-down measures based on national laws, decrees and legally binding 'guidance' to infrastructure operators that outlines exactly which plans they should develop.

SAIV provides the framework for defining and implementing security measures for the protection of vital points of importance (PIV). PIVs are understood as national establishments, facilities or structures which, if damaged or destroyed, would seriously weaken national economic, military or security capacity, or else seriously damage the health and wellbeing of the population (Secrétariat général de la défense et de la sécurité nationale 2014a: 21).[2] We see, therefore, a concern with both physical infrastructure including military and security apparatuses, and something more akin to governmentality in its concern with what is vital to society and the wellbeing of its citizens. On this point the French approach, like the German, is notably more pro-European than the UK approach, advocating a 'social model' understanding of what is vital to society rather than a neo-liberal focus on individual self-reliance. Following the 2006 European Programme for CIP of the critical infrastructure of the Member States, it is argued, is 'indispensable to the maintenance of vital societal functions, health, the safety, security and economic or social well-being of citizens' (Secrétariat général de la défense et de la sécurité nationale 2014a: 49, my translation).[3]

Another government body promoting resilience is the Ministry of the Environment and the General Commission for Sustainable Development. Launching the Integrated Assessment of Territorial Resilience initiative in 2012 it seeks to strengthen the capacity of local governments, communities and their infrastructure to respond to crises and disasters.

This is somewhat closer to the UK approach in looking at communities as well as infrastructure. Interestingly, it defines resilience, when

---

[2] Un PIV est un établissement, une installation ou un ouvrage sis sur le territoire national dont le dommage, l'indisponibilité ou la destruction par suite d'un acte de malveillance, de sabotage ou de terrorisme risquerait, directement ou indirectement - d'obérer gravement le potentiel de guerre ou économique, la sécurité ou la capacité de survie de la Nation; - ou de mettre gravement en cause la santé ou la vie de la population.

[3] Une infrastructure critique est un « point, système ou partie de celui-ci, situé dans les États membres, qui est indispensable au maintien des fonctions vitales de la société, de la santé, de la sûreté, de la sécurité et du bien-être économique ou social des citoyens, et dont l'arrêt ou la destruction aurait un impact significatif dans un État membre du fait de la défaillance de ces fonctions ».

applied to human societies, as maintaining a level of functioning, but also in the more dynamic sense of having the capacity to adapt in the face of hazards based on the capabilities and flexibility of the system (Commissariat Général au Développement Durable 2013: 2). A resilience strategy aims to encourage populations in vulnerable areas to take preventative measures, or to change their individual or collective behaviour. The project seeks to produce a guide that will help local actors – defined as local government and decentralised services, communities, the public sector, private companies, NGOs and associations – to analyse the causes of vulnerabilities, examine coping mechanisms and provide methodological assistance for shared solutions (Commissariat Général au Développement Durable 2013: 4).

Initiatives such as these suggest that away from official government policy, there is a more receptive attitude towards resilience thinking, particularly in relation to communities and civil society. Among research institutes, foundations and think-tanks we find positive promotion of the benefits of a resilience approach, perhaps most notably with the think-tank Haut Comité Francais pour la Défense Civile (HCFDC). Their position paper from 2010 promotes familiar themes such as BCM, coordination among stakeholders, public–private initiatives and the importance of local community involvement in resilience-building. It also notes how the idea of resilience is much stronger in the United Kingdom and that crisis management is carried out through local forums which enable essential actors to understand their requirements and to perform exercises in preparation. The legal framework and role of the state is 'lighter' with more responsibility falling on the actors themselves, whereas in France crisis management is controlled by the state (Haut Comité Francais pour la Défense Civile 2010: 13). Yet, apparently, resilience is an unavoidable modern societal condition and it is a growing international trend that populations be more involved in comprehensive crisis management (Haut Comité Francais pour la Défense Civile 2010: 15).

The approach of the HCFDC is to promote better coordination between public and private actors, encourage mutual understanding and, through training and exercises, gain better knowledge of reciprocal crisis management tools. Communities can be encouraged to better understand how to cope with a crisis even if the state remains in charge of crisis management and emergency response. It is necessary to move away from the view that the state's approach is the only possible understanding of a crisis. Different actors will have different perspectives and a comprehensive response requires a sharing of viewpoints. Communities too will often have a fuzzy understanding of the problems they face and will need better guidance and communication. The state cannot, indeed should not, plan everything. But it must manage priorities, plan for recovery of infrastructure and ensure restoration of essential services (Haut Comité Francais pour la Défense Civile 2010: 7).

Finally, the High Council for Strategic Education and Research, whose detailed report on resilience we shall discuss in the analysis section, argues for the benefits of adopting a resilience strategy as part of a wider change paradigm. This advocates a vision of sustainable development leading to greater economic security, based on social and ecological durability, flexibility and resilience. Risks are increasingly unpredictable and environments are highly uncertain, but a clear strategy should be able to anticipate such uncertainty through better preparedness and clearer decision-making (Conseil Supérieur de la Formation et de la Recherche Stratégiques 2011: 55).

These discussions give some indication of the different approaches being advocated by various research institutes, think-tanks and foundations. Their promotion of resilience is certainly more enthusiastic than the official government position, and it is perhaps closer to the Anglo-Saxon point of view. Nonetheless, it is the introduction of resilience into government policy-making that provides the opportunity for this further discussion and debate. This situation we will expect to continue, albeit with some of the reservations about the Anglo-Saxon understanding of resilience, as we shall outline later in the analysis section.

German Infrastructure Protection

The German Federal Ministry of the Interior (BMI) set up the CIP Working Party of Federal Ministries in 1997 and the issue of infrastructure protection has developed since then through various campaigns and special commissions to raise awareness. Initiatives have begun to coordinate infrastructure protection with the private sector, particularly in areas such as IT security. Germany is, however, still somewhat behind the Anglo-Saxon countries in formulating policy and guidelines.

The purpose of this section is to indicate how CIP is developing in Germany, while lacking the conception of resilience found in Anglo-Saxon discourse. Partly this is because the German approach gives a central role to government and the state with little or no emphasis on building resilience within communities. However, this does not mean that there are not some similarities in policy and argument. The most important government document in this field is the *National Strategy for Critical Infrastructure Protection (CIP Strategy)* published in 2009. While the arguments are somewhat technical, the setting of the context contains familiar assumptions. The context, indeed, can be found in UK, US and EU arguments about the need for global competitiveness and infrastructure protection is justified on this basis:

Infrastructure in general and critical infrastructure in particular are the life-blood of modern, efficient societies. Germany is among the leading industrial and technology-oriented nations. Germany's importance as a location for business and industry and ensuring the country's competitiveness in a globalized economic and technological setting are crucially dependent, as preconditions for prosperity and progress, on the availability of high-performance and well-functioning infrastructure. Therefore, ensuring the protection of this infrastructure is a key function of security-related preparedness measures taken by industry and government agencies, and is a central issue of our country's security policy. (Federal Ministry of the Interior 2009: 3)

While the importance of this infrastructure grows, so too does society's vulnerability due to the extent to which 'nearly all spheres of life are pervaded with, and dependent on, critical infrastructure' (Federal Ministry of the Interior 2009: 5). These changed conditions are seen as necessitating greater trust and cooperation across different government departments, industry, business and civil society.

Critical infrastructure is defined as 'organizational and physical structures and facilities of such vital importance to a nation's society and economy that their failure or degradation would result in sustained supply shortages, significant disruption of public safety and security, or other dramatic consequences' (Federal Ministry of the Interior 2009: 4). While the UK approach emphasises business and communities, the German approach makes more reference to society as a whole. Infrastructure is considered critical 'whenever it is of major importance to the functioning of modern societies and any failure or degradation would result in sustained disruptions in the overall system' (Federal Ministry of the Interior 2009: 7). Protecting critical infrastructure 'is a task of society as a whole, which calls for coordinated action supported by all players – government, business and industry, and the general public' (Federal Ministry of the Interior 2009: 10). The attention of the state and of society should be directed at two threats in particular – the threat of terrorism and the growing impact of natural hazards.

Infrastructure in Germany is divided into technical basic infrastructure and socio-economic services infrastructure. The technical side includes power supply, information and communications technology, transportation and water supply. The socio-economic services side includes public health, food, emergency and rescue services, disaster control and management, government, public administration, law enforcement agencies, finance, insurance business, media and cultural heritage objects (Federal Ministry of the Interior 2009: 7). Significant interdependency exists between these with socio-economic services largely dependent upon the technical basic infrastructure, but with the basic infrastructure dependent on socio-economic factors such as a stable legal system and functioning emergency service (Federal Ministry of the Interior 2009: 8).

The ownership and operation of this infrastructure, following most trends, is moving into the private sector. This is increasingly the case for public infrastructure services provided at local government level. With the private sector increasingly responsible for the security, reliability and availability of such infrastructure, the responsibilities and functions of the state or public authorities are mainly to ensure the safety and control of the supply of goods and services in times of crises when market mechanisms might not be reliable (Federal Ministry of the Interior 2009: 8). This approach takes privatisation policy for granted, deeming it an inevitable tendency, but does recognise that there are significant limits to what the market can do. It is also the case that there is significant intervention at the regional level with city and municipal public-utility companies (*Stadtwerke* and *Gemeindewerke*) subject to significant regional and municipal regulations.

Thus, the German approach continues to emphasise the central role of the state, but notes the need for better cooperation, on a partnership basis, with other public and private actors. The state may do this as a moderator, or by rule-making and regulating measures for safeguarding the 'overall system' and its procedures (Federal Ministry of the Interior 2009: 3). The guiding principles are 'to build trusting co-operation between the state and business and industry' (Federal Ministry of the Interior 2009: 12). The German approach is notable (and might be contrasted with the United Kingdom in this respect) in that this is backed up by a strong legal framework. It is noted that compared to other countries, Germany has a good record of security of supply because privately organized power supply companies are under a legal obligation to operate a secure, reliable and high-performance supply network (Federal Ministry of the Interior 2009: 4). As the guidance to companies and public authorities makes clear:

Public limited companies and limited liability companies (GmbH) are currently subject to overarching legal requirements for controlling risk and crises. The financial sector also has regulations which are obligatory in practice, such as minimum requirements for risk management (MaRisk). According to these regulations, the concept of enterprise security includes protecting persons and material goods such as buildings and facilities, maintaining operations through any kind of disruption up to a crisis, whether a stock market crisis, natural disaster or terrorist attack. (Federal Ministry of the Interior, 2008: 12)

The German approach to CIP is also affected by the federal structure of the German state. The Federation, the *Länder* and local governments are required to jointly act and there is a structured implementation procedure across these three levels of government. Parallel work packages relate to the definition of general protection targets; analysis of threats, vulnerabilities and management capabilities; and assessment of threats and identification of protection targets. Interestingly, it is emphasised that these work packages are implemented primarily by the public sector, while the Federal Ministry of the Interior coordinates at the federal level. Relevant companies and operators take responsibility for implementation of goal attainment measures, internal regulations, self-commitment agreements and risk assessment and communication (Federal Ministry of the Interior 2009: 16).

There is a neo-liberal element that creeps into the argument that suggests the way forward is to govern through risk. It claims that: 'No one-hundred percent protection of infrastructure and its operational effectiveness can be ensured by either the state or operators. The present security mentality must be converted into a new "risk culture"' (Federal Ministry of the Interior 2009: 11). Creating a risk culture is the closest the CIP Strategy comes to the Anglo-Saxon approaches. This 'novel risk culture' will be based on cooperation among stakeholders, 'risk communication among the state, companies, citizens and the general public', more self-commitment from operators to manage and prevent incidents and 'a greater and self-reliant self-protection and self-help capability of individuals or institutions affected by the disruption or compromise of critical infrastructure services' (Federal Ministry of the Interior 2009: 11). This risk culture will help make society more robust and resistant in the face of vulnerabilities.

What is interesting here, however, is the mixed message that reflects the fact that the German approach is torn between two different 'cultures'. The 'novel risk culture' promoted here is undoubtedly an Anglo-Saxon neo-liberal one that seeks to promote private initiative, while responsibilising operators and individuals. It represents governance from a distance by governing through risk assessment and risk awareness. This suggests resilience insofar as it is accepted that we must give up on the idea of one hundred percent protection and accept that crises are inevitable. However, rather than drawing the obvious conclusions – that we must instead promote a culture of dynamic adaptability and reorganisation, the argument concludes with what might be considered the 'conservative' view of resilience; that is, that the aim of the strategy is to make society more robust and resistant. This is the 'engineering view' of resilience criticised by Anglo-Saxon approaches – it seeks to protect things as they are and to resist rather than adapt. A similar 'conservative' view can be found in risk and crisis management guidelines for companies and government authorities: 'The aim of crisis management for critical infrastructure organizations is to deal with a crisis while maintaining the greatest possible ability to function, and/or recovering critical functions as quickly as possible' (Protecting Critical Infrastructures – Risk and Crisis Management: A guide for companies and government authorities, Federal Ministry of the Interior, 2008: 22). Indeed, these arguments advocate resistance, not resilience, and maintain the key role of the state as protector of society, rather than the Anglo-Saxon view of devolved governance through self-reliant individuals and communities.

To take this argument a little further, the strategy outlines three elements of risk management. First, Prevention – the identification of all existing and anticipated risks, critical elements and processes, so that severe disruption will be avoided. This will be done through 'comprehensive proactive (preparedness) arrangements' and 'efficient risk and crisis management'. The Response element seeks to minimise the consequences of severe disruptions through effective emergency and crisis management and 'effective self-help capabilities of the entities and establishments directly affected' (Federal Ministry of the Interior 2009: 12). The Sustainability element seeks the establishment of protection standards to be developed jointly with the operators and in accordance with international standards. This again differs from Anglo-Saxon approaches to resilience which place less emphasis on prevention and protection. While there is the phrase 'effective self-help capabilities', it seems clear that the main direction for this strategy will come from the state and that the state maintains chief responsibility for protection.

There are other attempts at promoting risk management through vulnerability analysis and developing a methodology for analysing critical infrastructure sectors – in one case developing a 'society-level criticality matrix' to determine processes of significant and high criticality (Federal Office for Information Security 2004: 8). Vulnerability analysis looks at how risk elements in sub-processes determine how an organisation is affected. Dependence on these risk elements demands a combination of risk reduction, risk avoidance, risk shifting and risk acceptance (Federal Ministry of the Interior 2008: 22).

The Federal Office of Civil Protection and Disaster Assistance produces guidance and commissions academic work to promote better understanding and practices in this field. The best example of this work is the work on flooding – a natural hazard that has had a significant impact on Germany and central Europe. This is one issue – as noted also in the EU's work – that has a cross-border impact requiring international cooperation. In one of the very few mentions of resilience in the German literature, it is suggested that:

The use of internationally applicable guidelines for assessing vulnerability at a community level can play a decisive role in achieving international cooperation in this area. Exchanging assessment data can lead to an improvement in flood management at a community and national level, as well as forming the basis for recommendations about resilience strategies. (Federal Office of Civil Protection and Disaster Assistance 2014: 24)

The 200-page guidance on flooding mentions resilience just this once, although the community focus is more central. This focus, however, is not on the role of community as understood in the UK documents, but as an object of measurement. The report's main aim is to develop key vulnerability indicators covering such things as exposure, susceptibility, capability, evacuation time, coping capacity, insurance time, flood experience and flood protection measures in private households. Alongside the standardised core indicators are community-specific indicators listed as flood sensitivity, level of information on flood hazards, actual insurance cover and flood protection measures. These contain some of the issues discussed in the UK guidance. For example, the flood sensitivity indicator looks at how those people who are aware of their own flood risk are likely to be better prepared and better informed about the correct behaviour in event of an emergency (Federal Office of Civil Protection and Disaster Assistance 2014: 73). Such discussions are interesting, and are compatible with approaches that seek to measure levels of resilience. But they are largely technical accounts that construct the community as an object of analysis rather than as pro-active actor in flood prevention.

The conclusion to be drawn is that there is a much weaker sense of communities and individuals as actors. This can be seen positively or negatively depending on point of view. It could be claimed that the UK approach places the resilience of communities and individuals centre stage, or it could be claimed that this is a strategy of devolving responsibility away from the state by governmentalising the population. The lack of discussion of community resilience in the German literature might be seen as indicating lack of dynamism. Or it might be that this lack of emphasis on the role of communities occurs because German policy-making retains its strong emphasis on the role of the state as the main responsible actor that people ultimately depend upon for protection and that the lesser emphasis on communities and individuals is due to a greater emphasis on society as a whole.

Resilience in EU Policy-Making

This section looks at how the EU is dealing with a number of trans-border challenges, particularly in relation to critical infrastructure, the civil protection mechanism and climate change adaptation. These challenges arise in relation to basic societal functions and needs such as energy, transport and food distribution. The process of European integration, combined with the general trends towards interconnectedness and interdependence renders member states more vulnerable to trans-border threats to such functions, exacerbated by the spread of communications and new technologies and by Europe-wide policies of market liberalisation. Hence threats to critical infrastructure are of particular importance in that they have an impact both on other member states and the European economy as a whole. These impacts affect such areas as agriculture, economic growth and the competitiveness of EU regions (European Commission 2009a: 4). The Commission is particularly concerned to promote better coordination and cooperation across different countries and between different stakeholders – member states, the Commission, industry and business associations, standardisation bodies, owners, operators and users. Stakeholders are required to cooperate and contribute to the development and implementation of CIP according to their specific roles and responsibilities (European Commission 2005: 4). Developing an EU-wide framework is therefore necessary to maintain levels of infrastructure protection, but it is also noted that this should support the rules of competition within the internal market. The Commission will support this by assuming the role of facilitator, identifying, exchanging and disseminating best practices for trans-border infrastructure protection which will provide the basis for a common framework (European Commission 2005: 5). We understand this as a good example of governance from a distance with the EU conceived of as facilitator, coordinator, regulator and occasional manager (Kirchner, Fanoulis and Dorussen 2015: 291).

The protection of critical infrastructure is described under the subsidiarity principle as being first and foremost the responsibility of member states, the owners and operators. The EU's role is to concentrate on those aspects of infrastructure protection that have trans-border effects. This form of indirect governance emphasises the responsibility and accountability of owners and operators to make their own plans and decisions for protecting their assets (European Commission 2005: 4). However, there are accompanying principles of collective responsibility where member states set up measures for prevention and preparedness and the principle of solidarity (Morsut 2014: 147). The Solidarity Clause is aimed at getting member states to act together to assist in the event of a terrorist attack and natural- or human-made disaster. It also encourages use of various EU instruments in areas of police and judicial cooperation and civil protection. However, despite being in place since the end of 2009, little use has been made of the solidarity clause and member states have proved reluctant to activate binding procedures (Fuchs-Drapier 2011: 184).

Because of this, approaches to disaster prevention, for example, continue to emphasise that primary responsibility to protect citizens remains with member states, but that the EU can, 'in the spirit of solidarity', be called upon to complement and support action taken at national, regional or local levels, while continuing to respect the principle of subsidiarity (European Council 2009: 1). Rather than strong compulsion, the Commission works through sharing and promoting various practices, lessons learnt and relevant data and information, raising awareness of the social, economic and environmental impacts of disasters and providing relevant information to policy makers. It encourages those involved in disaster prevention to work together and suggests developing a common legal framework if possible. However, it does not compel these things. Instead it seeks to make use of guidelines and methods to map risks, make assessments, raise public awareness, improve dissemination of forecasts, encourage exchange of policy makers and researchers and improve the links between existing early warning systems (European Council 2009: 7).

An important tool in the EU's response to crises and disasters is the Union Civil Protection Mechanism. This offers assistance to any member state that is struggling to cope with the aftermath of a crisis or disaster. The Lisbon Treaty recognises civil protection as a formal policy area with competences shared between the EU and its member states based on the principles of complementarity and promotion. The main role of the mechanism is to prevent or reduce the effects of crises through 'fostering a culture of prevention', improving cooperation, enhancing preparedness and facilitating rapid and efficient response as well as increasing public awareness and preparedness for disasters (European Council 2013). The EU approach is to offer coordination and facilitation from a distance, encouraging member states and other actors to respond in the most appropriate ways, coordinate efforts, share information and encourage public awareness. The principle of subsidiarity is particularly relevant here as this determines the most appropriate level of intervention – either at European, national or local levels – with the EU only intervening if it can do so more effectively than member states and local actors.

In the area of environmental policy, we will look at the measures the EU is taking in response to the threats posed by climate change. The EU's Adaptation Strategy for a more climate-resilient Europe focuses on how to respond to climate change at local, regional and EU levels through enhancing preparedness and capacity to respond. Again, most emphasis is placed on developing a coherent approach and improving coordination of actors. Of particular importance is the need to ensure coherence between national adaptation strategies and national risk management plans. It notes how many member states are developing such plans as cross-sectoral planning instruments to better prevent and prepare for disasters on the basis of comprehensive national risk assessments (European Commission 2013a: 5). The first phase of the adaptation strategy seeks to establish knowledge of the consequences of climate change and to integrate adaptation into key EU policy areas. It argues for a combination of policy-based and market-based instruments, guidelines and public–private partnerships to deliver on adaptation (European Commission 2009b: 7). Vulnerability assessment should be carried out across member states to best determine various adaptation measures. The Commission will develop vulnerability indicators and means of monitoring both impacts and adaptation measures and to better understand the costs and benefits of adaptation (European Commission 2009b: 8).

Again, emphasis is placed on member states as having primary responsibility for protecting existing and future infrastructure from the impact of climate change. The EU's role is to develop common standards and promote best practices, carry out risk assessments and assess the effectiveness of different adaptation measures while monitoring and evaluating past adaptation efforts (European Commission 2013a: 7). Looked at from the perspective of climate change, then the main aim of these approaches is to emphasise the need for adaptation. The main climate change paper, *Adapting to Climate Change: Towards a European Framework for Action*, is aimed at getting policy makers to understand climate change impacts with emphasis on policies with the optimal level of adaptation. The emphasis placed on climate change-resilient ecosystems means not simply trying to resist change, but working with nature's ability to absorb or control impact. This is considered more effective and efficient than simply focusing on enhancing physical infrastructure (European Commission 2009b: 5).

The Commission is examining ways to improve the monitoring of impacts and adaptation measures so as to develop a set of vulnerability indicators. It is also seeking quantified information on the costs and benefits of adaptation while also analysing past efforts (European Commission 2009b: 8). The implementation of benchmarking is voluntary and non-binding, relying on self-assessments. It is intended, through negotiations, to develop a framework with a set of standards and mechanisms that, while remaining non-binding, can be used to ensure that different actors can be held accountable for their actions. As a form of governance, it works by providing incentives for commitments to be met while ensuring ownership of the implementation process.

Standardisation is one technique by which the EU promotes a particular type of governance. The Commission began standardisation activities to better deal with adaptation considerations through European standardisation organisations (ESOs) to identify and map industry-relevant standards in the three designated priority areas – energy, transport and buildings. It also seeks to improve the market penetration of natural disaster insurance and insurance pricing and other financial products for risk-awareness prevention and mitigation which are seen as crucial for business and investment resilience (European Commission 2013a: 9). The ESOs will develop tools and guidance for standardisation, identify existing European standards and European standardisation deliverables most relevant for adaptation to climate change and draft new ones if necessary (European Commission 2014b: 3). The strategy sets out a framework and mechanisms for raising preparedness and resilience and does so by 'encouraging and supporting action by the EU Member States on adaptation', providing for better-informed decision-making on adaptation and making key economic and policy sectors more resilient to the effects of climate change (European Commission 2013a: 11).

It is argued that standardisation efforts should also cover the overall actions relevant to risk management and that this should be supported by systematic actions to raise public awareness of risk and improve risk and crisis communication (education, involvement of media, networks). The main EU document on the Hyogo Framework for Action argues that:

The new framework should further contribute to enhance governance for disaster management at all levels and across all sectors, building effective coordination mechanisms and sustainable partnerships between different public authorities and relevant stakeholders (civil society, academia and research institutions, private sector). Involvement of relevant actors and communities in decision-making processes should be ensured through inclusive participatory mechanisms and the promotion of a right-based approach. Strong local structures and enhancement of local authorities' capacities are essential to improve planning and resilience of cities and ensure local political commitment and effective implementation of existing legal and policy frameworks. (European Commission 2014a: 8)

The need to involve communities and other relevant actors is a feature of EU strategy to shift emphasis away from reliance on physical infrastructure, particularly in relation to climate change. For example, coastal zone management strategy seeks a shift away from hard structures such as seawalls to protect coastlines and on to management policy to take into account adaptive local capacity. While engineering measures can improve the robustness and reliability of installations, more robust operational and maintenance procedures, demand management, forecasting and early-warning may prove more effective (European Commission 2013c). Perhaps the clearest statement of the promotion of the private sector comes in the Commission Communication *The post-2015 Hyogo Framework for Action: Managing risks to achieve resilience.* Here it is argued that the Hyogo Framework must be developed and implemented in close partnership with the private sector, international financial institutions and major investors. It argues for new initiatives to engage businesses and build partnerships across public, private and other stakeholders. It also places strong emphasis on the role of insurance and suggests that market-based instruments should be used to help those vulnerable to disasters create effective financial contingency mechanisms (European Commission 2014a: 10). Similar suggestions for cooperation are contained in the EU's response to the Sendai framework (European Commission 2016).

However, use of private insurance against risks is unevenly distributed across the EU with risk transfer varying by country. Most states are hesitant to outsource core tasks in crisis management to private companies although they do increasingly establish informal coordination mechanisms with private companies in areas like cyber-security and critical infrastructures (ANVIL 2014: 13). Primary emphasis on the private sector remains an Anglo-Saxon rather than European concern even if this is now increasingly promoted by EU bodies, particularly with the European Network and Information Security Agency (ENISA), the body responsible for information technology and cyber security. In other areas, to take a strong neo-liberal approach would be to create significant political and ideological tensions and thus undermine the EU's stated objective of better coordinating activities among member states.

Analysis: Infrastructure, Disasters and Governmentality

Resilience features among all countries and organisations as a way of providing a more coherent approach to critical infrastructure. A good example of this is the UK's Critical Infrastructure Resilience Programme which is concerned with promoting better communication, cohesion and planning across different sectors of government, society and infrastructure. In Germany and the US, promoting a more integrated approach also reflects the federal political structure while in the EU such coordination must occur across member states.

Additionally, the Anglo-Saxon approach is marked by a concern with the role of individuals and communities. UK guidelines on emergency response and recovery invoke 'all individuals and organisations' as having a role to play and a responsibility to act (Cabinet Office 2013a). In the US responsibility of preparing for recovery 'starts with the individual' and integrates with the wider responsibilities of the community and local government. The National Preparedness Goal argues for the need for the whole community to work together. Government, therefore, plays a supporting role, encouraging local initiative and installing a sense of responsibility among various actors. In the recovery phase, the best results are said to occur when communities can exercise a significant degree of self-determination. In the UK and US local communities are said to have opportunities for revitalising their environment through improving skills and knowledge and developing new commercial opportunities. This presents a more dynamic conception of resilience as transformative rather than simply reactive to crises.

One aspect of dynamism relates to the ability to embrace risk – indeed, it might be called governing though risk. UK guidelines describe this as 'identifying, understanding, managing, controlling, monitoring and communicating risk' with effective risk management the key to building resilience. This is particularly important in relation to investments and business continuity, promoting 'organisational resilience' in relation to uncertainties and disruptions to operation (Cabinet Office 2011b: 14). A similar language is used in the US (Department of Homeland Security 2013: 7) where the NISS approach emphasises risk acceptance, avoidance and transfer across various sectors of infrastructure. Risk is seen as a way of bringing together local and regional actors including public, private and non-profit organisations in order to develop various initiatives to support local resilience (Department of Homeland Security 2013: 22).

In Germany we saw that a risk-based strategy is also developing and that the Federal Ministry of the Interior (2009) calls this a 'novel risk culture'. Indeed, some of the conceptual arguments for resilience in Germany might actually better be understood as a more conventional argument for the development of a risk culture (Baban 2014). As with the US, there is also promotion of the private sector and private initiative. It is accepted that ownership and operation of critical infrastructure is passing into the private sector and that state responsibilities must be reformulated accordingly.

However, Germany differs from the Anglo-Saxon approaches by advocating strong state responsibility and legal protection as well as having strong public or semi-public Stadtwerke and Gemeindewerke at the city and municipal level. The term Daseinsvorsorge refers to the requirement of these to serve the public purpose. Germany is therefore caught between the Anglo-Saxon promotion of private initiative and individual responsibility and a 'whole of society' and 'public purpose' approach emphasising robustness, resistance and protection. The government's research framework for civil security contains the following passage:

Civil security can only be guaranteed in the long term if the resilience of society is strengthened. For example, this would include improving the robustness and security of critical infrastructures and increasing the ability of the population to overcome crisis situations. (Federal Ministry of Education and Research 2016: 13)

From a governmentality perspective, this places emphasis on enhancing the resilience of populations, but it invokes all of society and it emphasises robustness in relation to security strategy, something at odds with a neo-liberal approach.

The introduction of resilience into discussions of French infrastructure protection follows a similar path. Following Bourcart (2015), we can say that significant privatisation of infrastructure provision means that the state and central government needs to justify the new situation. In particular, it works to legitimate public–private partnerships, business continuity planning and a certain amount of stepping back by the state through better involvement of local governments, individuals and infrastructure providers.

However, this is not really governance from a distance as understood by the governmentality account. Perhaps even more than in Germany, the French state remains the central actor with private companies and local actors having either little ability or showing little interest in decision-making. As the main documents illustrate, the state has devolved some powers, but it continues to operate through decrees and legally-binding guidelines with the state showing little inclination towards promoting greater local autonomy (Bourcart 2015: 42). For their part, the private sector and municipalities show only partial engagement in the process with only 15 per cent of municipalities developing local emergency plans (Bourcart 2015: 49).

There are some similarities to the UK situation insofar as the UK's Civil Contingencies Act also operates in a top–down prescriptive way, albeit with more interaction from those required to implement resilience plans. By contrast, the French private sector plays a largely passive role, encouraged by the belief that the state will continue to decide what is to be done. Most of all, while there is some devolution to private companies and the local government, there is not the same discourse of community and individual resilience present in Anglo-Saxon approaches to infrastructure protection.

Such differences are well-illustrated in a scientific report by the High Council for Strategic Education and Research. In the section headed 'Nothing is possible without genuine decentralisation', it argues for a properly decentralised approach based on networks and locally situated and engaged actors. It goes on to note that France is the most centralised European country at a time when most problems require ever more localised solutions. Decentralisation is promoted as a more realistic way to harness the proliferation of social assets and French societal capacities. Indeed, the most important social dynamics run on complexities that are often ignored because of their informal, human character (Conseil Supérieur de la Formation et de la Recherche Stratégiques 2011: 29). In a later section of the report it is suggested that the resilience of a technical system, whether human or social, lies not in any simple capacity for robustness or 'resistance' to the threatening element, but in its agility, both human and systemic, in order to initiate the necessary changes (Conseil Supérieur de la Formation et de la Recherche Stratégiques 2011: 69).[4]

The consequences of such a view are, however, politically complex. While it looks like this is advocating the Anglo-Saxon view of resilience as adaptation rather than resistance, the report goes on to defend aspects of the French system against Anglo-Saxon 'individualism' while also noting that the Anglo-Saxon approach is not necessarily compatible with French forms of capitalism. It is argued that it is not easy to change centuries of doing things a certain way, especially when centralisation brings certain benefits, such as equal access to public services. Indeed, the report – echoing a wider feeling in France and indeed in other European countries – says that it is still necessary to reaffirm the importance of this social model of equal access (rather than individual rights), emphasising the fundamental difference between this approach and the Anglo-Saxon model (Conseil Supérieur de la Formation et de la Recherche Stratégiques 2011: 10, 29).

We might say that this reflects a wider distrust of Anglo-Saxon models of individual behaviour, something we also found in French responses to the use of resilience in the White Paper on Defence and National Security. It reflects a continued belief in the role of the state as providing security and protection. Instead of neo-liberal

---

[4] La résilience d'un système technique, humain ou social ne réside pas dans sa simple capacité de robustesse ou de « résistance » à des phénomènes menaçant son intégrité et sa pérennité. La résilience d'un système réside dans son agilité, aussi bien humaine que systémique, proper à engager les transformations nécessaires avant la rencontre de ses points de rupture.

governance through denial of its obligations, this might be said to reflect a more progressive European tradition that sees the state as still obliged to protect people. In actual practice, however, this may not necessarily be the case. Further policy development acknowledges the need for the state to devolve powers, but this might create a more confusing situation whereby the state seems to express its will to take a step back from its protective role while not really being prepared to properly do so.

While still not particularly prominent in its policies, the emergence of resilience in EU policy-making does raise questions about the purpose of EU strategy in these areas. In the case of European infrastructure protection, we see resilience playing a limited role that is often synonymous with protecting the actual infrastructure and restoring its functioning in the case of a disaster. The trans-border nature of infrastructure highlights the difficulties the EU faces in trying to coordinate collective action across the different member states. Not surprisingly, the main emphasis in the policy documents is for better, more coherent and more coordinated actions. In terms of the role of the European Commission, it sees itself mainly as a facilitator that encourages such coordination through suggestion, policy recommendation, good practice, peer review, standardisation, evaluation and other measures that we have described as representing 'governance from a distance'.

In the case of environmental policy, we find resilience promoted as a response to climate change with the emphasis on the need for adaptability in the face of developments that are increasingly difficult to control. More prominent here is the need for adaptability, making these arguments for resilience more like those of the Anglo-Saxon countries. This view tends to accept systemic crises and change as inevitable and, therefore, emphasises adaptation as the only realist response. Attention is shifted away from large-scale state intervention to protect and prevent in favour of government support to help citizens prepare and adapt in order to better cope with adversity. Emphasis is placed on pragmatic and 'best fit' solutions.

Some of the arguments relating to climate change response contrast with other arguments in favour of resilient infrastructure and highlight tensions in the EU's understanding of resilience. Looking at some of the EU's arguments about CIP, it is clearly not the case that the EU has abandoned the state's role to protect and prevent. However, the adaption strategy for climate resilience does place greater emphasis on acquiring better understanding, involving the private sector, and better informing the community about how to deal with crises. Rather than putting more money into physical infrastructure protection, there is an emphasis on management programmes. This goes some way towards the Anglo-Saxon approach without fully abandoning the idea that the role of the state is to protect people rather than to 'help them to help themselves' as the UK approach argues (Cabinet Office 2011a: 4).

As it gets promoted more ardently, resilience will surely become more prominent within the already-existing mechanisms of governance from a distance. What is questionable is whether this form of governance is really neo-liberal in character as the governmentality critics would suggest is the case in the Anglo-Saxon approach to resilience. Hence while we find the *mechanisms* of governance or governmentality present in the way the EU seeks to work through the 'conduct of conduct', we do not really find a strong neo-liberal *rationality* that attempts to instil in this conduct neo-liberal values of enterprise and competitiveness. While EU policy accepts and promotes things like the private provision of infrastructure and services and seeks to build a network of private and quasi-private bodies, the strategy of distant coordination is more a product of the peculiar nature of the EU and the relation to member states rather than a stronger, more assertively neo-liberal form of governance.

Summarising the situation of the EU's uptake of resilience, it can be seen as based less on ideological commitment to Anglo-Saxon or neo-liberal values than to pragmatic considerations of infrastructure and civil protection and coordination issues relating to the member states and other actors. Nevertheless, this does result in a form of 'governance from a distance' that shares features of the Anglo-Saxon and neo-liberal approaches to governance and might indeed even be described as governmentality. The EU's approach is to give preference to 'conducting conduct' through facilitation and suggestion wherever this is possible. This less direct form of governing is nevertheless backed up with regulative techniques, notably benchmarking, monitoring, best practice and peer-review.

The term has recognisability and it is seen as worthwhile to emphasise resilience in certain areas of policy-making. But, this fails to go much beyond using it as a fashionable buzzword and it fails to really acquire a deeper meaning. In the United Kingdom, policy in these areas invokes notions of individual and community responsiveness, awareness and preparedness, but these elements are under-developed in the EU's arguments for resilience even if they have some presence in the area of environmental politics and the need for climate change adaptation. Nor is there any of the dynamism found in Anglo-Saxon approaches which go beyond the idea of protection and returning to normal to emphasise how crises provide opportunities to build new relationships and generate new ways of operating (Arnold, Mearns, Oshima and Prasad 2014: 5).

Instead, a considerable amount of the EU's concern is directed at problems of coordination, both across different member states and over different areas and scales. Attempts to develop an EU approach are channelled through questions concerning areas of competence and subsidiarity. While there is a strong emphasis on cooperation, learning and shared practice, this raises questions about the purpose of cooperation and whether this is undermined by differences of priority and understanding. For example, member states may have different national security priorities, different expectations and a different relationship with their citizens, civil society and the private sector. This is particularly the case with a notion like civil protection which combines a security dimension with a relationship with civil society or community – something that various significantly across Europe and which is also affected by different legal systems and constitutional settlements.

Nevertheless, the Commission has for a long time been emphasising Europe's global challenges, particularly in relation to new threats, a more competitive global environment and Europe's less-secure position in the world. While not presented in a particularly innovative or dynamic way, the connection between resilience and adaptation is slowly developing, set within the context of the neo-liberal tendencies of Europe 2020 and its arguments for socio-economic restructuring. For this reason, and regardless of the difficulties in presenting the Anglo-Saxon 'vision' of resilient Europe, the EU is gradually putting in place the kind of framework that would allow resilience to come to the fore as a major idea. Due to the dynamics of governance from a distance with its dissemination of policy proposals, standardisation procedures, use of indicators, benchmarks and more compelling forms of obtaining compliance, we might, despite opposition, expect the EU to move in the direction of the Anglo-Saxon view of resilience, albeit with significant internal tensions.

Conclusion

We can summarise the differences in cases in the following way. The UK and US share an Anglo-Saxon approach to resilience in infrastructure, disasters and emergencies. We can describe this approach as governmentality because it seeks to govern from a distance, devolve responsibility to individuals and communities, place heavy emphasis on the role of the private sector, invoke innovation and enterprise and combine emphasis on adaptation with a view of resilience as transformation of communities. By contrast, the French and German approaches to infrastructure and domestic emergencies has only just started to talk of resilience, often without the above connotations. Hence resilience does not play the same role as a tool of governmentality – indeed, its place in the wider discourse causes certain tensions and contradictions. This is also the case with the EU, although we saw that the EU has its own reasons for developing the idea further.

This leaves us to return to the UK approach in order to raise the question of whether there are, in fact, some contradictions and tensions in the Anglo-Saxon approach itself. While the UK approach looks like neo-liberal governmentality, does it actually meet all of the elements of governmentality mentioned above? We might say, first of all, that the UK approach is perhaps not so 'distant' as it first seems. This is not so contradictory since our understanding is that neo-liberalism seeks to 'create' free subjects. It should, therefore, not be a surprise to find the UK state playing a leading and directing role in trying to do this. Although the UK's Critical Infrastructure Resilience Programme encourages 'voluntary cooperation', it admits that stricter legislative powers may also be used. We also noted how the preferred form of 'governance from a distance' is supported by extensive monitoring techniques, information gathering and various forms of assessment and performance measurement. Hence the notion of community resilience should be tempered with the knowledge that the state continues to play the dominant role and that it maintains considerable powers of intervention and enforcement. This is particularly the case, as we saw in Chapter 2, where questions of national security are involved. Counter-terrorism measures are coercive, regardless of appeals to community resilience. However, while there is less need for coercion – as in cases like flood protection – there is still a strong top–down element to the 'devolution' of responsibilities.

We will pick out a couple of critical interventions to make this point. First, the work of Tudor Vilcan can be used to examine the practices of flood protection in the UK and to question whether community resilience really is a genuine thing. Vilcan notes the aim of the strategy is to 're-orchestrate' the distinction between the state as protector and the passive public as one between 'state as enabler and individuals as active participants' (Vilcan 2017: 33). Paradoxically, of course, it is the state that does the re-orchestrating. How does empowerment of the community work? Who is to be listened to? Vilcan's study of resilience-building for flood protection finds that the government 'frames' empowerment in a certain way that narrows the voices of the community which is effectively reduced to members of flood groups. These flood groups rely on a few key people and are certainly not representative of the whole community. Moreover, the government's flooding Evaluation Report avoids political questions, framing engagement with the community in terms of an awareness-raising exercise, fed down to the community level in the manner of an outreach programme (Vilcan 2017: 39–40). This suggests that community resilience is more of a government fabrication, rather than an organically emergent community concern. Moreover, as Geoff O'Brien and Paul Read suggest (2005: 359), public-awareness campaigns often have little impact on preparedness at the individual and local level.

The critical intervention by O'Brien and Read is also useful in challenging some other aspects of the UK approach to resilience in this field. They question the government's priorities in a number of ways. They argue that many of the changes claimed under the framework of the Civil Contingencies Act are really codifications of existing practices with the most responsibility continuing to fall upon emergency responders. Where the government has made significant structural changes to civil protection, they raise questions of whether the government really has taken a more holistic approach, or whether it is actually focusing on selected areas (O'Brien and Read 2005: 356). In particular, they note that while the amount spent on civil defence has increased, the figure is miniscule in comparison to the amount spent on the UK's counter-terrorism activities (O'Brien and Read 2005: 358).

As we move on to look at overseas interventions we might conclude, therefore, that building local, national and trans-border resilience is certainly a developing field. But, it is an uneven field with many of the old practices, discourses and government priorities still evident and with significant tensions over both understanding and implementation of resilience-building measures. This clearly applies to France, Germany and the EU, but it is also evident in the Anglo-Saxon approach, despite this being the dominant one in this area.

4 | Resilience in Development Strategy and Humanitarian Intervention

Introduction

In this final comparative chapter, we turn our attention to overseas strategy to look at how countries are building resilience into their humanitarian and development strategies. There is a wider context to consider here insofar as countries are seeking to combine short-term interventions with longer-term strategy. Therefore, some of the issues covered in Chapter 3 on disaster and emergency planning are also relevant to the discussion here. A significant issue for this chapter is how resilience is seeking to link short-term emergency response to longer-term development strategy. This is an argument that is present in all the literature covered and suggests that different countries are seeking a more coherent and holistic approach to their overseas strategy. While coherence and 'joined up' approaches are a prominent feature, we also suggest that resilience strategy helps justify a governmentality strategy and, indeed, that in this area neo-liberal governmentality is far more entrenched and far less contentious than in other areas of policy-making.

Indeed, resilience has been taken up by the majority of international organisations and aid donors, driven in particular by thinking coming out of the World Bank and United Nations as well as the EU and the Department for International Development (DFID) in the United Kingdom. The discourse is particularly prominent in disaster risk reduction (DRR) and environmental hazards as can be found, for example in this early definition of resilience from the UN/ISDR, defining it as:

The capacity of a system, community or society potentially exposed to hazards to adapt, by resisting or changing in order to reach and maintain an acceptable level of functioning and structure. This is determined by the degree to which the social system is capable of organising itself to increase

this capacity for learning from past disasters for better future protection and
to improve risk reduction measures. (UN/ISDR 2005)

It will be argued that such understandings promote a form of neo-
liberal governmentality that 'governs from a distance' through a
concern with threatened populations; they invoke civil society and
the private sector with the effect of responsibilising national governments and shaping their conduct. In particular, resilience works to
place increased emphasis on the need for local populations and governments to develop learning, self-awareness and the ability to adapt.
It is suggested here that resilience draws on neo-liberal market-based
technologies, but also gets at something slightly different, concerning itself with the limits of purely economic calculation. But this, it
can be argued, is ultimately consistent with a neo-liberal critique of
liberal universalism and is also consistent with, and strengthening
of, the specific methods and technologies of contemporary governance such as monitoring, benchmarking, information-sharing and
peer review.

To outline this approach, the chapter starts with a focus on the
UK and the role of DFID in shaping the international agenda, but
will also extensively examine ECHO, the main EU body responsible
for promoting resilience. It will then briefly compare United States
Agency for International Development (USAID), Germany's Federal
Foreign Office and Federal Ministry of Economic Cooperation and
Development (BMZ) and the French Development Agency (AFD).
The latter has the weakest uptake of the strategy, with resilience
being more prominent in French private bodies. However, the overall argument of this chapter is that, unlike other areas covered in
this study, resilience-building is regarded as much less controversial
in relation to overseas development strategy and that the Anglo-
Saxon approaches of DFID and USAID enjoy widespread international support. Following an examination of the different bodies,
starting with DFID, the chapter will offer an explanation for why
resilience is more prominent in this area of policy-making before
pointing towards some overall conclusions about the uptake of resilience approaches among different international bodies and making
some suggestions for why resilience is proving popular in the United
Kingdom and EU approaches in particular.

The UK's Department for International Development

DFID was established in 1997 as part of a rebranding of British overseas aid and development policy conducted by Tony Blair's Labour Government. Its first White Paper announced the government's intention to refocus international development efforts around the elimination of poverty through encouraging economic growth that benefits the poor. Priorities are the promotion of international sustainable development policies that create sustainable livelihoods for poor people while promoting human development and helping to conserve the environment (DFID 1997: 6). DFID commits itself to working closely with other donors and development agencies in order to build partnerships with developing countries as well as with the UK's private and voluntary sectors and the research community. The emphasis on capacity-building rejects the idea of a minimalist state and unregulated market, but accepts that the state has a key role to play in promoting markets and stimulating enterprise as the best means of encouraging human development and attracting foreign investment (DFID 1997: 12).

DFID's new approach to development might be associated with the then fashionable 'third way' approach of New Labour, promoting the market and private sector, but outlining a supporting role for the state. In actuality, this was consistent with a global shift as outlined by the World Bank in *The State in a Changing World* (World Bank 1997). Development strategy takes its lead from the World Bank's arguments for a turn to capacity-building, providing institutional support for markets, engaging civil society, building partnerships and promoting good governance. Although a later development, resilience is able to fit fairly closely with these concerns while offering a critical reflection on the institutional and capacity-building phase of development strategy and helping to fine-tune some of its mechanisms and rationalities.

Resilience was placed at the centre of the UK government's strategy following the 2011 Humanitarian Emergency Response Review (HERR) becoming a 'new and vital component of humanitarian and development work' (Béné, Godfrey Wood, Newsham and Davies 2012: 8). HERR reinforced the view that humanitarian work should take a more anticipatory approach, that DFID should link emergency response to longer-term development, that it should engage more with local people and institutions, continue its emphasis on capacity-building and show better accountability and transparency (Ashdown 2011). Resilience emerged as pivotal to all of these aims with DFID making it a core part of all its humanitarian work, both to provide a faster and more-efficient response to major disasters and to achieve longer-term development goals (DFID 2011c: 6).

The appeal of resilience in this field is that it appears as a new approach, indeed a 'new area for DFID', while not disrupting existing approaches insofar as 'much of what we do already is likely to feature in this new agenda' (DFID 2011c: 6).

The new resilience agenda will draw upon the skills, resources and ongoing work of different parts of DFID. Our climate change teams are the furthest advanced in understanding resilience, and we will draw on their work. Our new growth and resilience team will make a better analysis of the effects of various types of economic growth, and the best pathways for growth that mitigates risks. We will determine how to promote resilience to shocks and disasters. This will mean increased investment in longer term resilience-building such as social protection, livelihoods promotion, risk financing and insurance mechanisms and encouraging private investment strategies that provide sustainable long-term growth. (DFID 2011c: 8)

This approach is divided into four areas. Economic resilience is concerned with how economics can withstand shocks, physical resilience refers to vital infrastructure, social resilience builds on DFID's governance work to strengthen institutions while environmental resilience relates to the ability to cope with natural hazards (DFID 2011c: 8). In addition, DIFID talks of national resilience as 'helping governments and civil society prepare for and respond to disasters through training and equipping the relevant institutions' (DFID 2011c: 8). In the field of international intervention, where the discourse of fragile states is prominent, the new approach promises to replace a 'substitution service delivery' with a better understanding of how to support weak institutions and maintain life-saving services (DFID 2011c: 8).

As in other fields, resilience is seen as a key means of providing a joined-up or complementary approach, in this case in relation to humanitarian aid, disaster management and longer-term development strategy – particularly in relation to weak states in areas of strategic importance. According to DFID, this means coordinating such things as DRR, adaptation to climate change, social protection and humanitarian preparedness and response (DFID 2011a: 5). The understanding of resilience as the ability of countries, communities and households to manage change in the face of shocks and stress is divided into four core elements – context, disturbance, capacity and reaction (DFID 2011a: 7). Context relates to awareness of social groups, socio-economic political systems, institutional factors and environmental context. Disturbance relates to sudden shocks – including weather-related and geophysical events, disease outbreaks, conflict-related events and economic disturbances – and to longer term stresses – including resource degradation, demographic change, climate change and political instability. Capacity refers to the ability to deal with shocks and stress and depends on the level of exposure to risk, the degree to which a system will be affected and the adaptive capacities of actors. Adaptive capacities, whether of individuals, groups or institutions, depends on their ability to cope, adjust and take advantage of opportunities. This will depend on their ability to anticipate, plan and learn. Finally, reaction refers to the ability to 'bounce back'. This can be interpreted in different ways – to return to the normal, pre-existing condition or transform to a new, enhanced system better able to cope with future shocks (DFID 2011a: 8–9).

DFID has various operational plans in place in different countries and regions. For example, in Bangladesh, DFID has engaged in a programme to strengthen resilience to climate change through enhancing early warning systems, protecting villages from flooding, renovating roads and making crops more climate-resilient. In Pakistan, it is 'mainstreaming' DRR in school recovery programmes and working with communities on disaster awareness and training. Here, too, it promotes more resilient crops and addresses food storage as well as helping to build flood-resistant houses. In Ethiopia, DFID is involved in a Productive Safety Net Programme covering 7.8 million vulnerable people, breaking the need for emergency food programmes by providing those people with regular cash and food transfers (DFID 2011a: 12).

DFID Ethiopia is regarded as a leading example of embedding disaster resilience across DFID's support programme. Although Ethiopia is poor and vulnerable and located in an unstable region, it is regarded by DFID as a comparatively stable country with significant improvement in its provision of basic services and a degree of political stability provided through a system of decentralised regional government.

DFID notes its good record of pro-poor spending, sound financial management and commitment to fighting corruption. All this fits with the UK's poverty reduction and good governance agenda and the United Kingdom uses these opportunities to make its support 'more transformational' and 'accelerate Ethiopia's graduation from aid dependency' (DFID 2013a: 1). International support will be focused on building resilience to changing weather patterns, helping to develop the skills and tools needed to adapt to future change and also to benefit from opportunities for low-carbon growth. This will be done through the Ethiopian government engaging with the private sector and civil society while 'new climate programming will help leverage the benefits of international finance and link research to climate smart decisions for industry and investment' (DFID 2013a: 2).

Neighbouring Kenya is another country vulnerable to climate change, but is regarded by DFID as having East Africa's most diversified and innovative economy with strong human capacity and entrepreneurial capabilities. DFID's approach is therefore focused on service delivery and good governance combined with encouraging private sector provision of services. DFID Kenya provides support for the Kenyan government's Vision 2030 strategy which seeks to promote political and macro-economic stability, sustained economic growth and social development – underpinned by rapidly expanding infrastructure and private sector growth (DFID 2013b: 1-2). The aim here is a build a longer-term link between economic growth and service provision, reducing vulnerability and enhancing stability.

DFID's approach to these countries is part of a wider regional approach that combines humanitarian intervention and development strategy with regional security concerns. DFID has two major interventions of this nature in Africa – one in the Horn of Africa and another in the Sahel region of North West Africa. The Horn of Africa strategy is focused on resilience-building in Ethiopia and Kenya and prioritises the encouragement of institutional support and private investment. UK strategic interests are affected because poverty and instability in the Horn of Africa are seen as the causes of radicalism and fundamentalism, as well as causing migration to Europe (DFID 2013a: 1). The Sahel strategy was developed in response to the regional food crisis and the humanitarian crisis in Mali, 2012. It outlines three phases of the strategy: 'Early action and Preparedness' in response to the food and security crisis across the region; 'Response and Recovery' in response to any military intervention in Mali as well as wider humanitarian needs in the Sahel and; 'Building resilience to future shocks' as a longer-term objective (DFID 2013c: 7). As with the Horn of Africa region, so DFID's concern in the Sahel is to break the cycle of humanitarian crises, using arguments about resilience to reject the traditional focus on short-term humanitarian aid that does little to reduce people's vulnerability. In response to the HERR, DFID committed itself to a Sahel resilience strategy focused on supporting disaster resilience through multi-lateral partners and regional programs. This will inform subsequent phases of support in the Sahel region. Stabilizing the humanitarian situation linked to the conflict in Mali is seen as having a broader stabilization impact. Two key aims are to promote humanitarian preparedness and early action and to address the protection concerns of conflict-afflicted populations (DFID 2013c: 8).

This indeed is key to the UK's wider security strategy as outlined in the document *Building Stability Overseas Strategy* jointly produced by DFID, the Foreign and Commonwealth Office and the Ministry of Defence. The strategy is upfront about the need to focus on those fragile states and conflict-affected regions where British interests are most at stake (DFID, Foreign and Commonwealth Office and Ministry of Defence 2011: 18), thus connecting with the UK's National Security Strategy (see Chapter 2). In the cases above, concern is with the effects of resource scarcity, volatile food and energy prices, population growth and climate change. These increase the stresses on fragile countries and hence the potential for conflict. The regions under particular pressure form an arc running from West Africa, across the Sahel, through the Horn of Africa, the Middle East, up into South and Central Asia (DFID, Foreign and Commonwealth Office and Ministry of Defence 2011: 10).

The UK's strategy is based on anticipation of instability and early identification of crises, quick preventative action and response; and addressing the causes of instability, fragility and conflict upstream. Investing in upstream prevention is understood as helping build strong and legitimate institutions and robust societies so that crisis-prone countries are capable of managing tensions and shocks (DFID, Foreign and Commonwealth Office and Ministry of Defence 2011: 18). A successful strategy is considered more likely when short, medium and longer-term measures for prevention and stabilisation are coordinated by a country-owned strategy whose development and implementation is assisted by partner countries like the UK (DFID, Foreign and Commonwealth Office and Ministry of Defence 2011: 24). This returns us to the central role of resilience as a coordinated response. But it also raises questions about who is responsible for what?

DFID's stated motivation is how best to help countries prepare themselves to withstand shocks and disasters (DFID 2011b: 1). The key term here is 'themselves'. In line with critical thinking in this area (Abrahamsen 2004; Best 2007; Chandler 2014), it can be argued that this shifts the onus and responsibility away from the international community and onto the target country itself. This, of course, can be packaged positively as encouraging local ownership, while the international community provides guidance and expertise. It could, alternatively, be understood as the international community doing less while expecting more. If we take the following passage from a DFID strategy document then both interpretations are possible:

> Ultimately, it is a country government's responsibility to help protect its own population's capacity to resist and adapt to shocks. But the international community has a critical role to support national and local governments, civil society and other partners to help build resilience to future disasters. By doing so, we also safeguard our broader aid investments and the progress made in achieving the Millennium Development Goals. (DFID 2011b: 1)

A critical interpretation of this passage, as will be elaborated upon in more detail in the analysis section, would emphasise first that not only does this approach shift responsibility onto local actors, but also that it addresses the issue of development, not in relation to local needs, but in terms of whether British aid investment meets its targets. It will be suggested that both responsibilising local actors and measuring donor effectiveness are indicative of a governmentalising strategy.

Accessing the most appropriate skills and products requires new 'modalities of engagement' (Ashdown 2011: 36). We have seen that in particular resilience interventions such as the Horn of Africa, the role of the private sector is strongly emphasised as the most efficient and effective way of doing things. The HERR has been very explicit about this in its advice to DFID:

> The private sector can bring professionalism, leadership and management best practice, tools for driving efficiency and managing risk, and the use

of cutting edge technology and information. Such skills need to be con-textualized to the challenges of post-disaster situations through working in partnership with humanitarian organisations and building long-term collab-orative relationships that enable knowledge transfer. (Ashdown 2011: 37)

The private sector is seen here as a 'doer' and public–private partnerships are promoted as the best way to share risks, credit and investment. Such partnerships are seen as means for DFID to operate in an 'increasingly complex humanitarian system' (DFID 2011c: 1). In responding to the HERR, DFID reaffirms its commitment to work with the EU and US, emerging powers, NGOs, the military and the private sector. Clearly this is seen as the natural way of things even though it is the case that the private sector's involvement in resilience-building will have to be stimulated using public finances (DFID 2013d: 10). Engagement with the private sector is assumed to be a necessary strategy without any evi-dence being provided that this does actually work best. This, of course, is connected to a neo-liberal belief in free markets and the role of the global economy, but in terms of contemporary governance perhaps the more pertinent issue is the devolution of power and competences and the belief in the need to activate the 'doing' capacity of the private sphere as well as civil society.

This approach can be considered as a form of global governmentality – understood as an extension of governmentality in relation to governance of the global, international, regional and other extra-domestic spaces (Larner and Walters 2006). This global governmentality works from a distance through invoking private and civil society actors, governing through the market and the competences of the private sector, lowering expectations of what international organisations and Western govern-ments will do directly, while promoting the need for capacity building to enhance practices of good governance. This is transmitted through a normative and normalising discourse that transfers responsibility to local governments, donors and private and civil society actors. This can easily be promoted as agent-centred and empowering as we have seen in the language of the policy documents. The resilience approach operates by placing emphasis on governing through an appeal to the freedom and autonomy of the governed, promoting the ideas of responsibility, self-awareness and self-regulation. However, the global sphere is char-acterised by inequalities in power and resources and poorer states that are in need of international support are deemed to lack the adequate capacities and institutional resources to adequately promote resilience and self-regulation.

This establishes a power relationship between donor and recipient whereby those states receiving 'assistance' from the international community must follow the advice and implement the 'correct' policies. Hence countries receiving assistance are subjected to a system of monitoring and assessment to measure progress in implementing resilience measures. DFID is pushing ahead with developing progress indicators for embedding resilience, with country offices and DFID offices deciding on which indicators are appropriate measures (DFID 2011a: 14). DFID also uses a number of performance indicators to measure its own work (DFID 2013d). Again, this indicates governance from a distance and the shaping of conduct through indicators, peer review and good practice – although given the vagueness and ambiguity in the meaning and use of resilience, international organisations are faced with a difficult task in deciding just how unmeasurable qualities like resilience are to be measured. DFID itself has commissioned a report to look at ways to do this, particularly in relation to levels of exposure, sensitivity and adaptive capacity (Brooks, Aure and Whiteside 2014). This suggests that resilience is, indeed, becoming a tool of global governmentality although not without some debate.

The Resilience Approach of ECHO and the European Union

The EU has a long history of assisting with disaster management and humanitarian response in developing countries. In the main, the European Commission coordinates this through the Directorate General for Humanitarian Aid and Civil Protection (DG ECHO). ECHO was created in 1992 as the European Community Humanitarian Office but has been through several changes, becoming the Directorate-General for Humanitarian Aid in 2004 and incorporating responsibility for civil protection in 2010. It is responsible for emergencies, rehabilitation and reconstruction and longer-term assistance. ECHO takes the lead in formulating policy and managing aid to those non-EU countries suffering from natural or human-made disasters. ECHO is also responsible for the management of civil protection within the EU. Its role has grown in importance as member states increasingly pool resources and channel their aid through the EU. Greater emphasis is placed on the need to coordinate policy and harmonise results, orientation, ownership and coherence. Resilience-building therefore comes into the picture as a means of doing this, emphasising coordination between actors across different levels or scales, perhaps offering a bridge between crisis response and longer-term development planning, and applying DRR as a development, humanitarian and climate change issue (European Commission 2009c: 11).

The EU's definition of resilience combines recovery and restoration with a more radical emphasis on adaptation and change: 'Resilience is the ability of an individual, a household, a community, a country or a region to withstand, adapt, and quickly recover from stresses and shocks such as drought, violence, conflict or natural disaster' (European Commission 2012a: 1). This is said to have two dimensions: the inherent strength of an entity to resist stress and shock and its capacity to bounce back from the impact (European Commission 2012b: 5). A 'multi-faceted strategy' to increase strength and reduce impact aims at both reducing possible risks and improving coping and adaptation mechanisms at local, national and regional levels.

EU documents present resilience strategies as addressing the root causes of crises, by embedding longer-term action in local and national policies. Key components of the strategy are listed as anticipating crises by assessing risks, greater focus on risk reduction, prevention, mitigation and preparedness and efforts to enhance quick response and recovery (European Council 2013: 2). These are seen as playing an essential role in resilience-building based on preventing recurrent crises through tackling root causes via local communities. However, it is also noted that as well as local actors, this agenda must engage with other development partners and multi-lateral actors, notably the United Nations system (European Council 2013: 3).

This fits with accepted development practice across other international organisations and allows for the continuation of capacity-building and strengthening institutions, but fine-tuned to deal with how communities respond to crises. This is done through the promotion of awareness and preparedness – 'in order to empower people to protect themselves and make their livelihoods more resilient to disasters' (European Commission 2009c: 8). Preparedness activities should also link naturally with response and recovery activities. There should be coherence between disaster management activities, often falling within the remit of civil protection organisations, and humanitarian and development activities aimed at capacity building and recovery planning (European Commission 2009c: 10). This is emphasised across all relevant sectors with solutions rooted in local communities, countries and regions. Rather than reflecting a new paradigm, this is consistent with existing state-building approaches, but it does place more emphasis on the 'bottom–up' role of local communities, civil society, local authorities, research institutions and the private sector (European Council 2013: 3).

This is reflected in the EU's 2013 Action Plan for Resilience in Crisis Prone Countries which talks of people-centred approaches that address individual life-cycle risks (European Commission 2013: 3). This places emphasis on the need for individuals themselves to address their resilience strategies in order to make themselves less vulnerable and prone to poverty. At another level up, the plan talks of country-ownership claiming that it is 'primarily a national governments' responsibility to build resilience and to define political, economic, environmental and social priorities accordingly' (European Commission 2013: 3). These national strategies require firm political commitments and accountability, and may require not only technical support but institutional change. As with the DFID approach, it is clearly stated that ultimately individual countries have the responsibility to progress towards resilience (based on meeting key development standards that are decided by the international community) (European Commission 2013: 3). This builds on existing practice that is focused on capacity-building that works by targeting local institutions and actors. Organisations like the EU will help through development 'partnerships', but this will be done from a distance through offering advice and expertise and by setting various standards and benchmarks that should be implemented by the recipient state. The indirect nature of these projects is also reflected in the way that they work through a range of different international organisations and NGOs.

The EU's Action Plan sets out an operational framework for multi-agent partnerships for development cooperation with particular focus on peace and state-building, climate change and DRR, food security and social protection. This plan builds on existing work being done and seeks to consolidate existing initiatives within a holistic approach, ensuring complementary of interventions across different sectors and learning best practice from the effective development of resilience strategies in different regions (European Commission 2013: 5). Of particular importance, therefore, are two major projects being piloted in Africa that form the backbone of the EU's new approach. One is the *Alliance Globale pour l'Initiative Résilience* (AGIR) partnership in the Sahel, the other is Supporting the Horn of Africa's Resilience (SHARE). It should be noted that these are the exact same areas targeted by DFID and are also areas being engaged with by USAID.

The Sahel region of West Africa is a logical place for the EU to get involved in resilience-building. Although a remote and relatively isolated region running below the Sahara Desert, the Sahel has long been a concern for the EU countries because of close geographical and historical ties and continuing relevance to a security strategy focused on terrorism, illegal arms flows, migration, human trafficking and drug trafficking. The AGIR was launched in 2012 after a severe drought and poor harvest affecting eighteen million people in the three core Sahelian states of Mauritania, Mali and Niger as well as Senegal, Gambia, Burkina Faso and Chad. Among the causes identified by the EU were poor access to basic services and education, acute poverty, environmental degradation and rapid population growth. Conflicts in Libya, Côte d'Ivoire and Mali have severely affected the region with the Libyan conflict causing 200,000 Tuareg migrants to return to the region and the Mali conflict displacing 320,000 people (Gubbels 2012a: 3). This has placed huge strain on a region already struggling to provide basic needs in food and protection.

The main EU strategy paper on the region identifies governance as the key issue, suggesting that the Sahel countries struggle to provide basic protection, assistance, development and public services to local populations. The blame is placed on insufficiently decentralised decision-making and the inequitable sharing of revenues of capital-intensive economic activities. It is argued that weak governance in areas like justice, social exclusion, corruption and a lack of education and employment opportunities all contribute to insecurity and drive people either to crime or to terrorist activities (European External Action Service 2011: 3). States in the region are said to have insufficient operational and strategic capacities in the wider security, law enforcement and judicial sectors to control their territory, enforce the law and prevent and respond to the security threats. The EU strategy paper also identifies weak legal frameworks and law enforcement capacity, ineffective border management, and means of gathering, and exchanging information (European External Action Service 2011: 3). The approach of the EU is to try and strengthen security and law enforcement capacities to deal with immediate threats while providing basic social needs to the most marginalised groups with a longer-term aim of building societal resilience against extremism (European External Action Service 2011: 7).

The AGIR initiative also talks of resilience-building in relation to preparedness and response to natural shocks. This includes improving information and early warning systems, the promotion of seasonal social safety nets and pilot projects and activities designed to encourage greater commitment to strengthening resilience and malnutrition reduction by governments (ECHO 2013: 9). Among the problems urgently needing addressing are lack of household resilience to scarcity, over-use of food and water, unregulated soil and water pollution and corruption, particularly in the supply of water (Simon, Mattelaer and Hadfield 2012: 22). Natural and human-made shocks can be dealt with through a combined strategy of enhancing political stability, improving security, good governance, social cohesion and economic and education opportunities, in order to create the conditions for local and national sustainable development.

The SHARE project, focused on Ethiopia, Kenya, Djibouti and Somalia has significant commonalities with AGIR. Like the Sahel, the Horn of Africa combines natural disasters with human conflict. Like AGIR, the SHARE project promotes the combination of emergency response with longer-term solutions. Launched following the 2011 food crisis, the project is aimed at the world's largest refugee crisis, high mortality among both people and livestock as well as rising food and water costs. The EU packages this as a major adaptation of its policy, promoting the SHARE and AGIR projects as important test cases in coordinating humanitarian and development assistance through focusing on resilience (European Commission 2012a: 1). More to the point, it might be noted that this region is still a reminder to Western states of the dangers of direct military intervention. The EU does engage in military activities such as counter-piracy operations (Naval Force Operation Atlanta, NAVFOR). But this is relatively easy to coordinate in comparison to land operations. Indeed, strategy for both regions might be said to be based on limited military operations where necessary and indirect forms of intervention wherever possible.

The EU encourages the development of national resilience strategies, disaster management plans and efficient early-warning systems as well as encouraging innovation in risk management (European Commission 2012a: 2). There is a focus on providing safety nets for the most vulnerable involving work and training, community-based disaster preparation projects, developing early-warning systems and working with the insurance industry (European Commission 2012a: 2). Specific projects include a canal-building programme in Somalia and a productive Safety Net Programme in Ethiopia that provides income for vulnerable people in return for their contribution to infrastructure programmes. A programme against drought in Kenya has contributed to a new early-warning system, while offering institutional support to bodies like the National Drought Management Authority as well as various community-level livelihood projects (European Commission 2012a).

As with Sahel policies, these hardly constitute a ground-breaking new strategy. The EU's *Humanitarian Implementation Plan for the Horn of Africa* might talk of longer-term strategic objectives to strengthen local resilience through disaster preparedness, stronger engagement with DRR stakeholders and encouragement of best practice (European Commission 2012b: 10). However, this does not go much beyond sharing information, encouraging best practice and making assessments (European Council 2008c: 3). The EU's strategy does commit it to working closely with partners in the field. But where this has occurred, the results have been far from satisfactory. For example, the Humanitarian Policy Group reports that the activities of project staff in the Horn of Africa have been undermined by poor knowledge of existing institutions and the various risks and vulnerabilities faced by people in everyday life (Pavanello 2010: 4). Another report on community-based warning systems in Somalia and Ethiopia concludes that participation, coordination and partnerships across different sectors and institutions relied too heavily on external intervention and failed to take account of actual local capacities and skills. This undermined local attempts to build resilience through contributing to decision-making and information-distribution (Issak and Yusef 2010: 6). This highlights the problems of externally imposing 'good governance', however well-meaning such interventions may be. Similar criticisms have been made by Gubbels (2012a, b) in relation to Sahel strategy.

These questions about the EU's application of resilience overseas are accompanied by questions of whether the EU is a divided actor. Most obvious are the differences between member states that have dogged attempts to develop a common foreign and security policy. There are also divisions between different parts of the EU apparatus. While ECHO is the main focus of this section, much of the policy in the Sahel is led by the European External Action Service which has the wider ambition of developing a dynamic European foreign policy. Furthermore, as resilience-building links humanitarian intervention to longer-term strategy it also runs into the area covered by the Directorate General for International Cooperation and Development (DevCo). These bodies have their own strategic interests linked to institutional incentives, bureaucratic conditioning and role identities. ECHO also contains internal divisions between short-term and long-term objectives and between internal and external protection mechanisms. While ECHO claims to focus on providing apolitical emergency assistance and civil protection, the introduction of resilience, in linking emergency aid to longer-term preparedness may cause more problems than it solves.

We can, nevertheless, conclude this section by giving two principal reasons for the EU's uptake of the resilience approach. The first relates to the problems just mentioned and the very clear perception that the EU needs a far more coordinated strategy to disaster management and humanitarian aid. A resilience approach fits with some core concerns of what the EU wants to do and, in theory at least, it emphasises a coordinated approach and the bridging of short-term intervention with longer-term strategy.

Secondly, resilience-building strategies fit neatly with the self-identity of the EU and Commission as special types of actors that take a more facilitative and advisory approach, exercising a 'softer' sort of power which we have described throughout this book as a form of governmentality 'from a distance'. The perceived weaknesses and divisions within the EU over common foreign and security policy can be turned into positive forms of justification for alternative expressions of 'actorness' such as 'civilian' and 'normative power Europe' (Manners 2002). Resilience-building fits with the image of EU interventions as exercising a special type of power while also helping to disguise strategic divisions that inhibit other types of action. The idea of normative power Europe emphasises the EU's international role and identity based on the values of peace, liberty, democracy, rule of law and respect for human rights. Indeed, all these can be found in Article 177 of the original Treaty Establishing the European Community along with the goal of integrating developing countries into the global economy. Other normative aspects of the approach focus on such values as social solidarity, anti-discrimination and, increasingly, good governance. Resilience-building is therefore consistent with such aspirations while helping to disguise, and perhaps ultimately resolve, some of the deeper internal tensions and contradictions. These are strong dynamics that are worth exploring further and which suggest that the EU's motivations for developing a resilience approach are not purely attributable to neo-liberal governmentality.

USAID

The USAID is the main body responsible for US foreign assistance. It defines resilience to recurrent crisis as 'the ability of people, households, communities, countries, and systems to mitigate, adapt to and recover from shocks and stresses in a manner that reduces chronic vulnerability and facilitates inclusive growth' USAID (2012c). An USAID mission statement[1] links the eradication of poverty to the creation of 'resilient, democratic societies that are able to realize their potential'. Eliminating poverty, it is argued, requires inclusive, sustainable growth, promoting self-reliant societies, effective and legitimate government and developing human capital. This weaves together most of the themes already discussed, seeing resilience both in terms of governance, sustainability and a more human-centred set of capacities. Resilient societies are democratic, with 'healthy, well-nourished, and educated populations; and environmental sustainability'. They have 'legitimate, inclusive, and accountable institutions', they respect human rights and they 'advance freedom, human dignity and development'. They are able to manage conflict, mitigate the impact of disasters and forestall crises. There is, of course, a bit of everything in these statements, so an examination of more specific USAID strategies is required.

In *Building Resilience to Recurrent Crisis,* USAID sets out its policy and programme guidance on resilience. As already noted, such an

---

[1] See www.usaid.gov/who-we-are/mission-vision-values.

approach is regarded as combining short and long-term humanitarian assistance, reducing vulnerability while establishing the basis for longer-term development (USAID 2012a: 6). Resilience plays a central role in coordinating strategic planning between development and humanitarian assistance, with objectives set out as:

1. *Joint Problem Analysis and Objective Setting* so teams have a common understanding of the underlying causes of recurrent crisis.
2. *Intensified, Coordinated Strategic Planning around Resilience* to ensure that we anticipate risks, vulnerabilities, and probable humanitarian need when deciding on development strategies.
3. *Mutually Informed Project Designs and Procurements* to enable the layering, integrating, and sequencing of humanitarian and development assistance.
4. *Robust Learning* so we can develop the appropriate indicators, make midcourse corrections, and share lessons learned across the Agency and with external partners. (USAID 2012a: 66)

The resilience strategy is aimed at reducing barriers to organisational change, aiming to build leadership at all levels, empowering 'solution-holders close to the problem' and 'addressing unnecessary roadblocks' that frustrate these objectives (USAID 2012a: 66). Such approaches, as we have already seen, connect humanitarian assistance to development programmes through country-led strategies to build resilience.

This sounds empowering for all sides. But it is premised on the equally familiar fatalism characteristic of the way resilience policy is framed. Hence: 'While we cannot stop shocks from occurring, we can do much more to help people withstand and recover from them, creating a platform for their continued development. By layering, integrating, and sequencing humanitarian and development assistance, we can further the objectives of each to a greater extent than by programming in isolation' (USAID 2012a: 68). Given that the main resilience strategies govern through a denial of the possibility to stop shocks from happening and also by denying the responsibility of the international community to provide major assistance in preventing or alleviating such shocks,

[USAID instead] strives to build resilience so that, in the face of stresses and shocks, the communities where we work are prepared and able to take anticipatory action to avoid major losses, and in the event that crisis results, they are able to respond effectively and build back better than before. This continued path of growth – even in the face of potential setbacks – is a critical component of our work. (USAID 2012a: 69)

The main way of achieving this is to enhance the adaptive capacity of communities. Adaptive capacity is here understood as 'the ability to quickly and effectively respond to new circumstances [based on] ... ensuring that social systems, inclusive governance structures, and economic opportunities are in place' (USAID 2012a: 61). As in any complex system, the components of adaptive capacity are numerous and wide-ranging. Hence there is an attempt to conceptualise 'adaptive facilitators', here understood as 'intangible elements of social capital and patterns that create an enabling environment for institutions and resources to mitigate shocks, recover from them and potentially "bounce back better" after a shock occurs' (Bujones, Jaskiewicz, Linakis and McGirr 2013: 12). More specifically, adaptive facilitators in the political subsystem includes those actions, linkages and behaviour that that allow communities and institutions to actively engage with one other and, in a somewhat conservative definition, 'positively contribute to the stability of the political order, processes, decision-making and transfer of power' (Bujones, Jaskiewicz, Linakis and McGirr 2013: 17). This contradicts an early claim that variation in context and the relative importance of different facilitators means resilient institutions and resources require the creation of an environment that is 'adaptable, collaborative, innovative, and responsive' (Bujones, Jaskiewicz, Linakis and McGirr 2013: 12). Unless we understand a stable political order as one that is always adaptable, these arguments reflect some uncertainty in terms of who or what it is that should adapt and what it is that should remain stable.

More likely the USAID approach is still finding its way in deciding whether to place more emphasis on the adaptive capacity of communities and individuals, or to take a more established line of defending existing institutions and practices. The latter remains prominent in the USAID approach as seen in the promotion of good governance measures. These reflect existing concerns of state-building and development strategy:

Functioning institutions of good governance and democratic accountability are essential to developing a country's adaptive capacity and its ability to address and reduce risk. Good governance requires institutions and processes that are transparent, accountable, and responsive to the people they serve and that promote positive state-society relationships (including a strong civil society and a vibrant private sector). Governance capacity determines the ability of the state to respond effectively to crises and to address the long-term development needs required to effectively address recurrent issues. Furthermore, good governance is crucial to prevent and mitigate conflict, which plays a detrimental role in many of the communities where we are applying a resilience approach, and which has, in past efforts to build resilience, stood decisively in the way of sustainable progress. (USAID 2012a: 612)

Such statements are worth emphasising in the face of claims that resilience represents a radically new agenda. In this instance, resilience fits in with existing practice. In the field of climate change too, the USAID approach is very much focused on a governance agenda. The main solutions are to be found in good practices in democratic governance, hence USAID will prioritise capacity building and developing robust institutions at the appropriate governance level (USAID 2012b: 9). Mitigation requires inclusive and transparent decision-making with USAID helping enhance government capacity to promote clean energy and low emission development through policy, regulatory and market reforms (USAID 2012b: 12). Success of the strategy depends upon host country enablement, local ownership, good governance and political will to enable countries to take the lead in their own development. This requires an inclusive dialogue between stakeholders at all levels, promoting inclusive and accountable governance and linkages between different levels of governance. The idea behind country-owned strategies for development can create a 'double compact' between the government and the international community and between government and citizens (USAID 2012a: 616). Resilience programming is said to be rooted in society and responsive to community needs.

USAID has been involved in a range of initiatives to promote its resilience strategy. In particular, it has followed the EU's initiatives in the Sahel and Horn of Africa regions. This is justified because of a clear and significant commitment from partner countries and the international community to implement a resilience building approach and undertake operational changes (USAID 2012a: 613). It is believed that concentrating efforts in certain areas will increase the ability of these regions to respond quickly and effectively to new circumstances, improve their ability to deal with risk, and improve the socioeconomic conditions of vulnerable populations. Over the longer-term, it is believed that this will both reduce humanitarian need in these areas and help USAID measure its own progress (USAID 2012c).

The strategic plan for the Sahel region repeats familiar arguments for combining humanitarian and development assistance to reduce risk, build resilience and facilitate inclusive economic growth. Its first component is 'to increase sustainable economic wellbeing defined by income, food access, assets (broadly conceived) and adaptive capacity' with sub-components focused on diversifying economic opportunities, improved livestock and crop production, better access to financial services and more competitive food value chains. There is strong focus on private sector investment. A development credit authority mechanism will encourage private sector investment in the financial services sector. The second component aims to strengthen institutions and governance. This relates to natural resources and conflict and disaster risk management. This component emphasises the need to strengthen government capacity to coordinate and build resilience. The third component concerns health and nutrition (USAID 2013b).

A somewhat similar plan for the Horn of Africa talks of increasing adaptive capacity to resist shocks such as drought, improving ability to address and reduce risk and improving the social and economic conditions of vulnerable populations (USAID 2013a: 3). As with similar initiatives, the stated aim is to join humanitarian work to longer-term development plans. USAID's report talks of a shared resilience building framework between its experts in development and humanitarian relief, looking in particular at the dynamics of change in pastoralist systems (USAID 2013a: 6). It identifies five priorities – economic opportunities, livelihood strategies, nutrition and health services, environment, water, sanitation and management and, access to education (USAID 2013a: 8).

Staying in this region, USAID's Kenya programme talks of empowering communities and putting local stakeholders in charge of identifying opportunities and threats, mapping local resources and identifying their development needs. This is done through community development action plans which address issues such as diversification of livelihood opportunities, community management of natural resources, improving market access, conflict resolution, DRR and improving nutritional outcomes (USAID 2013a: 16). In Ethiopia USAID supports the Building Resilience Project, supporting resource mapping and cash-for-work natural resource rehabilitation activities such as work on grazing land and water schemes. There is also support for a vaccination campaign for livestock (USAID 2013a: 22). Ethiopia's Country Development Cooperation Strategy, supported by USAID in alignment with the Ethiopian government's National Transformation Plan, promotes resilience and local-level development strategies with a particular focus on climatic and economic shocks, aiming for the sustainability and expansion of relevant economic, social, political and agricultural systems (USAID 2012a: 621). All these programmes will be closely monitored before USAID decides on committing more significant resources. Resilience-building initiatives in the Sahel and Horn of Africa are ongoing processes, part of a learning curve for combining humanitarian and development work (USAID 2013a: 27).

As well as these projects, USAID also has significant involvement in the Global Resilience Partnership which was established in 2014 by USAID, the Rockefeller Foundation and the Swedish International Development Cooperation Agency (Sida). The approach of the partnership can be considered through the lens of global governmentality with emphasis placed on such techniques as 'the adoption, scaling and integration of information tools, methods and machines that promote evidence-based decision-making and/or accelerate the deployment of innovative solutions'. Measurement approaches to 'quantify and qualify the financial and social impact of resilience efforts', tools that can 'help measure, visualize and predict resilience needs'. It seeks to promote innovative and unconventional financing instruments and to fill knowledge gaps in areas relevant to resilience such as gender and social capital. The approach talks of the world's 'complex and interrelated resilience challenges', arguing that these can be tackled by better use of data and information, evidence-based tools and innovations and by connecting governments with civil society and the resources and expertise of the private sector.[2] For all USAID actions datasets play a dual role, first as the basis for assessment of the effectiveness of its own actions, second in order to determine the effectiveness of institutions, monitor performance and enforce regulations

[2] See www.rockefellerfoundation.org/our-work/initiatives/
global-resilience-partnership/.

(USAID 2012b: 16). The launch of a Sahel resilience learning programme is one such case where resilience programming will be driven
by certain objectives and assessment criteria produced by resilience
models (Mosel and Levine 2014: 7).

Therefore, it seems that there is not anything particularly exceptional about USAID's resilience strategy and that it represents a fairly
conventional approach to global governance. If seen from a governmentality perspective, it represents a familiar case of 'governing from
a distance' by emphasising local ownership while using techniques of
monitoring and performance measurement, promoting good governance and institutional capacity-building and merely repackaging existing aid and development programmes. However, this misses some of
the nuance present in the USAID approach as the meaning of resilience
is still being worked out. For example, a more complex framework is
outlined in a paper that, while not officially representing the views of
USAID, has been developed for USAID's office of Conflict Management
and Mitigation. Here there remains a focus on issues of poor governance, security and legitimacy within fragile states. However, from the
outset, the focus emphasises the role of communities as much as institutions, seeking to strengthen community resilience and the gaps in societies vis-à-vis shocks and stressors. This is promoted as 'an alternative
to the traditional root cause approaches by looking into strengthening communal, societal or institutional abilities to withstand or better
cope with different stresses that they experience' (Bujones, Jaskiewicz,
Linakis and McGirr 2013: 5). Community, as the main unit of analysis, is understood as 'a group of individuals that share similar characteristics and levels of exposure to certain shocks and stressors' while
shocks are understood as sudden events that impact on communities
and stressors as longer-term pressures that increase vulnerability while
undermining stability. A country's resilience is ultimately, it is suggested, 'an aggregate of its communities' (Bujones, Jaskiewicz, Linakis
and McGirr 2013: 4).

The framework adopts a combination of contextual and factor
analysis that examines a country's history, key actors, structures, and
communities and how they might be subject to various shocks and
stressors while also looking at the community's access to mechanisms
that allow it to mitigate these, adapt to them or recover. The approach
remains concerned with established governance issues like institutional performance and legitimacy, but adds adaptive facilitators

comprising networks, behaviour, values and norms, innovation and institutional memory. They influence how shocks are absorbed and how stressors develop within a society. The combination of these leads to an assessment of community resilience.

Institutions provide the rules and regulations that govern communities; resources are the tangible assets available to them; and adaptive facilitators are intangible elements of social capital and patterns. Institutions, resources and adaptive facilitators are critical because together they constitute the means by which all actors are able to mitigate, adapt and recover from shocks and stressors. (Bujones, Jaskiewicz, Linakis and McGirr 2013: 6)

These intangible elements are crucial to the distinctiveness of the resilience approach because they rely on human and social qualities that cannot be reduced to calculative behaviour. However, as we shall argue in Chapter 5, the understanding of these remains caught within a logic reminiscent of the social capital approach of Putnam and others that tries to fill the gaps in market rationality with a more social element.

Through informal structures and networks, people engage with one another, with social and political groups as well as with the government and political institutions. Attitudes and innovativeness are considered important human attributes. Within the political subsystem, attitudes are important since these include trust in politicians and government and feelings of fair treatment and inclusion. The less formal aspects of this process may provide a better basis for the legitimacy of a system, particularly when contrasted with external attempts at formal institution building (Bujones, Jaskiewicz, Linakis and McGirr 2013: 17). Innovation addresses how people can learn from experiences and adapt their behaviour in response to shocks and stressors. It is argued that innovation 'allows institutions, communities, and individuals the opportunity to think critically and to challenge existing structures that are in place and create new ideas in order to "bounce back better"' (Bujones, Jaskiewicz, Linakis and McGirr 2013: 13). These human attributes are especially important when service delivery is absent and communities need to think critically and develop new coping mechanisms. This supports the more 'transformational' view of resilience which sees crises as an opportunity to modernise. For example, in the write-up of a USAID workshop on the Horn of Africa, lip service is paid to the need to strengthen traditional coping mechanisms, but in fact the aim of resilience is stated as transformation of communities through moving people and resources out of traditional agriculture and herding as well as the need to modernise these traditional sectors, their technologies and their physical and human capital (Headey and Kennedy 2005: 5).

In summary, our discussion reflects a challenging element in USAID's thinking that moves beyond a purely institutional approach by introducing informal networks and intangible human capacities. It does not go as far as to challenge the institution-building approach – indeed, it supports it – but it introduces an important emphasis on community resilience that is far more characteristic of Anglo-Saxon approaches that devolve responsibility downwards onto populations and individuals.

German Overseas Policy

In Germany, the Federal Foreign Office (Auswärtiges Amt, AA) is mainly responsible for humanitarian aid and immediate disaster response while the BMZ focuses on longer-term measures. The Germany Agency for International Cooperation (Deutsche Gesellschaft für Internationale Zusammenarbeit (GIZ) is the main implementing agency, responsible for implementing development projects in agreement with BMZ. In 2011, reform of the ministries gave the Federal Foreign Office control of emergency aid and BMZ responsibility for what became known as 'Transitional and Development Assistance' (TDA) which takes a longer-term approach to building the resilience of populations in affected areas. There was actually a large shift of resources in favour of emergency aid and away from BMZ's TDA budget. New strategy papers outlined the objectives of TDA with a focus on fragile states, countries at risk from climate change and natural disasters and support for reconstruction projects.

The Federal Foreign Office works within a board framework for humanitarian assistance, seeking to offer quick, effective and flexible assistance in accordance with international standards and through international cooperation, notably through UN-led humanitarian assistance (Federal Foreign Office 2012: 4). However, it also noted that while humanitarian needs rise, budgetary constraints are also increasing and that greater coordination between actors is required.

One way of doing this is to place greater emphasis on preparedness and improved response capabilities. These would include better risk analysis, assessment and management, more early warning systems, quicker response to warnings, better training for aid workers and other enhanced humanitarian response capabilities (Federal Foreign Office 2012: 5). At the centre of this emerging new strategy is resilience. As the main strategy of the Federal Foreign Office states:

The Federal Ministry for Economic Cooperation and Development has at its disposal the newly developed recovery and rehabilitation instrument, which being part of development cooperation follows the principles of that sphere. Recovery and rehabilitation is aimed at strengthening the resilience of local communities, civil society players and (state) institutions at the dynamic interface between the Federal Foreign Office's humanitarian assistance and long-term development cooperation through recovery and rehabilitation. (Federal Foreign Office 2012: 7)

This restates many of the resilience themes discussed and is outlined in detail in the new approach to Transitional Development Assistance, outlined in a BMZ strategy paper. The need to strengthen the resilience of individuals, local communities, civil society actors and state institutions is reiterated in relation to natural hazards and climate change. The context is set out as one of complex crisis of a non-linear character (BMZ 2013: 5). The multi-dimensional nature of these crises requires effective coordination of inter-connected measures bridging the short, medium and longer-term in line with the established approach of Linking Relief, Rehabilitation and Development (LRRD). This policy, initiated in the 1990s, is related to sustainability and, in the new formulation of transitional development assistance, links such assistance to longer-term structures and programmes developed by state and civil society actors (BMZ 2013: 8). TDA is seen as a comprehensive and holistic approach that seeks to integrate national approaches into the Hyogo Framework for Action 2005, covering all aspects of mitigation, prevention and preparedness (BMZ 2013: 12).

The argument for resilience takes a capacity-building approach, combining an emphasis on people's capacity with the more traditional focus on institutional capacity-building. Local capacity-building requires longer-term measures, allowing people to improve their livelihoods through their own efforts. This is in order to enable people and institutions 'to cope with situations and adapt accordingly' (BMZ 2013: 8). TDA seeks to strengthen the capacities of state, civil society and private-sector actors and facilitate their better working together. We also find the theme of a flexible and pragmatic approach, taken in response 'to the uncertainty and challenges that affect planning and implementation in fragile contexts' (BMZ 2013: 8). In this sense, the arguments for resilience are rather similar to other organisations, although it is presented as a radical reorganisation of German overseas policy. BMZ openly acknowledges that it takes its definition of resilience from DFID (2011a), arguing that it is 'the ability of people and institutions – whether individuals, households, local communities or states – to withstand acute shocks or chronic stress caused by fragile situations, crises, violent conflict or extreme natural events, and to adapt and recover quickly without compromising their medium and longer-term prospects' (BMZ 2013: 7). This is a rather banal definition of resilience, but its entry into the German discourse has opened up some space for a discussion of where the emphasis should lie.

BMZ commissioned the Humanitarian Policy Group to write a paper on the challenges of promoting resilience in places where strong institutions and governance practices are absent. In such cases, resilience must focus much more on the role of people rather than at the level of systems. The starting point is to look at people's exposure, vulnerabilities and coping abilities. This raises issues such as how people adapt to problems, their ability to maintain an acceptable level of well-being and how they might recover an acceptable level of welfare following a crisis (Mosel and Levine 2014: 3). This focuses more on the social, political and economic aspects of people's lives, rather than purely technical issues of DRR and development (Mosel and Levine 2014: 7).

However, this response to BMZ's work reflects tensions in the resilience debate. On the one hand, it is quite critical of technical and institutional approaches that overlook genuine human needs. On the other hand, this human turn is still caught within a governmentality of populations. On the former, critical approach the paper argues:

Much programming is based on a naïve belief about how a project will play out institutionally, failing to take into consideration the way in which resources and power are contested – and that the people whose resilience needs building are precisely those with the least ability to contest. This requirement is true in all situations, but is most crucial – and hardest to do well – in difficult places. (Mosel and Levine 2014: 14)

Resilience is therefore seen as opening up new human potential by examining how people make choices and what constraints they might be under. However, this still tends to fall under the framework of individual autonomy and human capital. It looks at vulnerability at the micro level, while macro conditions are considered an 'enabling environment' (Mosel and Levine 2014: 11). Wider conditions are considered in terms of constraints on human capacities and the solution is to turn from generic institutional solutions to more of a focus on local institutions, particular governmental agencies and human capacity-building. Ultimately this human turn is also a pragmatic turn, realist in the sense of 'having less ambitious objectives, being more modest about the ability of external actors to effect change on their own and being much more open about the degree of risk that must be run' (Mosel and Levine 2014: 16).

This turn reflects a governmentalisation of populations insofar as it remains narrowly focused on human capacities and indeed, an even narrower focus on adaptive capacity. The broader context is understood as 'ensuring that development policy and interventions support people's own ability to deal with unknown futures (or, to use the current jargon, their "adaptive capacity"' (Mosel and Levine 2014: 12). As Irina Mosel and Simon Levine elaborate:

Adaptive capacity means people's ability to make and realise well-informed decisions in the future. Adaptive capacity is important in all development situations, but it is especially critical in difficult places, which are typically rapidly changing situations, where the ability to cope with change is key – and where people may not be able to rely on others (e.g. their state, elites) without exploitation. Supporting adaptive capacity is slower and more difficult than transplanting new technologies or providing assets, and it needs very different skills from the ones technicians generally possess. It will thus have significant implications for staffing and resources. (Mosel and Levine 2014: 12)

Elsewhere the adaptive capacity approach is understood as 'self-help', so the Federal Foreign Ministry talks of measures to boost self-help capabilities through the involvement of local stakeholders and aid recipients (Federal Foreign Office 2012: 4). The German Red Cross (GRC), a major partner in German resilience strategy also emphasises self-help, but talks of this in relation to the 'underlying general social, cultural, environmental, physical, financial and political conditions' (German Red Cross 2014: 15).

All these discussions point to a complex picture in Germany where the Anglo-Saxon language of capacities and self-help, normally understood as a means of governmentalising populations through shifting responsibility on to communities and individuals, is being gradually introduced. Yet at the same time, there remains a focus on people's real needs, on social conditions and on the need for protection. This comes out in debates about the role of civil society where again there is a clash between the more established socio-cultural framework, and the new Anglo-Saxon discourse.

The BMZ approach emphasises the importance of civil society's active involvement in political decision-making. It argues that state structures can only be resilient if they are in constructive dialogue with society, responding to people's needs. These relations should be understood as 'inherently political processes' rather than purely technical ones (BMZ 2009: 15). To summarise:

German development cooperation therefore does not limit its support to state institutions, but also regards their roots in society, the legitimacy of state actions, society as a whole and the interfaces between state and society as central elements in sustainable state-building processes. In this sense it is linked to the promotion of political involvement in all its dimensions of cooperation. (BMZ 2009: 15)

This is important and reflects the social turn in thinking about these issues, placing greater emphasis on 'different political and social situations, the socio-cultural settings and the individual needs of the partner countries' (BMZ 2009: 13). However, alongside this social understanding lies a much more instrumental account of civil society:

Strengthening civil society enables it to better fulfil its role as a critical but constructive watchdog and as a lobby. It also promotes democratic consciousness among the citizens, promotes the integration of disadvantaged groups and helps to bring greater transparency to policy-making. (BMZ 2009: 8)

Here civil society, rather than being an important socio-cultural context, becomes an instrumental means for ensuring that states adhere to a good governance agenda as determined by international organisations like the World Back. Civil society is regarded as a 'watchdog' for holding the state to account in such areas as democracy and the rule of law, efficiency and transparency and cooperation with the international community (BMZ 2009: 14). This is ironic given that the same document later notes the problematic relationship between certain civil society actors and external funders where dependence on external funds leads such groups to assume the priorities of the donors rather than representing the concerns of the local people in political processes (BMZ 2009: 25). Again, we might note the tensions in German overseas policy between a genuine concern for social and political processes, and a more instrumental approach that reflects the pervasive influence of neo-liberal governmentality within the wider field of international development and the Anglo-Saxon dominance of the main international organisations and donors.

Finally, we can highlight some of the tensions between neo-liberal governmentality and a more sympathetic understanding of socio-cultural context by looking at the approach of the GRC which is a major player in the development of German resilience strategy in this area. GRC's Resilience Framework outlines its main objectives which, in line with BMZ strategy, focuses on building resilient communities and enhancing their ability to overcome shocks, adapt and recover. The GRC looks at how these resilient communities can develop by looking at their coping mechanisms and capacity to identify and deal with problems. The interesting point here is that it is suggested that communities already have traditional coping mechanisms for reacting to crises and emergencies so that stress should be on local ownership. As the GRC says: 'people know precisely what needs they have in their community and what measures to take in order to further strengthen their coping capacities' (German Red Cross 2014: 318). This is in contrast to the arguments found in the USAID paper in the Horn of Africa which questions traditional coping mechanisms and suggests people develop a more entrepreneurial approach in dealing with local problems (Headey and Kennedy 2012: 2).

The GRC approach also places emphasis on building networks with external stakeholders while also recognising the way communities are able to organise themselves through self-help measures in order to optimise their coping capacities (German Red Cross 2014: 318). Access to knowledge is recognised as another important factor in building resilience among communities, allowing people in less developed countries to understand their vulnerabilities and risks and develop appropriate strategies to adjust and adapt (German Red Cross 2014: 318). Although the emphasis is on communities, there is a recognition of the importance of robust physical infrastructure and access to the services (German Red Cross 2014: 319).

As with other German arguments about resilience, there is a tension between the more social emphasis of established policy and the individualist, neo-liberal language characteristic of much Anglo-Saxon resilience discourse. When the GRC talks of 'the strengthening of the self-help capacities and coping mechanisms of particularly vulnerable individuals and groups in developing countries' we find a peculiar use of neo-liberal language, if not intentions. Elsewhere, the GRC says that the strengthening of resilience means not only providing protection against natural hazards, but 'comprehensively reducing the underlying factors of vulnerability' such as health risks, food security, access to water and sanitation and to social services. These social measures are regarded as at least as important as adaptation to the consequences of climate change and DRR measures. Indeed, strengthening resilience has political, socio-cultural, economic and ecological dimensions. It is therefore necessary to work with governmental authorities to strengthen health systems, land use and disaster management (German Red Cross 2014: 329). It is stressed that we cannot replace the role of governmental structures and that donors must work with political decision-makers, who are called upon to support the population in strengthening resilience. This responsibility may not be delegated to civil society actors (German Red Cross 2014: 330).

This is particularly interesting because in effect such delegation lies at the heart of Anglo-Saxon governmentality. In particular, the Anglo-Saxon approach wishes to govern through a denial of the responsibility of the international community by governmentalising the behaviour of national governments and civil society groups. This sums up the tensions in the German approach to resilience. As it becomes an increasingly influential idea, it brings with it Anglo-Saxon arguments about devolving responsibility to civil society. Yet German discussions of resilience understand this slightly differently and still talk about such things as the need to recognise that the process of change should come from within society that we ought to value those initiatives that come out of civil society, rather than just seeing them as a means to achieve a larger strategy (BMZ 2014: 5).

But in other ways the emergence of resilience in this sphere of German policy-making is in line with dominant trends within the international community. BMZ writes that the quality of transitional development assistance is maintained though compliance with international standards and principles of cooperation, particularly those of the OECD. This covers mechanisms of planning, implementation and evaluation based on an analysis of needs, effectiveness, efficiency and sustainability. Moreover, these are in line with the Post-Hyogo Framework for Action and the Global Platform for DRR, on the basis of the Principles of Good Humanitarian Donorship (Federal Foreign Office 2012: 5; BMZ 2013: 9). TDA compliance with international standards requires detailed analysis of its effectiveness, efficiency and sustainability with all results and impacts subject to an ongoing monitoring process (BMZ 2013: 9).

French Efforts to Build Resilience Overseas

The main French development agency, the Agence Française de Développement (AFD) goes along with the idea of resilience, but not in any meaningful way. It participates in events with partners like DFID that discuss resilience-building in various regions and it is a supporter of the AGIR project discussed above, mainly due to French interests in the region. Otherwise, discussion of resilience is sporadic, although there is reason to believe that usage of the term will increase.

The Strategic Orientation Plan for 2012–16 provides some familiar contextualisation, arguing that we live in a rapidly changing international environment requiring long-term development activities that help communities build sustainable conditions to meet their priority needs. AFD projects must pay particular attention to social and environmental dimensions with an emphasis on sustainable development and impact on climate change. France's development seeks 'differentiated geographical partnerships' with priority given to sub-Saharan Africa and the Mediterranean. AFD has a targeted approach, particularly towards fragile States (AFD 2012a: 1). In such countries, AFD's declared strategy is to focus on preventative measures to reduce vulnerability and to promote resilience. This relates to insecure environments in both post-conflict countries and to those places faced with major natural disasters. AFD will work to gain a comprehensive understanding of situations, tensions and stakeholder interests seeing to combine rapid results with longer-term institution strengthening (AFD 2012a: 10).

An examination of AFD's annual reports gives an indication of just how much, or little, resilience has affected thinking. The 2014 report mentions resilience just twice. It is used to confirm that we live in an increasingly interdependent world where challenges need to be addressed through new growth and development models. These must be 'more resilient, less emissive, and even better able to fulfil the world's economic and social aspirations' (AFD 2014: 7). Elsewhere the report talks of support for a project in the Eastern part of Burkina Faso to develop resilience to both climate change and economic vagaries among residents (AFD 2014: 22). The 2013 report mentions resilience just once and this is in relation to psychosocial services that aim to increase the resilience of individuals, families and communities affected by conflicts or natural catastrophes (AFD 2013: 35). This reflects the much stronger influence of psychology on French conceptions of resilience (Cyrulnik 2009) as opposed to the ecological or systems approach mainly discussed here. The 2012 report mentions how AFD does not intervene directly in humanitarian emergencies, but funds projects that can alleviate the causes of fragility and reinforce the resilience of societies (AFD 2012b: 34).

If we go back a few years further we can see that although resilience is absent from discussions, the context for a more resilience-friendly approach is clearly already outlined. AFD, in *Adapting French Aid to the Challenges of a Changing World*, talks of how development assistance is undergoing fundamental change and that it 'is increasingly called on to help each developing country to design and implement public policies that address today's national and international challenges' (AFD 2008: 11). As with the other approaches discussed, this is founded on a fatalistic view of global change in 'a world of limited resources', where 'each country needs to find its proper place in the "new deal" of globalisation' (AFD 2008: 11). Strong emphasis is placed on research, knowledge and information as the means to help countries capitalise on their assets. As we have seen with other approaches to resilience, the French justifications now recognise the challenges of coordination, claiming that the increasing number of international aid providers – and an acceptance of the primary role of the private sector – requires the strengthening of donor coordination and more innovative partnerships and alliances. The strategy also emphasises the importance of measuring results and impacts to ensure accountability. These indicators will be harmonised and aggregated with those of other international donors as AFD radically develops its monitoring strategy and evaluation mechanisms in line with international partners (AFD 2008: 6).

Understandably, work in the area of environmental sustainability is caught up in the discourse of resilience and adaptation. It is noticeable that the French Global Environment Facility (FFEM), with its strong focus on sustainability, has argued for the importance of adaptation. FFEM was created in 1994 to finance development projects and has contributed to such projects in areas such as climate change, biodiversity and land degradation. It has representatives of five government ministries on its steering committee including AFD, Foreign Affairs and International Development (MAEDI) and Ecology, Sustainable Development and Energy (MEDDE). Through their focus on mitigation and adaptation initiatives all these bodies have had some engagement with the idea of resilience. In providing finance for various projects, FFEM states that it will prioritise those that improve the resilience of ecosystems or help combat desertification. A priority area is the development of sustainable agricultural production systems. Where resilience is mentioned, it is in the context of either the resilience of societies to climate change or the resilience of ecosystems. The meaning of these or potential differences between the resilience of systems and the resilience of societies is not discussed. This suggests that resilience remains a term rather than a significant concept in its own right. In dealing with priority challenges such as land degradation, sustainable agriculture and integrated costal and maritime zones management, FFEM's common theme is 'mitigation, adaptation and resilience to climate change' (FFEM 2014: 10).

Elsewhere the Commissariat general au développement durable (2012) has taken up resilience in some of its work, for example, in the protection of counties under risk of natural disaster, emphasising the importance of working with local actors to identify the best forms of individual and collective behaviour likely to strengthen resilience. It has launched a project on integrated territorial resilience to help different actors – such as states, communities, NGOS and the private sector – best analyse the source of vulnerabilities and coping mechanisms. It notes the importance of flexibility and adaptation and the need to maintain basic functioning in the face of threats.

In summary, the uptake of the resilience discourse in France is slow, but unavoidable given the other international actors in this field. It is safe to predict that it will become more visible year by year. Overseas policy is an area where perceived Anglo-Saxon ideas are less contentious, indeed they are implicitly accepted in most existing work. This is certainly the case in Germany where BMZ has readily borrowed ideas from DFID and other international agencies. The French approach follows national traditions of scepticism towards the Anglophone sphere which explains the lukewarm uptake of resilience-thinking. However, there are few other obstacles to the notion become more prominent and it is likely that French overseas policy will follow that of Germany in become more and more resilience-friendly. Other groups in France have been quicker to embrace resilience that AFD. However, as far back as 2008, AFD was laying out a new strategic framework within which a notion of resilience could develop. The diversity of development situations, issues, stakeholders and relationships, and the rapid pace of change are said to be presenting beneficiary countries and donors with increasingly complex situations. In this context, AFD has noted the need to develop a new strategy backed by a wide range of technical and financial instruments (AFD 2008: 12). More frequent use of the term resilience will complement this perspective while probably not making much difference in practice.

Analysis: Resilience as Global Governmentality

In this analytical section we set out why resilience should be considered an emerging part of a system of global governmentality, understood in relation to governance of the global, the international and other extra-domestic spaces. We have seen how resilience thinking in the area of international intervention is dominated by an Anglo-Saxon point of view that can be summarised as: (1) governance from a distance through facilitation and monitoring, (2) the attempted devolution of responsibility for being resilient and managing crises, (3) the promotion of civil society and the private sector, (4) the encouragement of initiative and enterprise in the face of challenges and (5) the idea of crises and disasters as transformative opportunities, particularly as argued in the documents of USAID.[3] We look at some of these issues in relation to the UK's DFID before considering whether other countries – or in this case, the EU – have their own reasons for adopting resilience. Indeed, it will be argued that although the EU has largely adopted DFID's approach to resilience, it has its own specific reasons for doing so.

Resilience has emerged as an important way to articulate certain overseas policy objectives, in particular as a way to link short term emergency intervention with longer-term development. All countries and organisations make this argument and use resilience to support a more-integrated and coordinated policy. This is clearly articulated in the UK government's approach which emphasises the need for better coordination of different partners – governments, NGOs, the UN and others – in order to integrate resilience and DRR with work on climate change and conflict prevention, improving the coherence of links between development and humanitarian work (DFID 2011d: 10–11). Yet at the same time as the UK government emphasises greater coordination and integration, it also uses resilience to stress the need for devolved responsibility and local ownership, two key elements of contemporary global governmentality. The coordinated action of the international community of which the UK plays a central role is in fact 'limited' to a support role with the main emphasis now placed on local, national and regional actors including governments, civil society and the private sector. While the international community supports these 'partners', we saw that it is ultimately a particular government's responsibility to build the capacity of its population to resist and adapt to shocks (DFID 2011b: 1).

Global governmentality, like domestic governmentality, works from a distance through invoking private and civil society actors while lowering expectations of what international organisations and Western governments will do directly. Governments are given the opportunity direct their own national development and emergency prevention strategies while engaging with local groups and stakeholders. While governance is devolved, international actors appear to be engaged as 'partners' offering a certain amount of aid and investment as well

---

[3] Or as the World Bank puts it: 'As the world changes, new opportunities and possibilities, as well as risks and complications, continually arise. Rejecting or ignoring change can lead to stagnation and impoverishment. In contrast, embracing change and proactively dealing with risks can open the way to sustained progress' (World Bank 2014: 58).

as providing knowledge and expertise in return for commitments to good governance. The dominant discourse in international intervention claims to have learned the lessons of past failures of intervention and state-building by switching to a less direct strategy of intervention with an emphasis on building or supporting local capacities. This argument simultaneously responsibilises local actors and governments while also lessening the responsibilities of the international community. Now the prevailing view is that the international community has neither the ability nor the obligation to intervene and that its best role is to encourage responsible local agency. This does not mean an outright rejection of previous approaches to global governance. It is more like a recalibration of the techniques of global governmentality that places more emphasis on local agency backed up with mechanisms to ensure compliance with international norms and standards. Resilience helps in the argument that local agents need to adapt their behaviour and expectations in the face of complex problems that the international community either cannot, or does not, want to deal with itself. Past failures of humanitarian intervention and state-building are used to justify retreat from certain global and domestic obligations, while reinforcing the need for a certain type of governance in the face of significant shocks and threats (Joseph 2016).

Hence governing from a distance by shaping the conduct of conduct – here understood as the conduct of national and local governments, officials and key actors – can be seen in policy areas like development, poverty reduction, and disaster preparedness. These approaches regulate the behaviour of states – or the key societal and governmental actors – from a distance through encouraging them to 'freely' act in a responsible way. Responsibility is defined in relation to the norms of the international community (governments, donors, international organisations and INGOs), civil society and the private sphere. This situation might be described as an example of multi-level governmentality. Normally we would expect governmentality to work directly on populations or communities in order to responsibilise their conduct through embedding a series of societal norms. In the case of global governmentality populations are invoked as the intended beneficiaries, their health, wellbeing and prosperity being achieved through the right types of governance and responsible engagement with the global market. By invoking populations, it is actually states that are governmentalised with the wealth, welfare and wellbeing of populations being of secondary concern. This has been suggested by some governmentality scholars working in this field. For example, Laura Zanotti writes of how states have become the subject of international scrutiny and intervention aimed at regulating them as 'governments' concerned with the well-being of their populations (Zanotti 2005: 480) while Tore Fougner is concerned with how states are constituted according to neo-liberal norms of entrepreneurial and competitive behaviour (Fougner 2008: 308). Whether states actually do provide for the well-being of their populations is perhaps secondary to their adherence to a set of international processes and norms through which such states are constituted, monitored and assessed (Joseph 2010, 2012).

To relate this most generally to development policy, humanitarian intervention and DRR, this can be considered an effective form of governmentality insofar as recipient countries willingly enter into agreements with a range of partners and open up their institutions and political practices to external scrutiny and review. As Abrahamsen notes, this appears to empower recipient countries but in fact is a means of conferring various obligations and duties in relation to development targets, levels of performance and objectives of social development (Abrahamsen 2004: 1461). The effect is to reinforce global economic and security strategies and we have seen that countries like the United Kingdom are clear about their pursuit of their own strategic interests in return for scaled-back development assistance. However, they can describe this in positive terms as 'partnership' in promoting human security (well-being of populations) and helping build resilience in particular strategically important regions of the world to the benefit of all parties.

Whether the promotion of resilience actually does make a difference on the ground, or is more of a means of reinforcing global governmentality is a matter for debate. Gubbels, a co-founder of the NGO Groundswell International, raises a number of highly significant issues. First, in relation to general coordination problems he notes that the numerous groups involved on the ground often lack overall coherence and effectiveness because of the lack of a systematic, comprehensive approach (Gubbels 2012b: 12). This is ironic given the emphasis on coordination and integration. Organisations tend to compete with one another for resources, rather than coordinating activities. This is a problem commonly raised about NGO activities and is compounded by the prevailing logic of privatisation and outsourcing. However, it is particularly damaging to the credibility of a strategy that relies on the claim that resilience-building fosters a more coherent and comprehensive approach. Second, looking specifically at work being done in the Sahel region, Gubbels notes a number of practical failings. These include failure to properly target the livelihood needs of the most vulnerable people or strengthen the productive capacity of households, develop capacity for effective action at community and district government levels, adequately prepare for, and mitigate the risk of drought and more generally fail to deal with underlying dynamics and structural causes (2012b: 29). We have suggested this can be attributed to the logic of global governmentality which, rather than trying to make a difference on the ground, is more concerned with the regulation of states, governments and elites. A cynical view would be to attribute failure to the dual logics of a global governmentality that targets states while ignoring people, and an approach that does target people, but relies on the wholly inappropriate neo-liberal logic of privatised interventions.

The field of global governmentality, in contrast to the other fields examined is more strongly dominated by the Anglo-Saxon perspective with international organisations like the World Bank, United Nations Development Programme (UNDP) and OECD-Development Assistance Committee having a significant influence over policy-thinking. This allows national bodies like USAID and DFID to have a strong influence on the field and the UK plays a leadership role in international development and disaster reduction that is certainly more difficult in other policy areas. DFID also argues that actors such as the World Bank Global Facility for Disaster Reduction and Recovery and the United Nations International Strategy for Disaster Reduction are necessary partners in effective resilience-building, perhaps as convenors who can help network together a range of other actors such as national governments, civil society, communities and the private sector (DFID 2011b: 16).

We have seen that the permeation of Anglo-Saxon thinking into the main international organisations even influences French and German development agencies. Overseas intervention is less of a contentious issue than domestic politics and so is more amenable to Anglo-Saxon ideas that might be contested in other policy fields. We saw that German humanitarian thinking has come under DFID's influence and that while resilience has had little impact on German domestic politics, it has emerged within the transitional development assistance strategy. As with the DFID approach, we find arguments for strengthening the resilience of individuals, communities, civil society and institutions to face complex crisis situations and to bridge medium and long-term measures (BMZ 2013: 5) with emphasis on efficiency, effectiveness, coherence and complementarity (BMZ 2013: 9). DFID is also clearly a significant influence on the EU and its DRR and development work coordinated by ECHO. DFID can also be seen as a major driving force in areas like the Horn of Africa and Sahel where it has its own in initiatives, but is also driving ECHO's work.

It has been argued that the EU's approach to governance reflects a neo-liberal rationality that promotes market mechanisms and uses competitiveness as a benchmarking tool. However, the situation inside the EU is somewhat different to Anglo-Saxon countries like the United States and United Kingdom insofar as neo-liberal policies are not fully hegemonic inside the EU and are up against powerful counter-models. Therefore, EU policy-making reflects a fight going on inside the EU between different models of governance. The EU and its member states are divided over neo-liberal strategy and what are perceived as Anglo-Saxon methods of governance when applied to areas of internal EU policy. This is clear from disagreements over financial regulation and economic reform, tensions on employment reform to flexibilise labour practices and, in particular, the significant failure by member states to comply with the Lisbon strategy. But with overseas action, these divisions are less significant while the EU is more influenced by the global governance discourse which has a decidedly more neo-liberal and Anglo-Saxon tone. The EU's resilience turn can therefore largely be explained as a result of a combination of two factors – the dominance of neo-liberal thinking in areas of development policy, and the relatively easier task of making such policies acceptable to member states (although the 2016 Global Security Strategy suggests a more pragmatic approach might be needed in the more immediate neighbourhood).

The historical shift in forms of international aid and intervention and the turn from grand strategy to a capacities and capabilities approach also neatly coincides with the way that the European Commission understands its role as one of networked facilitator that directs and coordinates from a distance. It is consistent with internal EU governance strategies such as the Lisbon strategy and Open

Method of Coordination. These work by attempting to tighten up mechanisms and procedures, while also appearing more *laissez faire* and distant in their manner of intervention. In promoting the idea of resilience, the EU and other organisations are taking a somewhat new turn that places limits on intervention while encouraging local agency, capacity-building and pragmatic solutions as an alternative to large-scale project-building.

It is worth pausing here to consider an underlying issue about acting and 'actorness'. It is common in the literature to find discussion of the EU as an actor with perhaps a question about what type of actor it is, but if the above discussions tell us anything, it is that in actuality there are different actors inside the EU, each with their own interests and agenda. It might therefore be argued that the ability to act is an emergent social feature insofar as 'actorness' at one level – for example as a transnational or global entity – is emergent out of the activities of groups of people at a different level of interaction.[4] This partly explains the difficulties of coordinating EU action given the different strategic interests not only of member states, but also the EU's own actors. The discussion of resilience reveals divisions with the EU between actors belonging to different departments such as ECHO and DevCo as well as divisions within departments like ECHO over its role and function. Now we find resilience emerging as a strong element in the strategy of the European External Action Service. These various actors have their own strategic interests linked to institutional incentives, bureaucratic conditioning and role identities. Particularly given its claims to be a bridging approach, the EU's resilience strategy actually reveals divisions of actors and interests that are multi-scalar and institutionally complex.

This is not to say, however, that there cannot be attempts to convey a sense of 'actorness' constructed around a particular identity regardless of the actual state of affairs. The resilience turn perhaps fits with this and does give new meaning to the 'special actor' argument. It is of course common to find this argument in the EU literature and particularly in relation to foreign policy. It is noted by certain analysts (e.g., Sicurelli 2010: 33) that the EU places greater emphasis on things like regional integration, local ownership and structural integration,

---

[4] This is a critical realist argument, the implications of which for international relations are elaborated in Wight (2006) and Joseph (2012).

all things that fit with a resilience approach. Discussions about EU foreign policy often highlight the distinctiveness of European motives. However, it is often the case with the EU that some of its perceived weaknesses and divisions both as an actor and an entity are turned into positive forms of justification for particular ways of acting or viewing the world. Notions like civilian and normative power Europe (Manners 2002) can often be found justifying the idea that EU interventions are of a special type while also helping to disguise strategic divisions that inhibit other types of action. The notion of Europe as a civilian power tries to turn the evident military weakness of the EU and its inability to coordinate sustained military intervention into a positive argument for the EU's role as a civilian actor. It can be used to contrast EU interventions with the actions of other powers, prioritising civilian ends, collective action and the social values of equality and justice. Likewise, the idea of normative power Europe, although a more complicated notion (Whitman 2006) would emphasise an international role and identity based on the values of peace, liberty, democracy, rule of law and respect for human rights. Indeed, all these can be found in Article 177 of the original Treaty Establishing the European Community along with the goal of integrating developing countries into the global economy. Other normative aspects of the approach focus on such values as social solidarity, anti-discrimination and, increasingly, good governance. As well as emphasising international law, Article 214 as modified by Lisbon claims the EU's humanitarian assistance is based on the principles of humanity, neutrality, impartiality and independence.

Thus, one perspective on the EU's resilience turn is that it can be seen as a product of an international organisation whose exercise of power is more normative in character and which is seeking to prove itself a global actor of a special type. Nathalie Tocci, now an advisor to the EU on their Global Security Strategy, is right in noting how EU treaties emphasise the preservation of peace in line with both the EU's own self-conception as a peace project and the more general liberal peace argument which emphasises longer-term institutional building, international law and the role of economic markets (Tocci 2011: 16). Hence the EU is interested in conflict transformation rather than just conflict management and its missions have medium to long-term aims that place more emphasis on the structural features of conflict. For Tocci (2011: 16) this means placing emphasis on civil society. This includes engaging with CSOs, giving financial assistance, offering training programmes and building organisational capacity. But, while she may be right to note that this produces a more bottom–up, structural approach, this can also fail according to what she calls the 'disembedded civil society thesis' where interventions may misidentify CSOs, lend undue support to those that are of a liberal, technical, and urban character and which can end up being excessively politicised (2011: 20). This chimes with Gubbels' arguments about failures on the ground.

This returns us to a more negative view of the reasons for EU foreign policy and the emphasis on humanitarian and emergency aid, it might be suggested that by engaging in such projects a view of the EU can be projected that helps disguise or even resolve some of its own internal tensions and contradictions. Developing a more coherent foreign policy, even if only in certain areas of activity, builds confidence in the idea of the EU as global actor and in doing so, develops a greater degree of internal coherence. In Chris Bickerton's view, foreign policy functions as a site for reflections on the ontology of the EU and its identity and purpose as an actor (Bickerton 2011: 7). Indeed, his view is that EU foreign policy functions as a way of legitimising Europe's retreat from power politics (Bickerton 2011: 35). This might well be so, and humanitarian intervention and disaster response seem like safe options. However, in regions like the Sahel, they are not so easily separable from political and military interests and the possible divisions among member states, particularly in the aftermath of the military intervention of France and the UK in Libya. Given these difficulties, a notion like resilience can perhaps play a role in conceptualising EU intervention as something that operates more cautiously though working with others and encouraging local initiative.

Therefore, while we have suggested that the EU's arguments for building resilience overseas are consistent with a widely accepted neo-liberal discourse on forms of governance, there are distinctive reasons for an EU strategy that relates to existential and organisational problems faced by the EU as an actor. The following issues to be dealt with here are: (1) EU 'self-identity' in relation to the EU's ability to act coherently, (2) humanitarianism and gaining support for the EU, (3) strategies of neo-liberal governance, (4) offering technical support and (5) the effect of austerity policies.

Firstly, the adoption of resilience-building as a strategy reflects both the actual weakness of the EU and an awareness of this among key actors. The EU position appears to be contradictory. The documents analysed above reveal an obsession with developing a more-integrated, better-coordinated, more-connected and better-engaged approach. There is considerable emphasis on implementing the correct procedures and tightening coordination while establishing longer-term strategies of monitoring and review. Yet at the same time, the EU's policy on resilience moves in a different direction by advocating that the EU plays a somewhat distant role, operating at arm's length, cutting back on financial commitments, working through NGOs and existing international coordination frameworks and arguing that affected states need to take responsibility for developing their own national resilience plans. The EU notes that the problems in the Sahel are cross-border and closely intertwined and that only an integrated and holistic strategy can allow progress to be made. It makes the familiar argument about the need for reinforced security and law enforcement capacity, more robust public institutions and more accountable governments (European External Action Service 2011: 2). The previous section raised doubts as to whether the EU's actions have done anything to achieve this. Notwithstanding such doubts, the uptake of resilience allows the EU to claim this as a stated aim, while placing the onus on local authorities to carry it out. Resilience gives the impression of being part of an integrated and holistic strategy without there actually being one. The resilience discourse is paradoxically more holistic and less engaged.

The EU is better able to do this because it is possible to hide its inability to act coherently on military matters behind more plausible claims to be exercising civilian or normative power. This leads to our second point concerning the appeal of the humanitarian aspect of resilience building which allows the EU to project itself in a particular way. It gives the impression that the EU is exercising a form of civilian power that is consistent with its own nature as an entity. Even if not true, it can give the appearance of being a form of soft power that differs from US approaches. This power works from a distance through persuasion rather than compulsion and it appears to do so as an indirect form of power that works through civil society and partnerships. The humanitarian angle is important to the EU's identity and is seen as one of the most popular areas among the European public.

External projection is necessary for the EU's own self-understanding and as Holland (2002: 244) argues, development policy has an important effect on improving the EU's image among its own citizens.

It has been argued that the EU's approach to governance reflects a neo-liberal rationality that promotes market mechanisms and uses competitiveness as a benchmarking tool. However, the situation inside the EU is somewhat different to Anglo-Saxon countries like the US and UK insofar as neo-liberal policies are not fully hegemonic inside the EU and are up against powerful counter-models as well as the notion of 'social Europe'. Therefore, EU policy-making reflects a fight going on inside the EU between different models of governance. Having said this, the consensus on development is far more straightforwardly neo-liberal than it might be in other EU policy areas. International organisations are dominated by an Anglo-Saxon way of thinking while national agencies like USAID and DFID are highly influential international actors. EU policy in this area is therefore more coherent and openly supports the view that governance should take place through engagement with the private sector, by devolving power and by capacity building in order to better engage with global markets. This is done through neo-liberal governance mechanisms that are consistent with the development approach of other international actors like the International Monetary Fund (IMF), UNDP and World Bank and which use tools of monitoring and benchmarking to try and secure compliance with international liberal norms.

Finally, there is one other, not to be underestimated, reason behind the turn to resilience which is the need for greater austerity measures. Resilience is a cheap option. The approach is realist and pragmatic in both a political sense, and in an economic one. It is consistent with a general retreat from grand strategy that is taking place in foreign policy and in development terms it lowers expectations of what kind of support can be expected. Mark Davies, head of the Centre for Social Protection in the UK, argues that DFID has been pushing resilience because it is seen as better investment and it 'ticks all their boxes' (IRIN 2012). DFID itself notes the 'growing evidence that building community resilience to shocks and stresses saves money as well as lives' (DFID 2011b: 2). The EU's own assessment concludes that investment in resilience is cost effective and that preparedness and planning is not only more effective than disaster response, but cheaper. As the EU puts it, when the world experiences an economic downturn, the pressure is to deliver maximum impact from minimum funds (European Commission 2012a: 3). More generally this might be said to mark the end of the period of ambitions grand projects. As Haldrup and Rosn (2013: 130) have noted, the financial costs of such projects have led to a scaling back of such involvement. Putting emphasis on resilience is a more pragmatic or realist approach with downscaled goals based on 'best fit' solutions.

Resilience captures the current moment, both for the EU and the world at large. Not in a particularly positive sense, but as a conservative idea for a cautious age. This captures the global political momentum as large powers scale down their grand strategies while the EU, starting from its very weak Common Foreign and Security Policy (CFSP), tries to scale up its international presence while dealing with significant internal divisions.

In promoting resilience and strengthening local capacities, the EU can be presented as exercising a special form of power that is in line with the existing norm of concentrating on civilian missions. This would seem to fit with the comprehensive security model outlined in the Lisbon Treaty while causing fewer tensions between member states. However, the policies themselves are entirely consistent with what other international organisations and governments are doing which somewhat gives the lie to the notion that the EU is a special kind of actor. Indeed, if the US is regarded as the hard power or realist counterpart to normative power Europe, then why is it doing exactly the same thing as the EU in promoting resilience in exactly the same regions (the Horn of Africa and Sahel)?[5] The main difference would seem to be that other global actors like the US have strategic capabilities that EU does not possess; not that the EU has a civilian power approach that is different from the rest.

Nor is it the case that the EU really has as 'nicer' approach compared to other actors. It is simply following the trends on governance that we have characterised as operating from a distance while locking governments and their populations into a regulative network of external monitoring that seeks to ensure compliance on key economic and security issues. It works through the responsibilisation of their

---

[5] Details of the newly launched Sahel RISE initiative can be found at: www.usaid .gov/news-information/press-releases/feb-3-2014-usaid-announces-rise-new-initiative-build-resilience-west-africa-sahel. The Horn of Africa initiative can be found at www.blog.usaid.gov/2011/12/building-resilience-in-the-horn-of-africa/.

action using, in particular, the promotion of partnership, ownership, stake-holding, appeal to civil society, calls for good governance and an engagement in networks and peer reviews. This is a politics that presents itself in terms of persuasion rather than coercion, enablement rather than constraint, partnership rather than command. It operates from a distance through policy suggestion backed up with a complex array of quasi-disciplinary techniques of monitoring and assessment.

In conclusion, the resilience turn is mainly about projection. While the approach of the EU fits with a general turn in global governance, resilience is particularly useful in helping to project an image of the EU as a special actor with a coherent strategy. Unfortunately, while it is good at projecting an image, resilience does little to address the underlying divisions among member states and between different actors inside different EU departments. While succeeding in making the outside world look more complex, it probably lacks the strategic tools necessary to deal with the EU's own complexity.

Conclusion

We can conclude that the field of development, humanitarian intervention and DRR is the most receptive to resilience promotion and that this idea has permeated the policies of all the major actors discussed here. It is still the case that the Anglo-Saxon countries lead the way, but in this field, other countries do tend to follow. The field as a whole is much more open to the Anglo-Saxon way of thinking. Consequently, it is easier for the term to spread – indeed it is hard for it not to do so because most of the influential actors, notably the World Bank, UNDP and OECD, are already strongly promoting resilience. DFID and USAID also enjoy strong influence and it is noticeable how these bodies have influenced thinking in other countries such as Germany. Nevertheless, thinking in such countries – France in particular – has not really developed significance in itself. Rather, it fits in with existing strategy without causing too many disruptions. The EU, as we have just outlined, also follows the Anglo-Saxon lead, but it has its own reasons for doing so.

In the next chapter, we will consider general issues about the difference resilience makes to thinking about various forms of intervention. However, there are some field-specific issues that we will conclude with here. Certainly, critical scholars of resilience like David Chandler are correct to point out that the discourse surrounding resilience reflects a shift away from some key concerns of a classical liberal framework for intervention which believes that strong measures and planning can manage and control global problems and crises. This should be qualified insofar as this problematisation of some key components of classical liberalism is not so radically new if considered in the context of UK domestic policy-making where the two waves (Bevir 2013: 162) of policy revision have substantially questioned many core liberal assumptions about the relationship between state, market, society and individual. However, in the international sphere this does come across as a significant retreat from the grand scale ambitions of liberal intervention and state-building projects. About DFID's stance on this there is less doubt with a clear emphasis on the reduced costs of a resilience approach compared to existing strategies (DFID 2011b: 2).

Resilience turns instead to the subjective capacity for learning and self-awareness as part of a strategy of adaptation, taking for granted that we have little or no control over wider circumstances and that all attempts at large-scale intervention are doomed to failure. Instead DFID looks to the 'adaptive capacities of actors – individuals, communities, regions, governments, organisations or institutions' and considers how these are determined by 'ability to adjust to a disturbance, moderate potential damage, take advantage of opportunities and cope with the consequences of a transformation … [and] allow actors to anticipate, plan, react to, and learn from shocks or stresses' (DFID 2011a: 8). Although fatalistic about wider circumstances we can see that this is couched in the language of opportunity.

Hence while it appears that we have less control over systemic shocks and crises, these actually work to justify certain strategies of governance that work though the responsibilisation of behaviour at lower levels. Thus, it would be wrong to see resilience as a rejection of neo-liberal logic; instead it can raise awareness of the limits of markets while actually working to further embed this rationality in a system of variegated practices. It is actually through failures and crises that this can be done – naturalising crisis while responsibilising governments and key actors. Although resilience works to give the appearance of a new strategy, the emphasis placed on complexity and social embeddedness is part of an overall approach to governance that actually works to reinforce, rather than undermine, an instrumental rationality and associated methods of monitoring and evaluation. Rather than constituting a shift away from the calculating logic of neo-liberalism, or a form of 'governmentality after neoliberalism' (Bevir 2016), it combines neo-liberal practices and logic with other technologies. In the field of the international, it remains consistent with what Jacqueline Best calls 'the non-juridical logic of international standards, the calculating metric of transparency and the entrepreneurial ethic of self-responsibility' (Best 2007: 102).

However, despite scepticism about the motives, it might be the case that a resilience approach that recognises the limits of liberal intervention and market logic may, willingly or not, create space for local politics and fulfil the potential for some sort of hybrid approach (see Chandler and Richmond 2015). While this would require a lengthy analysis of such possibilities, from the point of view of this chapter, the interesting question is not whether resilience will lead to more local politics, but whether there are sufficient gaps in the approaches of the different international actors to present certain possibilities. To take as an example an argument from DFID:

Humanitarian assistance should be delivered in a way that does not undermine existing coping mechanisms and helps a community build its own resilience for the future. National governments in at-risk countries can ensure that disaster risk management policies and strategies are linked to community-level action. Where governments are already building resilience in at-risk countries, the UK will support them through its development programmes. (DFID 2011d: 10)

There is a degree of sensitivity in this understanding that maybe does offer some scope for local or hybrid solutions to various problems. Indeed, it might be a hope that while resilience is influential in this policy area, in relative terms, the influence of NGOs and civil society actors might soften the interpretation of resilience with less strident emphasis on the transformative element as might be found in some World Bank and USAID documents. Perhaps the issue is the degree to which 'softer' actors in the field are able to influence the direction of such government strategies and, of course, the degree to which local actors are really allowed to have a say, rather than them just being told that they should 'bounce back better'.

5 | Analysing the Anglo-Saxon Approach to Resilience and the Alternatives

Introduction

Having assessed the emergence of resilience across a range of policy areas in different countries, the task of this chapter to bring together the analysis sections in order to address the extent to which resilience varies from place to place, and whether this has an impact on our understanding of resilience as an expression of neo-liberal governmentality. We will therefore run through some of the findings of Chapters 2–4, but will do so through the conceptual framework of governmentality. This chapter will set out the core characteristics of the Anglo-Saxon approach as found in the UK and US and will assess the extent to which French, German and EU conceptions of resilience differ from this approach. We have already seen that non-Anglo-Saxon usage of resilience leads to alternative understandings, although how conscious these variations are, is a matter to be addressed.

The Anglo-Saxon Approach to Resilience

The findings of the three previous chapters clearly suggest that there is a distinctive Anglo-Saxon approach to resilience. Outlined below are some central features of this as understood through the lens of neo-liberal governmentality. It should be stressed that resilience itself is too much of a floating signifier to bear the description neo-liberal governmentality. Rather, its character derives from the dominant discourses and practices within which it is located which, in the Anglo-Saxon case, means the discourses and practices of embedded neo-liberalism. This is not its only meaning, as we shall go on to demonstrate. It is, however, the dominant one. We have already outlined the arguments for governmentality. It should be emphasised that resilience's relationship to governmentality – as both shaped by and as helping to shape its practices – can be said to have two key dimensions. The first element of resilience in relation to governmentality refers to the way that it helps to frame the world in a certain way. Secondly, resilience helps in the creation of certain types of (responsible) subjects. It helps frame the world in such as way that its complex and unpredictable character comes to the fore. This allows problems to be articulated in certain ways and helps legitimise practices of governance that seek to manage populations and the way of dealing with these problems. Subjects are expected to think and act according to the norms of values of such framings – hence the embedding element of resilience as governmentality. These subjective features include, reflexivity, resourcesfulness and ability to cope with adversity. We have seen that in countries like the United Kingdom and United States, this subject-construction is achieved through the active intervention of the state into society. Subjects have to be created and the state plays an active role in this process.

Proceeding with what we can consider the Anglo-Saxon approach, we can look at the processes of context framing and subject construction in the following way. First, governmentality works through the establishment of a system of governing from a distance where the states, governments and international organisations are seen to be playing a facilitative role that works through encouragement, the sharing of information, best practice and expertise and the empowerment of local agency. This leads to the second feature of the Anglo-Saxon approach which is the devolution of responsibilities that ultimately tries to reach right down to the individual and shape our subjectivity in terms of how we think and act in relation to stresses and crises. We see, in particular, how the Anglo-Saxon approach invokes the resilient individual and community. Thirdly, the Anglo-Saxon approach can be distinguished by its strong promotion of the private sphere as the sector most likely to find solutions to crises. Fourthly, governmentality encourages innovation and initiative with a strong emphasis on human attributes and capacities. Finally, the Anglo-Saxon approach to resilience takes a transformative view that rejects the idea of robustness and returning to normal, in favour of an approach that stresses ongoing adaptation and change in our ways of behaving and organising. These five elements of governmentality are not clear analytical distinctions; governing from a distance, for instance, clearly requires devolving responsibilities, while the transformative approach rejects traditional solutions in favour of more innovative and enterprising behaviour. However, they are useful for guiding our analysis.

We can now link these five elements of governmentality to the specific arguments of the Anglo-Saxon form of resilience. We have argued at length for how resilience contributes to 'governance from a distance', particularly with its emphasis on the improvement of the health, welfare and well-being of populations. We have seen how resilience is promoted as part of a form of facilitation, particularly in relation to capacities, claiming to help local communities through support and advice that will enable them to deal with risks and crises themselves. Rather than constituting a radical break from previous work, resilience is often promoted as embedding already existing practices, sharing experiences and learning from real events (Cabinet Office 2010b). That is because the technologies and techniques of governance from a distance are already well-embedded within the Anglo-Saxon societies allowing a resilience approach to fit in with and modify already-existing practices.

We have seen that the Anglo-Saxon approach is focused on building the resilience of individuals and communities, drawing on existing resources and practices, while intervening to enhance others. While this can be considered governance from a distance, it should be noted that some of this can be heavy-handed, particularly if we look at the focus on community cohesion in relation to UK counter-terrorism policy. It is also top–down insofar as governance from a distance is still directed by the state. The devolution of powers to individuals and communities is backed up with the use of indicators and monitoring tools. This can be presented as facilitative – for example using benchmarks to assess business continuity plans – but there is often no opt-out option. Those who are governed from a distance must conduct themselves in a responsible way, or be held to account.

This is also the case in the international domain where organisations like DIFD and USAID claim to want to help countries to help themselves in order that they are prepared and ready to withstand shocks and disasters (DFID 2011a: 1). This is governance from a distance insofar as it shifts responsibility away from the international community and on to the poorer countries themselves who must develop the capacity to resist and adapt to shocks (DFID 2011a: 1). If they do not develop such capacities, then the blame lies with them. The international community will provide assistance, less through direct help than by playing the role of facilitator and enabler. As with domestic policy, this is backed up with an extensive system of monitoring and assessment to ensure that countries receiving support make use of it in the proper way. Such disciplinary mechanisms are already in place and reinforce the existing strategies of international organisations like the World Bank.

The second and related aspect of governmentality is the strategy of devolving responsibility and attempting to reach right down to the individual. The UK government emphasises its role is to support, empower and facilitate other actors and actions and that residence work should be owned by the communities themselves (Cabinet Office 2010b: 14). This is consistent with the existing Anglo-Saxon discourse of partnership and stake-holding with resilience resting on the government's partnership with the private and voluntary sectors, communities and individuals (Cabinet Office Community Resilience for Practitioners 43). Facilitative practices involve encouraging the participation of different actors, offering guidance and sharing good practice and useful ideas.

In the United Kingdom, the Pitt Report argued for strengthening community resilience so that populations are better prepared and more self-reliant. The Strategic National Framework on Community Resilience has the aim of fostering emergency preparedness among communities and individuals. Various government guidelines directly target individuals, asking them to be more aware of the risks they face, to know how they can get involved in community planning and how they might better help themselves in an emergency. The same arguments apply in the United States. In the US communities should consider how they can contribute to the National Preparedness Goal through the knowledge and skills they possess and by improving awareness of the risks they face (FEMA 2015: 2). Both domestically and internationally, attention has shifted to building human capacities. This fits with a governmentality approach since, while there continues to be a concern with institutions, there is now a greater effort to reach right down to individuals and to encourage them to be more resourceful, show initiative, act reflectively, plan, learn and manage both risks and opportunities.

The third element of governmentality relates to the promotion of the free market and the role of private enterprise. The Anglo-Saxon approach to resilience emphasises the private sector's ability to get things done and actively promotes such things as public–private partnerships as the best way to share risks and encourage investment. The private sector is regarded as essential to the 'viability' of a community, being the main source of dynamism and providing the best means of solving local problems (Department of Homeland Security 2016: 14). Internationally, the role of the private sector is taken for granted as a more efficient and effective means of getting things done and as the only realistic way to operate in a complex humanitarian system (Ashdown 2011: 1). This partly connects to the more general development aim of making poorer countries more open to market forces, partly to the neo-liberal assumption that the private sector offers more dynamism, particularly in managing risk (Ashdown 2011: 37).

This links with a fourth element of governmentality which is to encourage innovation and initiative as well as a more pragmatic approach. Resilient subjects should be able to learn from experiences and adapt their behaviour in appropriate ways. The US approach to Homeland Security talks of the initiative and ingenuity of individuals, communities and the private sector (United States Government 2010: 16). This strategy is also intended to reinforce national values – American society is claimed as exceptional in its openness and diversity (United States Government 2010: 9), blessed with the ideas, values, energy, creativity and resilience of its people (United States Government 2010: 16).

It could be argued that resilience also works to keep people constantly on their toes. In other words, the worst thing that could happen would be an actual emergency because, as a form of governance, resilience really aims at keeping people in a state of constant preparedness. For example, Anderson and Adey look at how emergences, rather than being unique occurrences, are 'assembled' through specific acts and organisational forms (Anderson and Adey 2011: 26). Emergency is seen as an interval – with planning occurring in the gap between recognition of a threat and the threat emerging as an event. This allows emergency planning to occur continuously so that something like UK Civil Contingencies should be understood as a continuous state of preparing for a range of possible emergencies (Anderson and Adey 2011: 29). This encourages the population to be always aware to their situation, to the risks that they face and to their choices that they might make. Now intensified with fiscal entrenchment, this should allow for the creation of more pragmatic subjects.

We might contrast, however, the situation inside Europe and North America where populations are encouraged to be more creative and pragmatic in the face of *potential* threats, with that in poorer parts

of the world where populations are encouraged to be more pragmatic and innovative in the face of *actual* emergencies. Here we see
crises being promoted as opportunities. The USAID report discussed
in Chapter 4 promotes innovation as allowing people the chance to
think more critically and challenge their existing structures and ways
of life, while drawing on their human attributes in order to develop
better coping mechanisms and deal pragmatically with deficiencies in
service delivery (Bujones, Jaskiewicz, Linakis and McGirr 2013: 13).

This advice also represents the fifth element of the Anglo-Saxon
approach which is the transformative view of resilience as an opportunity to organise and rebuild. This is particularly in evidence in overseas interventions where resilience is used to encourage adaptation
and reorganisation. The same USAID report says that enhanced adaptive capacity means the ability to quickly and effectively respond to
new circumstances by means of enhanced governance structures and
economic opportunities. It also mentions 'intangible elements of social
capital' – something we will discuss at the end of this chapter (Bujones,
Jaskiewicz, Linakis and McGirr 2013: 12). The transformative view of
resilience looks to 'bounce back better' – not simply to preserve and
resist, but to adapt and evolve. There is, however, a neo-liberal bias
to the understanding of this, emphasising individual and community
enterprise and initiative. As argued by DFID, the aim of enhancing
adaptive capacities is not only to cope, but also to take advantages of
the opportunities of a transformation (DFID 2011b: 8). The Anglo-
Saxon approach to building resilience overseas takes the free market
as its model, arguing that traditional coping mechanisms are unable
to deal with new, complex challenges and that modernisation – i.e., a
more open approach to the global market, greater individual and community adaptability, more flexible working practices, greater individual initiative, etc. (Headey and Kennedy 2012: 5) – is necessary under
changing, more complex and uncertain conditions.

We will see that this transformative view – where transformation
is seen as an opportunity to embed neo-liberal norms of behaviour –
is not wholly accepted in France and Germany's discourse on building resilience overseas. This is, perhaps, the main difference between
Anglo-Saxon approaches to resilience, and the understanding of
resilience in non-Anglo-Saxon countries. In domestic policy-making
the difference is even more striking. In Germany and France, there is
hardly any discussion of resilience as transformation, whereas in the

UK and US community resilience is synonymous with 'seiz[ing] the opportunities to transform and revitalise' the neighbourhood and to improve such things as commercial activities, skills and people's aspirations (Cabinet office 2004b: 83).

In summary, we have a distinct set of features that constitute the Anglo-Saxon approach to resilience, understood here through the lens of neo-liberal governmentality based on the key factors of distant governance, devolved responsibilities, private sector initiative, pragmatism and innovation and finally a dynamic, transformative understanding of resilience. This can be observed in domestic policy-making as well as the overseas policies of DFID and USAID. In the next section we move on to examine how influential these features are outside the Anglo-Saxon sphere and whether the promotion of resilience should always be seen as synonymous with neo-liberal governmentality.

The European Varieties of Resilience

Having established what Anglo-Saxon governmentality looks like, we can look at French, German and EU arguments for resilience to see how these differ or vary from the UK and US approaches. To what extent do other countries try to build resilience within communities, or to try and create resilient subjects? To what extent do they question the central role of the state, or try to devolve powers to civil society and the private sphere? Do these societies embrace the transformative notion of resilience with an emphasis on learning and adaptation, or do they place greater emphasis on protection, resistance and robustness?

On the issue of governing from a distance we find that a range of arguments are developing in favour of a more distant and facilitative approach but that this often remains as an argument rather than a practice. France and Germany are distinct from the UK in having a more interventionist approach that is led by the state and the government. In France's case, the state is highly centralised, with the private sector and civil society playing a more passive role. Indeed, it is noted in France that the Anglo-Saxon approach has a stronger orientation to civil society, involving a wider range of local actors (Francart 2010). We have seen how resilience has nonetheless started to emerge in national security and civil protection discourse. However, the limited usage of the term is mainly in relation to the national security context rather than taking up the Anglo-Saxon theme of building individual and community resilience. The German approach also lacks emphasis on individual and community resilience. Instead it argues for a 'whole of society approach', in other words, a focus that is on all members of society, rather than encouraging the efforts of particular communities or individuals. This could be seen as being more inclusive and perhaps more contractual rather than individualist and certainly the state is seen as having a key responsibility in relation to society as a whole (Federal Ministry of Defence 2016: 60). So, while the entry of resilience into French and German domestic policy discourse allows for some limited sense of governing from a distance, there remains a key role for the state, legal system and an interventionist form of governance.

The EU approach is somewhat different given its organisational structure and the complexities of coordinating action. Its main emphasis is on better coordinated actions across member states with the European Commission acting as the main coordinator, facilitator and promotor of best practice, peer review and standardisation. In the field of disaster management, it encourages member states to respond to disasters and emergencies in the most appropriate ways, coordinate their efforts, share information and inform the public. In areas like climate change, the EU is looking to evaluate such things as adaptation measures. However, even if this implies a certain amount of support for Anglo-Saxon or neo-liberal values, these measures are mainly driven by more pragmatic considerations of things like infrastructure protection and response coordination.

In overseas policy the EU is more overtly neo-liberal. Its governance from a distance works by placing the emphasis on the need for individuals, communities and governments to develop their resilience strategies and make themselves less vulnerable and prone to poverty. Placing responsibility on national governments reinforces a system of global governance and various global standards. This requires accountability and political commitments and indeed may require institutional change (European Commission 2013: 3). Such arguments are consistent with those promoted by USAID, DFID and other leading bodies like the World Bank. This is a more Anglo-Saxon sphere of influence and the EU's approach accepts much of this discourse. However, resilience-building strategies also fit with the self-identity of the EU and Commission as special types of actors. Hence the EU already practices governance from a distance through its self-conception as a facilitator and advisor. The arguments for the EU as a global actor normally embrace the arguments for soft power like offering training and expertise, sharing information and good practice and promoting various norms and values. A resilience-building approach is consistent with all these aspects of the EU's strategy, while helping to camouflage actual difficulties in cooperation and coordination.

The German approach to overseas intervention supports the view of the international community as a facilitator, with emphasis placed on the role of civil society, communities and the private sector There are tensions in the German approach, but it is more amenable to the practices of governing from a distance than is the case in domestic policy. There is also strong support for monitoring and assessment. Both German and French approaches recognise the more Anglo-Saxon character of this field. It is also easier to govern from a distance from overseas, and this is probably the main reason for variation in approaches.

This division can again be seen if we consider the related issue of devolution of powers and responsibilities. We have concluded that French and German approaches to domestic policy are more overtly top–down with a focus on the role of the state as providing protection rather than encouraging local actors to protect themselves. In Germany there is mention of the European model and the needs of 'society as a whole'. In France the emphasis is on solidarity and national cohesion and consequently there is little encouragement for communities to be engaged in resilience-building. France has accepted some devolution of powers to private and municipal actors, however, these actors have shown only limited interest in taking over responsibilities from the state. The state on its part tends to operate through decrees and legally binding guidelines, creating passivity rather than devolving powers. Indeed, there is a degree of distrust in devolving such powers and encouraging local initiative. These are indeed associated with an Anglo-Saxon model that contrasts with the more social or collective approach found in Germany and France.

There is a different sort of devolution of powers in Germany due to the Federal model. This is also the case in the EU and the devolution of powers to member states. The EU deals with this through subsidiarity in order to determine the most appropriate level of intervention. This is a devolution of powers of sorts, but one based on existing actors rather than a conscious attempt to reach down to communities and individuals, of which discussion is largely absent from EU discourse.

Moving to international interventions, we find a different approach that is more willing to talk of devolution to local governments, communities and actors. However, we saw that this is largely a devolution of responsibility, with the international community emphasising the need for countries to take responsibility for their own development while developing appropriate measures to ensure resilience. Again, there are some tensions in France and Germany with the Anglo-Saxon discourse of individual and community resilience mixed up with a more European emphasis on social context and people's real needs (BMZ 2009: 15).

It is worth briefly mentioning promotion of the private sphere as something happening in all cases studied. In the Anglo-Saxon countries this is associated with a more neo-liberal form of capitalism and as something to be actively promoted. The discourse from France, Germany and the EU has more the tone of inevitability. Seen as part of a changing environment, private ownership of things like critical infrastructure is now taken for granted. Differences of opinion can be observed by comparing the positive Anglo-Saxon view of the private sector as more efficient and dynamic, with the view in France and Germany that state must be prepared to intervene to deal with market failures. The state is still seen as the main actor and the body most responsible for providing protection. But there is also recognition that privatisation is changing the role of state as well as its ability to intervene. So, there is an acceptance that the role of the state is more that of a coordinator, regulator and facilitator, rather than provider. Resilience helps justify this situation, promoting such things as business continuity, financial risk management and cooperation with the private sector as essential aims. Risk insurance is particularly important in relation to climate change policies, for example in German and EU policy in relation to climate risk insurance markets. The EU approach also encourages working with financial institutions and major investors, building business partnerships and developing financial contingency mechanisms.

Promotion of the private sector links with the fourth element of governmentality, the encouragement of innovation and initiative. The private sector provides the best means of sharing risks and encouraging investment. In France there is some talk of creating a risk culture while in Germany this is described as a 'novel risk culture'. However, the strong emphasis in Germany on the 'whole of society' and on social solidarity in France, acts against the Anglo-Saxon appeal to specific enterprising groups and individuals. It is fair to say, therefore, that the Anglo-Saxon emphasis on innovation and initiative has not really spread to Germany and France, nor has it had much success in EU policy-making despite the more active attempts by the Commission to promote such a culture. Overseas, the EU does encourage innovation in risk management and, following DFID's lead, sees the stimulation of enterprise as the best way to encourage human development while attracting foreign investment.

Finally, we saw that the Anglo-Saxon approach clearly encourages a transformative view of resilience, emphasising adaptation and behavioural change and even, in some cases, changes in means of living. This is not the case in France and Germany. In Germany, the dominant view is of resilience as a 'resolute approach' that emphasises robustness and resistance rather than adaptation. It is described as a term originating in cybernetics which accounts for 'a system's tolerance or capacity for resistance with respect to disruptive external influences' (Federal Ministry of Education and Research 2016: 51). A further research report on resilience by the Brandenburg Institute for Society and Security also describes resilience as resistance, arguing that it is about how a system can absorb disturbance, undergo change and still retain the same function, structure, identity and feedbacks (Baban 2014: 9). Like other German resilience literature, it recognises that there are two dimensions of civil security – social resilience and critical infrastructure protection (Baban 2014: 10). But critical infrastructure is understood in terms of ability to withstand and societal resilience in terms of retaining the same function.

The French understanding is similar, domestically at least, in viewing resilience as the restoration of the capacity to function (Présidence de la République 2008c: 60). National security aims at protection through enhancing the capacity for deterrence and intervention (Présidence de la République 2013: 67). This contrasts with the Anglo-Saxon view that a resilience approach takes the place of the now-unrealistic goal of full protection. The French domestic approach is state-driven rather than focused on communities and individuals, with little discussion of how the latter can prepare themselves. Instead resilience is based on a more formal relationship between central state, local government and strategic businesses sectors.

Our finding, therefore, is that there are indeed varieties of resilience, but not perhaps in the positive sense of real alternatives to the Anglo-Saxon model. Instead, the Anglo-Saxon model is far more developed in its understanding of such things as the role of civil society and the private sector, devolution of responsibilities and promotion of innovation and initiative among individuals and communities. It rejects the idea of resilience as resistance or robustness in favour of a transformative view with particular emphasis on building adaptive capacities. However, this approach has not spread its influence in an even way and we find arguments for resilience in France and Germany that are at odds with this dominant discourse. These alternative arguments derive from pre-existing national and cultural characteristics, different political traditions and policy objectives, a less individualistic approach to society and a greater emphasis on the role of the state. This leads, not to an alternative approach to resilience, but to significant tensions with the dominant Anglo-Saxon understanding. At present, resilience lacks deeper substance outside of the Anglo-Saxon context, but as arguments for resilience continue to grow, we need to consider whether genuine French, German and EU approaches to resilience are really starting to emerge, or whether the distinctive features of these 'variations' are simply variations on a dominant Anglo-Saxon theme.

The Distinctiveness of Resilience

The previous section emphasised the weakness of French, German and other non-Anglo-Saxon understandings of resilience. However, we argued that even the Anglo-Saxon approach has a certain emptiness to it and that its character derives from the dominant discourses and practices within which it is located. If this is true, then why should resilience be considered a significant development? If resilience is still more like a term than a concept, this begs the question, why would governmentality employ a resilience approach? What does it have to offer contemporary forms of governance? In this section, we outline why resilience does indeed offer something distinctive that helps develop and modify existing techniques of governance. Here we set out how resilience assists two particular attitudes to governance – governing through complexity and governing through failure and denial. These are then used to justify a changed attitude towards the social and, in particular, towards the human.

For David Chandler, the very notion of resilience would be impossible without complexity (Chandler 2014: 19). Complex life is interactive, relational and open-ended with no fixed laws or structures but rather, we find emergent human agency that expresses itself in multiple ways. Governing complexity is therefore about intervention in interactive social processes without the prospect of finding definite 'solutions' but instead, where feedback and adaptation are the key characteristics (Chandler 2014: 36–7). Contemporary governance is therefore networked, interconnected but uncertain and therefore adaptive to a continually changing environment. For Chandler, this means that people are considered better at governing than governments because they are more adaptive, more interactive, less formally constrained, and more self-organised in relation to the complexities of a shared world (Chandler 2014: 38–41).

This is a powerful argument that captures a great deal of contemporary conjuncture. However, this is not necessary reflective of policy-making as described throughout this book. Governance does indeed occur through complexity, but only partially in the way it is understood by Chandler. Moreover, this governance through complexity reinforces existing techniques of governance with the supposed shift from governments to people a reinforcement of governmentality and therefore the technologies and techniques of governance that are available to the state.

When we read justifications for resilience in policy statements, we often find quite simple arguments for complexity rather than elaborate philosophical statements reflecting a change in 'episteme'. The UK's National Security Strategy talks of a rapidly changing globalised world. Global events impact on events at home thus requiring new policies and partnerships and the development of new capabilities (Cabinet Office 2015: 10). The US National Security Strategy talks of a new era defined by long-term changes. These are listed as technological change, energy security, new terrorist threats and economic vulnerability. French, German and EU strategies make similar broad claims. There are indeed descriptions of complex situations, but these are hardly developed philosophical positions. They might invoke complexity and uncertainty and even some of Donald

Rumsfeld's 'unknown unknowns'. But they do not raise the need for complexity theory.

This argument is somewhat unfair because we do find more developed accounts of complexity depending on the area of policy. Certainly, we are likely to find a better argument for complexity in a field like ecology than in national security discourse. However, here as well it would be wrong to see this as confirming some radical philosophical or epistemic shift. Instead these arguments, where they do develop, draw, not on complexity theory, post-humanism or some other 'post-classical' perspective, but rather upon some variation of a complex systems approach as outlined in the ecology literature discussed in Chapter 2. This is well described in the USAID report mentioned earlier. It regards the complex systems approach as an integrated analysis of the various sub-systems and the manner in which processes within each of them interact. Complex systems are defined as having multiple parts that are interdependent and produce outcomes that are not necessarily predictable based on any one part's function, but by how the parts interact within the system. Instead of a linear cause and effect relationship, the complex systems approach examines the behaviour of interacting factors in response to a shock or stress. Hence the nature of the system is not predictable, but occurs through the interaction of multiple components (Bujones, Jaskiewicz, Linakis and McGirr 2013: 9). Emphasis is placed on the complex interconnections between political, security, economic, social and environmental sub-systems where shocks in one sub-system interact with the others. These then mutually adapt to each other in a non-linear manner. Institutions, resources and adaptive facilitators contribute to resilience by influencing feedback loops caused by shocks to the system (Bujones, Jaskiewicz, Linakis and McGirr 2013: 7).

Governing through complexity therefore means placing emphasis on changing conditions, difficult circumstances, multiple factors, interconnected issues and, as we shall see next, uncertainty and diversity. It is not, as Chandler and others might suggest, a radically new paradigm, although it does introduce certain ways of thinking about the world and our place within it. This is a continuation of trends in social theory rather than a radical alternative, an epistemic shift rather than an epistemological break. It contributes to the trend of blurring of the bigger picture and presenting the world as beyond our control and understanding. One way of understanding the fuzziness of this picture is through the notion of entanglement which captures both the inseparability of humans and things, and the inseparability or even disappearance of the distinction between thought and the world (Barad 2007). We might say that these theories work through an ontology of denial that rejects the idea that there is a knowable world 'out there' that science, at least in its modernist form, can adequately grasp. This means that interventions must be more pragmatic in nature, attuned to complex problems but not trying to gain some deeper understanding of them. A more pragmatic approach to a complex world looks for 'best fit' or 'good enough' solutions. Or otherwise, we might actually be better off embracing fuzzy thinking in order to better grasp (if not understand) complexity. This fuzziness has carried over into resilience thinking where some writers have welcomed the conceptual vagueness and malleability of the idea as if this allows us to better 'grasp the ambivalent character of boundary objects' (Brand and Jax 2007). Even some scholars who are critical of contemporary development strategy welcome the 'epistemic confusion' of resilience as a productive opportunity that illuminates those unresolvable tensions that make objective definition impossible (Walsh-Dilley and Wolford 2015: 177).

Governing though complexity might be better understood as *governing through failure and denial* (Joseph 2016). Resilience reinforces the view of a world of unpredictable events and uncertain outcomes. Given that we have very little control over and not much understanding of these, we have to take a pragmatic turn and learn better how we can govern ourselves, particularly through strategies of adaptation. Resilience thinking helps link complexity and uncertainty to failures of intervention and regulation. It rejects the established liberal framework of intervention whereby states and other institutions and organisations attempt to control and regulate their environment or provide comprehensive security and protection. Denying our ability to control the wider environment or global context combined with our historical record of failed interventions works to justify strategies of adaptation that shift responsibility on to poorer states, communities, and individuals who have to learn how to better cope with their risks and insecurities. We must enhance our adaptive capacities because we can no longer believe in the elimination of threats (Zebrowski 2016: 100). The success of resilience as an idea is therefore linked to this perceived failure of intervention both in terms of state intervention domestically and international interventions such as state-building and development strategy. This allows resilience to present itself as a radical critique. However, it actually reinforces rather than challenges existing governmentalising trends as outlined above. In particular, the perceived failure of state intervention allows for greater devolution of responsibility to those being governed.

There is an element of *governing through the social* present in resilience discourse, although this has a contradictory character. It might seem odd to talk of the social coming back into the equation, but it has certainly been missing from a lot of the instrumental logic of neo-liberal governance. In contrast, resilience gets at something intangible that cannot be reduced to such a logic. We noted that 'intangible elements of social capital' (Bujones, Jaskiewicz, Linakis and McGirr 2013: 12) creeps back into USAID discussions. Indeed, resilience, alongside well-being and sustainability might be considered social capital's new holy trinity. These terms get at the idea that we draw on human and societal resources in order to strengthen our ability to face challenges. Such thinking also fits with a capacities approach if this is understood as combining individual initiative with a favourable institutional environment in order to build societal resilience (DFID 2004: 2).

This is somewhat contradictory, however. On the one hand, there is recognition that people are embedded in a social context that is the source of their resourcefulness. Collectively people can build up societal resilience in order to meet the challenges they face. Individually, people can draw on their social networks, as is suggested in the social capital literature. On the other hand, the complexity arguments behind resilience-thinking emphasise the messy and entangled character of the social. Social relations are conceived of as fluid, contingent, even brittle (Edwards 2009), making it more difficult to engage in coherent social activities. Perhaps this is why the Anglo-Saxon discourse, while occasionally returning to the idea of the social, prefers to focus on community resilience. This can take a wider 'whole of community approach' that brings together, individuals, government and the private sector (United States Government 2015), or more commonly, it can target specific social groups and appeal to particular interests and motivations.

If the way that resilience relates to the social is contradictory, then perhaps it makes more sense to look at how resilience invokes the idea of the human.[1] After talking of society as 'brittle', Charlie Edwards' *Resilient Nation* goes on to talk of how we as humans have the capacity to learn, adapt and reorganise, change our habits and make different lifestyle choices (Edwards 2009: 17). Policy documents also make such arguments, the European Commission, for example, talks of the need for 'people-centred approaches that address individual life-cycle risks' (European Commission 2013: 3). This focus on human qualities and lifestyles is part of a common trend. If resilience-thinking has the effect of turning us away from the world by accepting systemic crisis as unavoidable, unpredictable and uncontrollable, then it makes sense for us to focus instead on how we deal with problems ourselves. We must also deal with these problems ourselves because past efforts at large-scale intervention are deemed to have been failures. Notwithstanding the points made above, this has the effect of turning away from society as well, not because the idea of society is rejected – our complex social embeddedness is indeed emphasised – but because 'traditional' attempts at social intervention are also deemed failures. Instead, *governing through the human* invokes certain human qualities that better allow us to deal with the complex problems we face. Here it is worth mentioning again the new trinity of resilience, wellbeing and sustainability along with a new interest in human capacities and capabilities. These notions invoke certain intangible human qualities that cannot simply be reduced to instrumental reason or calculative action. They are qualities that might be said to belong to life itself.

This certainly gives these ideas strong appeal and perhaps brings a more-nuanced approach to governance than was possible previously with the notion of social capital. But the arguments, while influential, are not necessarily true. Rather, they help fabricate certain norms of the social and the human. They appeal by giving the impression of being post-market or post-liberal while not actually breaking from such logic. This is to challenge interventions from David Chandler and Mark Bevir who both see new forms of governing as breaks from past practices. Chandler's argument is that resilience is post-liberal, breaking with the classical liberal view that government and the market are constructed upon the autonomy of the subject, understood as a rational self-determining actor (Chandler 2010: 25). Bevir's view is that a new

---

[1] Although, again, there might be some tension here given that some complexity arguments are founded on the idea of the post-human (see Chandler 2014).

wave of governance has become less market-oriented by promoting new networks and alliances (Bevir 2013: 162). According to such an account, resilience, wellbeing and sustainability would help constitute a new mix of practices or variegated governance that appears to be more aware of the limits of markets. However, our account of Anglo-Saxon approaches to resilience does not really support such a view. Instead, resilience can be seen as consistent with already existing forms of governmentality, while adding certain modifications and nuances. It does encourage a more social or human way of thinking though its focus on reflexive awareness of our embedded social context and precarious human position. However, as Michel Foucault's writings make clear (Foucault 2007, 2008), neo-liberal thinking has long held this view in its critique of neo-classical economics. While resilience does invoke various human qualities that do not appear to conform to a model of rational-calculative behaviour of a market type, we have seen that they are consistent with neo-liberalism and market-based technologies when understood in relation to practices of governance. As Philip Mirowski has argued, neo-liberalism revises what it means to be a (human) person with governance of the self, becoming the basis of social order and human capital as the basis of the self (Mirowski 2013: 58–9). And if neo-liberalism revises such things then perhaps resilience and other ideas that emphasise human qualities can be seen as helping in the revision of neo-liberalism itself.

Conclusion

Resilience has a number of distinctive features, notably promoting governance through complexity, governance through failure and denial and governance through invoking human qualities. All this makes it a useful policy tool, but it does not necessarily make it a strong concept and especially not a new governing paradigm. Indeed, its appeal might be said to lie in its vagueness (Brand and Jax 2007). As Zebrowski (2016: 7) notes, the vagueness of resilience actually enhances governmentality by allowing diverse actors and agencies to claim some semblance of a common objective under complex or contradictory conditions. This is not quite a case of meaning all things to all people since we can identify a number of core arguments, but not everyone fully shares such arguments and our study shows that, depending on country, context and field, resilience can mean somewhat different things to a range of different people.

The dominant view of resilience has been outlined as the Anglo-Saxon view. It is more the case that resilience derives its meaning from its place in UK and US policy-making rather than the other way around. This has been described as governmentality because of such features as governing from a distance and encouraging reflexivity and adaptability among subjects. It can be described as neo-liberal because of its promotion of individual initiative and enterprise and support for market solutions. In contrast to classical liberalism, it takes a more pragmatist and 'best-fit' approach to complex, often irresolvable problems. Thus, rather than this being indicative of 'governmentality after neoliberalism' (Bevir 2016), ideas like resilience help in the revision of neo-liberalism and its reconstitution 'after the crisis'. In promoting variegated governance, they do not necessarily offer an alternative to neo-liberalism precisely because neo-liberalism has always taken an imaginative approach to supposedly alternative ways of thinking about our social embeddedness. Of course, resilience and neo-liberalism are not synonymous. Both are ongoing projects, each with their own novel developments (Zebrowski 2016: 150). But there is enough evidence in policy-making to show that resilience and neo-liberal governance now work closely together.

Indeed, resilience and associated ideas like well-being and sustainability do not so much break with neo-liberal governance as enhance its ability to measure and evaluate human resources, capacities and behaviour. They also help constitute us in certain ways that are consistent with neo-liberal thinking – as innovative, enterprising and risk-taking. Rather than replacing market logic, these fill the social and human gaps in neo-liberal governance, thus ensuring its continuity.

Not entirely so, however. As this book shows, there are still significant gaps in policy-making even in the Anglo-Saxon approach. In other countries, we have seen that the tensions and contradictions between neo-liberal views and alternative approaches is even more pronounced. Certainly, the neo-liberal approach is not all-powerful. It clearly enjoys some dominance, and ideas like resilience help in its reinvention. But this does not mean that its inherent problems are being resolved – as critical political economists can, surely, demonstrate.

Conclusion

The findings of this book are undergoing change given the fast-moving discussions and applications of resilience. However, the main argument can be stated very clearly: The emergence of resilience in the fields of national security, counter-terrorism, civil protection, disaster risk reduction (DRR), critical infrastructure protection, development strategy and humanitarian intervention is dominated by a particular, Anglo-Saxon approach. This approach, allowing for subtleties, can be characterised as neo-liberal governmentality. By contrast, we find it difficult to make the case that there are distinctive French, German or European approaches to resilience. Instead, the arguments for resilience that are, indeed, emerging in France, Germany and the EU should be compared and contrasted with the Anglo-Saxon approach. They do not constitute distinct approaches in themselves, but provide evidence of variation from the Anglo-Saxon perspective. This variation is provided by a range of factors including different cultural understandings, different political traditions, different social pressures and priorities and, indeed, different motivations and reasons for the turn to resilience.

This study has been of a more empirical nature, taking its lead from the examination of actual policy documents. Its arguments take into consideration the uptake of resilience and development of related ideas within the wider policy discourse of the different fields and different countries studied. This does not mean that conceptual matters are not important. However, discussions of the philosophy of resilience that are divorced from actual policy-making run the risk of creating an imaginary world where discussions of resilience are not grounded in actualities.

Nevertheless, a conceptual framework is important for analytical purposes. Our approach in this book has been to start with the framework of governmentality in order to try and situate resilience within a wider set of practices and discourses. Our understanding is that resilience has little meaning in and of itself and we, therefore, resist the moves by some to claim that resilience represents a new episteme. Rather, it derives its significance from wider epistemic changes and from its position within existing practices.

These changes are not as developed as some believe. Describing resilience in relation to practices of embedding neo-liberalism (Joseph 2013) also highlights continuities and consistencies with existing practice. Indeed, our understanding of neo-liberalism itself is that it is a flexible set of practices and interventions that is reflexive in relation to its own character, social and cultural situated-ness and open-endedness. Resilience fits into this context, while bringing with it certain specificities about human resourcefulness and adaptability.

To describe the wider epistemic changes is therefore to talk of critique and revision within existing practices of intervention, both domestically and internationally. What resilience does within the Anglo-Saxon approach to governance is highlight the development of different technologies and techniques that manage populations 'from a distance', albeit with the back-up of strong coercive powers where necessary.

The coercive side has long been a characteristic of Anglo-Saxon neo-liberalism with its forceful 'roll-back' of alternative approaches combining with the more normative 'roll-out' phase of social and institutional embedding (Tickell and Peck 2003). While encouraging governance from a distance, neo-liberal governmentality also intersects with coercive and disciplinary practices, particularly so in areas where national security is an issue. We saw this at work in the UK's counter-terrorism practice and the use of statutory powers which makes forceful demands on communities and individuals. We also saw that despite claims to be *laissez-faire* and to 'empower' communities and individuals, the UK state often takes a top–down approach, as can be seen with the requirements in the Civil Contingencies Act.

In focusing on resilience in relation to strategies of governance, we paid more attention to the role of the state and the government. An important conclusion to draw is that although governmentality seeks governance from a distance, this is not about shifting power away from the state, but is about shifting or devolving responsibility. In fact it is by shifting responsibility that the power of the state is strategically enhanced. Rather than reducing the power of the state, devolution of powers is a state-led strategy that works by shifting responsibilities onto the governed while developing more subtle technologies and techniques of governance that sit alongside more overt state powers.

Despite the claims, resilience cannot therefore just be about creating active and responsible subjects who can ultimately be left to govern themselves. However, the subjective side of resilience is very important and we saw how this involves appealing to such things as the social, the human, the individual and the community. As we argued in Chapter 5, resilience does clearly bring something a bit different, although it is not alone in doing this and there is no reason why resilience should be held up as anything particularly special. It draws attention to human qualities and characteristics that can be useful in dealing with risks, threats and crises. These intangible human elements cannot be reduced to an instrumental rationality. However, as part of a wider governmentality, these arguments fill the gaps in neo-liberal strategies of governance rather than offering radical alternatives that do truly value being human.

Unfortunately, or fortunately perhaps, this is where the limits of the Anglo-Saxon approach are all too evident. In our analysis, we stated some basic elements of governmentality that feature in the Anglo-Saxon approach to resilience. Most important of these features are governing from a distance, devolving responsibilities, promoting the market, encouraging enterprise and initiative as well as adapting a transformative approach to resilience. These features are clearly evident in the UK and US approaches, particularly with their emphasis on the importance of building individual and community resilience, creating responsible subjects, promoting certain norms and values, encouraging initiative, stressing the need for adaptive capacities and holding to a transformational account of resilience that sees crises as opportunities to rebuild and reorganise. However, the ability to do such things is limited, even in the UK and US, and we saw that such things as encouraging local initiative is often replaced with top–down command and more direct forms of intervention.

The most severe limits, however, are found beyond the Anglo-Saxon sphere. In examining France and Germany as well as some of the EU's policy-making, we found much less focus on these elements of governmentality. The findings of this book are that resilience is emerging as a term in a number of areas of policy-making outside the Anglo-Saxon countries. However, lacking a lot of the Anglo-Saxon emphasis, the use of the term in policy discourse tends to be: (a) a buzzword with little if any substance; (b) highly technical, for example in relation to communications and critical infrastructure; or, (c) contradictory as evident in approaches to building resilience overseas or in relation to governing through risk.

Countries like France and Germany lack the individualism of their Anglo-Saxon counterparts and have a different understanding of the relation between state and society. People still expect the state to play a leading role in providing protection, backed up by a legal system and other protective infrastructure. Of course, neo-liberal ideas are influential outside Anglo-Saxon countries too, but we see in the tensions in the resilience discourse; that alternative, competing ideas, interests and beliefs also carry weight. This leads to the varieties of resilience that this book has been concerned to document. The spread of the Anglo-Saxon view of resilience is not as widespread as it might at first seem and there are clearly differences in the way that resilience is understood, interpreted and implemented – if it is indeed implemented at all.

These differences point to the future. There are varieties of resilience despite the Anglo-Saxon approach being more dominant. To understand these differences we should start, not from resilience itself, but from the different cultures, conditions and contexts within which it is situated. Tensions within the resilience discourse point to actual differences in the real world. In further exploring these different social conditions, institutional effects and differences in the ideas, understandings and motivations of agents, we might point not just to the limits of resilience, but also to its future possibilities.

Bibliography

Abrahamsen, Rita (2004) 'The Power of Partnerships in Global Governance', *Third World Quarterly* 25, 8: 1453–67.

Adger, Neil (2000) 'Social and Ecological Resilience: Are they Related?', *Progress in Human Geography* 24, 3: 347–64.

AFD (2008) *Adapting French Aid to the Challenges of a Changing World*, Paris: Agence française de développement.

(2012a) *Strategic Orientation Plan 2012–2016*, Paris: Agence française de développement.

(2012b) *Annual Report 2012*, Paris: Agence française de développement.

(2013) *Annual Report 2013*, Paris: Agence française de développement.

(2014) *Annual Report 2014*, Paris: Agence française de développement.

Aldrich, Daniel P. and Michelle A. Meyer (2015) 'Social Capital and Community Resilience', *American Behavioral Scientist* 59, 2: 254–69.

Anderson, Ben and Peter Adey (2011) 'Governing Events and Life "Emergency" in UK Civil Contingencies', *Political Geography* 31, 1: 24–33.

ANVIL (2014) *Civil Society and the European Union: A Survey of European Civil Security Systems and the Role of the EU in Building shared Crisis Management Capacities*, Stockholm: Swedish Institute of International Affairs.

Arnold, Margaret, Robin Mearns, Kaori Oshima, and Vivek Prasad (2014) *Climate and Disaster Resilience: The Role for Community-Driven Development, Social Development Department*, Washington, DC: World Bank.

Ashdown, Paddy (2011) *Humanitarian Emergency Response Review*, London: Department for International Development.

Baban, Constance (2014) *Gesellschaftliche Resilienz – Grundlagen für die zivile Sicherheit*, Potsdam: Brandenburgisches Institut für Gesellschaft und Sicherheit (BIGS).

Barad, Karen (2007) *Meeting the Universe Halfway: Quantum Physics and the Entanglement of Matter and Meaning*, Durham and London: Duke University Press.

Béné, Christophe, Rachel Godfrey Wood, Andrew Newsham, and Mark Davies (2012) *Resilience: New Utopia or New Tyranny? Reflection about the Potentials and Limits of the Concept of Resilience in Relation to Vulnerability Reduction Programmes*, IDS Working Paper 405. London: Institute of Development Studies.

Berkes, Fikret, John Colding, and Carl Folke (2000) 'Introduction' in Fikret Berkes, John Colding, and Carl Folke (eds.) *Navigating Social-ecological Systems: Building Resilience for Complexity and Change*, Cambridge: Cambridge University Press: 1–29.

Berkes, Fikret and Helen Ross (2015) 'Community Resilience: Toward an Integrated Approach', *Society and Natural Resources* 26, 1: 5–20.

Best, Jacqueline (2007) 'Why the Economy Is Often the Exception to Politics as Usual', *Theory, Culture and Society* 24, 4: 87–109.

Bevir, Mark (2013) *A Theory of Governance*, Berkeley: University of California Press.

——— (ed.) (2016) *Governmentality after Neoliberalism*, Abingdon: Routledge.

Bickerton, Christopher (2011) *European Union Foreign Policy: From Effectiveness to Functionality*, Basingstoke: Palgrave.

Bigo, Didier, Sergio Carrera, Elspeth Guild et al. (2015) *The EU and Its Counter-Terrorism Policies after the Paris Attacks*, Brussels: CEPS.

Biscop, Sven (2016) *The EU Global Strategy: Realpolitik with European Characteristics*, Security Brief 75, Brussels: Egmont – Royal Institute for International Relations.

BMZ (2009) *Promoting Resilient States and Constructive State-Society Relations – Legitimacy, Transparency and Accountability*, Bonn: BMZ.

——— (2013) *Strategy on Transitional Development Assistance: Strengthening Resilience – Shaping Transition*, Bonn: BMZ.

——— (2014) *Strategy on Government-Civil Society Cooperation in Post-2015 Development Policy*, Bonn: BMZ.

Boin, Arjen, Mark Rhinard, and Magnus Ekengren (2013) Managing Transboundary Crises: The Emergence of European Union Capacity. *Journal of Contingencies and Crisis Management* 22, 3: 131–142.

Boin, Arjen, Madalina Busuioc, and Martijn Groenleer (2014) 'Building European Union Capacity to Manage Transboundary Crises: Network or Lead-Agency Model?', *Regulation & Governance* 8, 4: 418–36.

Bourcart, Léo (2015) '"The State can't do Everything Any More": Understanding the Evolution of Civil Defence Policies in France', *Resilience: International Policies, Practices and Discourses* 3, 1: 40–54.

Bourbeau, Philippe (2015) 'Resilience and International Politics: Premises, Debates, Agenda', *International Studies Review* 17, 3: 374–95.

Bourgerie, Thomas (2009), 'Résilience: euphémisme sur nos faiblesses ou perspective de progrès?' Available from: www.ecoledeguerre. defense.gouv.fr/IMG/pdf/resilience_bourgerie-2.pdf [Accessed 29 July 2012].

Brand, Fridolin S. and Kurt Jax (2007) 'Focusing the Meaning(s) of Resilience: Resilience as a Descriptive Concept and a Boundary Object', *Ecology and Society* 12, 1: 23.

Brassett, James and Nick Vaughan-Williams (2013) 'The Politics of Resilience from a Practitioner's Perspective: An Interview with Helen Braithwaite OBE', *Politics* 33, 4: 229–39.

Brooks, Nick, Eunica Aure, and Martin Whiteside (2014) *Assessing the Impact of ICF Programmes on Household and Community Resilience to Climate Variability and Climate Change*, London: Evidence on Demand.

Bujones, Alejandra Kubitschek, Katrin Jaskiewicz, Lauren Linakis, and Michael McGirr (2013) *A Framework for Analyzing Resilience in Fragile and Conflict-Affected Situations*, Columbia University/USAID.

Bulley, Dan (2013) 'Producing and Governing Community (through) Resilience', *Politics* 33, 4: 265–75.

Cabinet Office (2004a) *The Lead Government Department and Its Role – Guidance and Best Practice*, London: Cabinet Office. Available from: www.gov.uk/government/uploads/system/uploads/attachment_data/file/61355/lead-government-departments-role.pdf [Accessed 29 July 2012].

(2004b) *Emergency Response and Recovery Non statutory guidance accompanying the Civil Contingencies Act*, London: Cabinet Office.

(2008) *Security in an Interdependent World: The National Security Strategy*, London: Cabinet Office.

(2010a), *A Strong Britain in an Age of Uncertainty: The National Security Strategy*, London: Cabinet Office. Available from: www.direct.gov .uk/prod_consum_dg/groups/dg_digitalassets/@dg/@en/documents/digitalasset/dg_191639.pdf?CID=PDF%26PLA=furl%26CRE= nationalsecuritystrategy [Accessed 29 July 2012].

(2010b), *Securing Britain in an Age of Uncertainty: The Strategic Defence and Security Review*, London: Cabinet Office. Available from: www.direct .gov.uk/prod_consum_dg/groups/dg_digitalassets/@dg/@en/documents/digitalasset/dg_191634.pdf?CID=PDF%26PLA=furl%26CRE=sdsr [Accessed 29 July 2012].

(2010c), *Strategic Framework and Policy Statement on Improving the Resilience of Critical Infrastructure to Disruption from Natural Hazards*, London: Cabinet Office. Available from: www.gov.uk/government/

publications/strategic-framework-and-policy-statement-on-improving-
the-resilience-of-critical-infrastructure-to-disruption-from-natural-
hazards [Accessed 18 April 2017].

(2010d) *Building the Big Society*, London: Cabinet Office. Available from:
www.gov.uk/government/publications/building-the-big-society [Accessed
18 April 2017].

(2011a), *Strategic National Framework on Community Resilience*, London:
Cabinet Office. Available from: www.cabinetoffice.gov.uk/sites/default/
files/resources/Strategic-National-Framework-on-Community-
Resilience_0.pdf [Accessed 29 July 2012].

(2011b) *Keeping the Country Running: Natural Hazards and
Infrastructure*, London: Cabinet Office. Available from: www.gov.uk/
government/publications/keeping-the-country-running-natural-
hazards-and-infrastructure [Accessed 18 April 2017].

(2013a), *Emergency Response and Recovery*, London: Cabinet Office.
Available from: www.gov.uk/government/publications/emergency-
response-and-recovery [Accessed 18 April 2017].

(2013b), *Responding to Emergencies: The UK Central Government
Response: Concept of Operations*, London: Cabinet Office. Available
from: www.gov.uk/government/uploads/system/uploads/attachment_
data/file/192425/CONOPs_incl_revised_chapter_24_Apr-13.pdf
[Accessed 18 April 2017].

(2013c), *Preparation and Planning for Emergencies: Responsibilities of
Responder Agencies and Others*, London: Cabinet Office. Available from:
www.gov.uk/guidance/preparation-and-planning-for-emergencies-
responsibilities-of-responder-agencies-and-others [Accessed 18 April 2017].

(2013d) *Enhancing the Resilience of Telecommunications*, London:
Cabinet Office. Available from: www.gov.uk/guidance/telecoms-resilience
[Accessed 18 April 2017].

(2014), *Resilience in Society: Infrastructure, Communities and Businesses*,
London: Cabinet Office. Available from: www.gov.uk/guidance/resilience-
in-society-infrastructure-communities-and-businesses [Accessed 18
April 2017].

(2015) *National Security Strategy and Strategic Defence and Security
Review 2015*, London: Cabinet Office. Available from: www.gov.uk/
government/publications/national-security-strategy-and-strategic-
defence-and-security-review-2015 [Accessed 18 April 2017].

(2016a) *Preparing for Emergencies: Guide for Communities*, London:
Cabinet Office. Available from: www.gov.uk/government/uploads/
system/uploads/attachment_data/file/552867/pfe_guide_for_communities
.pdf [Accessed 18 April 2017].

(2016b) *Community Resilience Framework for Practitioners*, London:
Cabinet Office. Available from: www.gov.uk/government/publications/

community-resilience-framework-for-practitioners/the-context-for-community-resilience [Accessed 18 April 2017].

Chandler, David (2010) *International Statebuilding: The Rise of Post-Liberal Governance*, Abingdon: Routledge.

(2014) *Resilience: The Governance of Complexity*, Abingdon: Routledge.

Chandler, David and Oliver Richmond (2015) 'Contesting Postliberalism: Governmentality or Emancipation?', *Journal of International Relations and Development* 18, 1: 1–24.

Commissariat Général au Développement Durable (2013) *Approche intégrée de la résilience des Territoires soumis aux risques naturels et technologiques*, Paris: Commissariat Général au Développement Durable.

Conseil Supérieur de la Formation et de la Recherche Stratégiques (2011) *Rapport du conseil scientifique du conseil supérieur de la formation et de la echerché stratégiques 2011*, Paris: CSFRS.

Cooper, Melinda and Jeremy Walker (2011) 'Genealogies of Resilience: From Systems Ecology to the Political Economy of Crisis Adaptation', *Security Dialogue* 14, 2: 143–60.

Cormier, Pierre-Yves, Alain Ferran, Christophe Rastouil, and Ian Turner (2010), '*Les principes de la resilience en France*'. Available from: www .ems.defense.gouv.fr/IMG/pdf/CCM-040.pdf [Accessed 29 July 2012].

Cyrulnik, Boris (1999) *Un Merveilleux Malheur*, Paris: Odile Jacob.

Dean, Mitchell (1999) *Governmentality: Power and Rule in Modern Society*, London: Sage.

Death, Carl (2013) 'Governmentality at the Limits of the International: African Politics and Foucauldian Theory'. *Review of International Studies* 39, 3: 763–87.

Department of Homeland Security (2012) *National Preparedness Report*, Washington, DC: Department of Homeland Security.

(2013) *NIPP 2013: Partnering for Critical Infrastructure Security and Resilience*, Washington, DC: Department of Homeland Security.

(2016a) *National Preparedness Report*, Washington, DC: Department of Homeland Security.

(2016b) *National Disaster Recovery Framework: Strengthening Disaster Recovery for the Nation*, Washington, DC: Department of Homeland Security / FEMA.

DFID (1997) *Eliminating World Poverty: A Challenge for the 21st Century*, London: Department for International Development.

(2004) *Disaster Risk Reduction: A Development Concern. A Scoping Study on Links between Disaster Risk Reduction, Poverty and Development*, London: Department for International Development.

(2011a) *Defining Disaster Resilience: A DFID Approach Paper*, London: Department for International Development.

(2011b) *Defining Disaster Resilience: What Does It Mean for DFID?*, London: Department for International Development.

(2011c) *Humanitarian Emergency Response Review: UK Government Response*, London: Department for International Development.

(2011d) *Saving Lives, Preventing Suffering and Building Resilience: The UK Government's Humanitarian Policy*, London: Department for International Development.

(2012a) *Minimum Standards for Embedding Disaster Resilience in DFID Country Offices*, London: Department for International Development.

(2012b) *Operational Plan 2011–2015 DFID Growth and Resilience Department (GRD)*, London: Department for International Development.

(2013a) *Operational Plan 2011–2015 DFID Ethiopia*, London: Department for International Development.

(2013b) *Operational Plan 2011–2015 DFID Kenya*, London: Department for International Development.

(2013c) *2013 UK Humanitarian Response in the Sahel*, London: Department for International Development.

(2013d) *2013 Accelerating Progress on Disaster Resilience in DFID Country Programmes: 'Catalytic Fund'*, London: Department for International Development.

DFID, Foreign and Commonwealth Office and Ministry for Defence (2011) *Building Stability Overseas Strategy*, London: Department for International Development.

Duffield, Mark (2013) 'How did we Become Unprepared? Emergency and Resilience in an Uncertain World', *British Academy Review* 21: 55–8.

ECHO (2013) *Humanitarian Implementation Plan (HIP) West Africa Sahel Region*, Brussels: ECHO.

Edwards, Charlie (2009) *Resilient Nation*, London: Demos.

emBRACE (2012) *Work Package 1: Early Discussion and Gap Analysis on Resilience.* Available from: www.embrace-eu.org/documents/emBRACE-D1%201-040412_Final%20docx.pdf [Accessed 27 April 2017].

European Commission (NDa) '*Resilient Europe Societal Challenge 6: Europe in a Changing World – Inclusive, Innovative and Reflective Societies*'. Available from: http://ec.europa.eu/programmes/horizon2020/en/h2020-section/europe-changing-world-inclusive-innovative-and-reflective-societies [Accessed 18 August 2015].

European Commission (NDb) '*External Advice and Societal Engagement: Towards the 2016 and 2017 Work Programme of "Inclusive, Innovative and Reflective Societies" of Horizon 2020*'. Available from: http://ec.europa.eu/programmes/horizon2020/en/h2020-section/europe-changing-world-inclusive-innovative-and-reflective-societies [Accessed 18 August 2015].

European Commission (2005) *Green Paper on a European Programme for Critical Infrastructure Protection*, Brussels: European Commission.

——— (2007) *Towards Better Protecting Citizens against Disaster Risks: Strengthening Early Warning Systems in Europe*, Brussels: European Commission.

——— (2009a) *A Community Approach on the Prevention of Natural and Man-Made Disasters*, Brussels: European Commission.

——— (2009b) *Adapting to Climate Change: Towards a European Framework for Action*, Brussels: European Commission.

——— (2009c) *EU Strategy for Supporting Disaster Risk Reduction in Developing Countries*, Brussels: European Commission.

——— (2010a) *Europe 2020 A Strategy for Smart, Sustainable and Inclusive Growth*, Brussels: European Commission.

——— (2010b) *The EU Internal Security Strategy in Action: Five Steps Towards a More Secure Europe*, Brussels: European Commission.

——— (2010c) *The EU Counter-Terrorism Policy: Main Achievements and Future Challenges*, Brussels: European Commission.

——— (2011) *Guidelines for Project Managers: Making Vulnerable Investment Climate Resilient*, Brussels: European Commission.

——— (2012a) *EU Approach to Resilience: Learning from Food Security Crises*, Brussels: European Commission.

——— (2012b) *Humanitarian Implementation Plan (HIP) Horn of Africa*, Brussels: European Commission.

——— (2013) *Action Plan for Resilience in Crisis Prone Countries 2013–2020*, Brussels: European Commission.

——— (2013a) *An EU Strategy on Adaptation to Climate Change*, Brussels: European Commission.

——— (2013b) *A New Approach to the European Programme for Critical Infrastructure Protection Making European Critical Infrastructures more Secure*, Brussels: European Commission.

——— (2013c) *Adapting Infrastructure to Climate Change*, Brussels: European Commission.

——— (2014) *Preventing Radicalisation to Terrorism and Violent Extremism: Strengthening the EU's Response*, Brussels: European Commission.

——— (2014a) *The Post 2015 Hyogo Framework for Action: Managing Risks to Achieve Resilience*, Brussels: European Commission.

——— (2014b) *Commission Implementing Decision of 28.5.2014 on Deciding to make a Standardisation Request to the European Standardisation Organisations in Support of Implementation of the EU Strategy on Adaptation to Climate Change*, Brussels: European Commission.

——— (2016) *Action Plan on the Sendai Framework for Disaster Risk Reduction 2015–2030 – A Disaster Risk-Informed Approach for all EU Policies*, Brussels: European Commission.

European Council (2003) *European Security Strategy: A Secure Europe in a Better World*, Brussels: European Council.

(2005) *The European Union Counterterrorism Strategy*, Brussels: European Council.

(2008a) *Report on the Implementation of the European Security Strategy – Providing Security in a Changing World*, Brussels: European Council.

(2008) *Council Directive 2008/114/EC of 8 December 2008 on the Identification and Designation of European Critical Infrastructures and the Assessment of the Need to Improve Their Protection*, Brussels: European Council.

(2008c) *European Consensus on Humanitarian Aid*, Brussels: European Council.

(2009) *Council Conclusions on a Community Framework on Disaster Prevention within the EU 2979th JUSTICE and HOME AFFAIRS Council Meeting Brussels, 30 November 2009*, Brussels: European Council.

(2010) *Internal Security Strategy for the European Union – Towards a European Security Model*, Brussels: European Council.

(2013) *Council Conclusions on EU Approach to Resilience*, Brussels: European Council.

European External Action Service (2011) *Strategy for Security and Development in the Sahel*, Brussels: EUAS.

European Parliament and European Council (2007) *Directive 2007/60/EC on the Assessment and Management of Flood Risks*, Brussels: European Parliament.

(2013) *Decision of 17 December 2013 on a Union Civil Protection Mechanism*, Brussels: European Parliament.

European Union Global Strategy (2016) *Shared Vision, Common Action: A Stronger Europe A Global Strategy for the European Union's Foreign and Security Policy*. Brussels: EUGS. Available from: http://eeas.europa.eu/archives/docs/top_stories/pdf/eugs_review_web.pdf [Accessed 10 May 2017].

Evans, Brad and Julian Reid (2014) *Resilient Life: The Art of Living Dangerously*, Cambridge: Polity.

Fairclough, Norman (2003) *Analysing Discourse: Textual Analysis for Social Research*, London: Routledge.

Federal Foreign Office (2012) *Strategy of the Federal Foreign Office for Humanitarian Assistance Abroad*, Berlin: Federal Foreign Office / Auswärtiges Amt.

Federal Ministry of Defence (2006) *White Paper on German Security Policy and the Future of the Bundeswehr*, Berlin: Federal Ministry of Defence.

(2011) *Defence Policy Guidelines: Safeguarding National Interests – Assuming International Responsibility – Shaping Security Together*, Berlin: Federal Ministry of Defence.

(2016) *White Paper on German Security Policy and the Future of the Bundeswehr*, Berlin: Federal Ministry of Defence.

Federal Ministry of Education and Research (2016) *Research for Civil Security 2012 – 2017: Framework Programme of the Federal Government*, Bonn: Bundesministerium für Bildung und Forschung / Federal Ministry of Education and Research (BMBF).

Federal Ministry of the Interior (2008) *Protecting Critical Infrastructures – Risk and Crisis Management: A Guide for Companies and Government Authorities*, Berlin: Federal Ministry of the Interior.

(2009) *National Strategy for Critical Infrastructure Protection (CIP Strategy)*, Berlin: Federal Ministry of the Interior.

Federal Office for Information Security (2004) *Analysis of Critical Infrastructures – The ACIS Methodology*, Berlin: BSI.

Federal Office of Civil Protection and Disaster Assistance (2014) *Assessing Vulnerability to Flood Events at a Community Level, Berlin: Federal Office of Civil Protection and Disaster Assistance*, Berlin: Federal Office of Civil Protection and Disaster Assistance.

FEMA (2015) *National Preparedness Goal Second Edition*, Washington DC: FEMA.

FFEM (2014) *Annual Report 2014*, Paris: Fonds Français pour l'Environnement Mondial.

Foley, Frank (2013) *Countering Terrorism in Britain and France: Institutions, Norms and the Shadow of the Past*, Cambridge: Cambridge University Press.

Folke, Carl (2006) 'Resilience: The Emergence of a Perspective for Social–Ecological Systems Analyses', *Global Environmental Change* 16: 253–67.

Foucault, Michel (1979) *Discipline and Punish*, Harmondsworth: Penguin Books.

(2004) *Society Must Be Defended*, Harmondsworth: Penguin Books.

(2007) *Security, Territory, Population*, Basingstoke: Palgrave Macmillan.

(2008) *The Birth of Biopolitics*, Basingstoke: Palgrave Macmillan.

Fougner, Tore (2008) 'Neoliberal Governance of States: The Role of Competitiveness Indexing and Country Benchmarking', *Millennium: Journal of International Studies* 37, 2: 303–26.

Francart, Loup (2010), 'What Does Resilience Really Mean?' Available from: www.diploweb.com/What-doesresilience-really-mean.html [Accessed 29 July 2012].

Fuchs-Drapier, Marie (2011) 'The European Union's Solidarity Clause in the Event of a Terrorist Attack: Towards Solidarity or Maintaining Sovereignty?', *Journal of Contingencies and Crisis Management* 19, 4: 184–97.

German Red Cross (2014) *The Resilience Framework of the German Red Cross Strengthening Resilience through the International Cooperation of the GRC*, Berlin: German Red Cross.

Giddens, Anthony (1990). *The Consequences of Modernity*, Cambridge: Polity Press.

Gunderson, Lance (2003) 'Adaptive Dancing: Interactions between Social Resilience and Ecological Crises' in Fikret Berkes, John Colding, and Carl Folke (eds.) *Navigating Social-Ecological Systems: Building Resilience for Complexity and Change*, Cambridge: Cambridge University Press: 33–52.

Gunderson, Lance, C. S. Holling, L. Pritchard, and G. D. Peterson (2002) 'Resilience' in Harold A. Mooney and Josep G. Canadell (eds.) *Encyclopaedia of Global Environmental Change Volume 2, The Earth System: Biological and Ecological Dimensions of Global Environmental Change*, Chichester UK: Wiley: 530–1.

Gubbels, Peter (2012a) 'A New Drumbeat for the Sahel', *Humanitarian Exchange*, 55: 3–6. Available from: www.odihpn.org/humanitarian-exchange-magazine/issue-55/a-new-drumbeat-for-the-sahel [Accessed 9 May 2013].

(2012b) 'Ending the Everyday Emergency: Resilience and Children in the Sahel', London: Save the Children and World Vision. Available from: www.savethechildren.org.uk/resources/online-library/ending-everyday-emergency-resilience-and-children-sahel [Accessed 2 February 2015].

Haldrup, Sren Vester and Frederik Rosn (2013) 'Developing Resilience: A Retreat from Grand Planning, Resilience', *International Policies, Practices and Discourses* 1, 2: 130–45.

Haut Comité Francais pour la Défense Civile (2010). Gestion des crises complexes, quelles interactions et quels processus entre secteurs public et privés?, Paris: Haut Comité Francais pour la Défense Civile.

Headey, D. and Kennedy, A. (2012) *Enhancing Resilience in the Horn of Africa*, Washington, DC: USAID and International Food Policy Research Institute.

Hecker, Marc (2015) 'Antiterrorisme: nul système n'est infaillible', *Libération*, 11 January. Available from: www.liberation.fr/planete/2015/01/11/antiterrorisme-nul-systeme-n-est-infaillible_1178529 [Accessed 8 June 2016].

Henretin, Joseph (2010) *La résilience dans l'antiterrorisme: Le dernier bouclier*, Paris: L'Esprit du Livre Editions.

Holland, Martin (2002) *The European Union and the Third World*, Basingstoke: Palgrave.

Holling, C. S. (1973) 'Resilience and Stability of Ecological Systems', *Annual Review of Ecology and Systematics* 4: 1–23.

Home Office (2011) *CONTEST: The United Kingdom's Strategy for Countering Terrorism*, London: Home Office. Available from: www.gov.uk/government/uploads/system/uploads/attachment_data/file/97995/strategy-contest.pdf [Accessed 1 April 2013].

—— (2015) *Counter Extremism Strategy*, London: Home Office. Available from: https://assets.publishing.service.gov.uk/government/uploads/system/uploads/attachment_data/file/470088/51859_Cm9148_Accessible.pdf [Accessed 25 May 2018].

IRIN (2012) 'Resisting the Mantra of Resilience'. Available from: www.irinnews.org/report/96549/aid-policy-resisting-the-mantra-of-resilience [Accessed 25 July 2014].

Issack, A.A. and Yusef, A. (2010) *Save the Children UK Experiences on Piloting Community Based Early Warning Systems in 3 Districts of Somali and Afar Regions of Ethiopia: What Worked and What Didn't*, Brussels and London: European Community Humanitarian Aid and Civil Protection (ECHO) and Save the Children.

Jessop, Bob (2007) *State Power*, Cambridge: Polity.

Joseph, Jonathan (2010) 'The Limits of Governmentality; Social Theory and the International', *European Journal of International Relations* 16, 2: 223–46.

—— (2012) *The Social in the Global: Social Theory, Governmentality and Global Politics*, Cambridge: Cambridge University Press.

—— (2013) 'Resilience as Embedded Neoliberalism: A Governmentality Approach', *Resilience: International Policies, Practices and Discourses* 1, 1: 38–52.

—— (2016) 'Governing Through Failure and Denial: The New Resilience Agenda', *Millennium: Journal of International Studies* 35, 2: 342–59.

Juncos, Ana (2017) 'Resilience as the New EU Foreign Policy Paradigm: A Pragmatist Turn?', *European Security* 26, 1: 1–18.

Larner, Wendy and William Walters (2006) *Global Governmentality: Governing International Spaces*, Abingdon: Routledge.

Keck, Markus and Patrick Sakdapolrak (2013) 'What Is Social Resilience?: Lessons Learned and Ways Forward', *Erdkunde* 67, 1: 5–19.

Keohane, Daniel (2006) 'Implementing the EU's Counter-Terrorism Strategy: Intelligence, Emergencies and Foreign Policy' in Dieter Mahncke and

Jörg Monar (eds.) *International Terrorism: A European Response to a Global Threat?*, Brussels: P.I.E. Peter Lang: 63–72.

Kirchner, Emil J., Evangelos Fanoulis and Han Dorussen (2015) 'Civil Security in the EU: National Persistence versus EU Ambitions?', *European Security* 24, 2: 287–303.

Kundnani, Arun (2009) *Spooked: How Not to Prevent Violent Extremism*, London: Institute of Race Relations.

Kurki, Milja (2013) *Democratic Futures: Re-Visioning Democracy Promotion*, Abingdon: Routledge.

Lijphart, Arend (1971) 'Comparative Politics and the Comparative Method', *The American Political Science Review* 65, 3: 682–93.

Lowe, David (2016) *Policing Terrorism: Research Studies into Police Counterterrorism Operations*, Boca Raton, FL: CRC Press.

MacKinnon, Danny and Kate Driscoll Derickson (2012) 'From Resilience to Resourcefulness: A Critique of Resilience Policy and Activism', *Progress in Human Geography* 37, 2: 253–70.

Mann, Bruce (2007), *Protecting the UK's Critical Infrastructure*, London: Cabinet Office/Contingency today. Available from: www.contingencytoday.com/online_article/Protecting-the-UK_s-Critical-National-Infrastructure/416 [Accessed 29 July 2012].

Manners, Ian (2002) 'Normative Power Europe: A Contradiction in Terms?', *Journal of Common Market Studies* 40, 2: 235–58.

Martin-Breen, Patrick and J. Marty Anderies (2011) *Resilience: A Literature Review*, Brighton: Bellagion Initiative, Institute for Development Studies and The Rockefeller Foundation.

Manyena, Siambabala Bernard (2006) 'The Concept of Resilience Revisited', *Disasters* 30, 4: 433–450.

Miller, Peter and Nikolas Rose (1990) 'Governing Economic Life', *Economy and Society* 19, 1: 1–31.

Ministry of Defence (2007) *Operations in the UK: The Defence Contribution to Resilience*, Shrivenham: Ministry of Defence, UK.

Mirowski, Philip (2013) *Never Let a Good Crisis Go to Waste*, London: Verso.

Morsut, Claudia (2014) 'The EU's Community Mechanism for Civil Protection: Analysing Its Development', *Journal of Contingencies and Crisis Management* 22, 3: 143–9.

Mosel, Irina and Simon Levine (2014) *Remaking the Case for Linking Relief, Rehabilitation and Development: How LRRD can become a Practically Useful Concept for Assistance in Difficult Places*, London: Humanitarian Policy Group / BMZ.

Müller, Uwe (2013) 'Implementation of the Flood Risk Management Directive in Selected European Countries', *International Journal of Disaster Risk Science* 4, 3: 115–25.

Norris, Fran H., Susan P. Stevens, Betty Pfefferbaum, Karen F. Wyche, and Rose L. Pfefferbaum (2008) 'Community Resilience as a Metaphor, Theory, Set of Capacities, and Strategy for Disaster Readiness', *American Journal Community Psychology* 41, 1–2: 127–50.

O'Brien, Geoff and Paul Read (2005) 'Future UK Emergency Management: New Wine, Old Skin?', *Disaster Prevention and Management* 14, 3: 353–61.

O'Malley, Pat (2010) 'Resilient Subjects: Uncertainty, Warfare and Liberalism', *Economy and Society* 39: 4: 488–509.

Pavanello, Sara (2010) 'Working across Borders: Harnessing the Potential of Cross-Border Activities to Improve Livelihood Security in the Horn of Africa Drylands', *Policy Brief 41*, London: Humanitarian Policy Group.

Présidence de la République (2008a) *Défense et sécurité nationale: le livre blanc*, Paris: Odile Jacob.

  (2008b) *Défense et sécurité nationale: le livre blanc – les débats*, Paris: Odile Jacob.

  (2008c) *The French White Paper on Defence and Security: Press Kit*, Paris: Présidence de la République.

  (2008d) *Un concept nouveau: la resilience*. Available from: www .livreblancdefenseetsecurite.gouv.fr/IMG/pdf/02.2-Unconceptnouveau-laresilience.pdf [Accessed 29 July 2012].

  (2013) *The French White Paper on Defence and Security*, Paris: Présidence de la République.

Richards, Julian (2012) *A Guide to National Security: Threats, Responses, and Strategies*, Oxford: Oxford University Press.

Secrétariat général de la défense et de la sécurité nationale (2014a) *L'instruction générale interministérielle n 6600 est relative à la sécurité des activités d'importance vitale*, Paris: Secrétariat général de la défense et de la sécurité nationale.

  (2014b) *L'organisation*. Available from: www.sgdsn.gouv.fr/site_rubrique70 .html [Accessed 4 August 2016].

Selby, Jan (2007) 'Engaging Foucault: Discourse, Liberal Governance and the Limits of Foucauldian IR', *International Relations* 21, 3: 324–45.

Seery, Mark D., E. Allison Holman, and Roxane Cohen Silver (2010) 'Whatever Does Not Kill Us: Cumulative Lifetime Adversity, Vulnerability, and Resilience', *Journal of Personality and Social Psychology* 99, 6: 1025–41.

Selchow, Sabine (2016) 'Resilience and Resilient in Obama's National Security Strategy 2010: Enter Two Political Keywords', *Politics* 37, 1: 1–16.

Sicurelli, Daniela (2010) *The European Union's African Policies: Norms, Interest and Impact*, Farnham: Ashgate.

Simon, Luis, Alexander Mattelaer and Amelia Hadfield (2012) *A Coherent EU Strategy for the Sahel*, European Parliament: Brussels.

Sum, Ngai-Ling and Bob Jessop (2013) *Towards a Cultural Political Economy: Putting Culture in its Place in Political Economy*, Cheltenham: Edward Elgar.

Tickell, Adam and Jamie Peck (2003) 'Making Global Rules: Globalisation or Neoliberalisation', in Jamie Peck and Henry Wai-chung Yeung (eds.) *Remaking the Global Economy*, London: Sage: 163–82.

Tocci, Nathalie 'The European Union, Civil Society and Conflict: An Analytical Framework' in Nathalie Tocci (ed.) *The European Union, Civil Society and Conflict*, Abingdon: Routledge, 2011: 1–27.

UN/ISDR (2005) *Towards National Resilience: Good Practices of National Platforms for Disaster Risk Reduction*, Geneva: United Nations Secretariat of the International Strategy for Disaster Reduction.

United States Government (2010) *National Security Strategy*, Washington DC: The White House.

(2014) *The 2014 Quadrennial Homeland Security Review*, Washington DC: The White House.

(2015) *National Security Strategy*, Washington DC: The White House.

USAID (2012a) *Building Resilience to Recurrent Crisis USAID Policy and Program Guidance*, Washington: USAID.

(2012b) *USAID Climate Change and Development Strategy 2012–2016 Clean Resilient Growth*, Washington: USAID.

(2012c) *The Resilience Agenda: Helping Vulnerable Communities Emerge from Cycles of Crisis onto a Pathway Toward Development*, Washington: USAID.

(2013a) *Horn of Africa Joint Planning Cell Annual Report*, Washington: USAID.

(2013b) *Sahel Joint Planning Cell Strategic Plan Reducing Risk, Building Resilience, and Facilitating Inclusive Economic Growth*, Washington: USAID.

(2012b) *USAID Climate Change and Development Strategy 2012–2016 Clean Resilient Growth*, Washington: USAID.

(2012c) *The Resilience Agenda: Helping Vulnerable Communities Emerge from Cycles of Crisis onto a Pathway Toward Development*, Washington: USAID.

(2013a) *Horn of Africa Joint Planning Cell Annual Report*, Washington: USAID.

(2013b) *Sahel Joint Planning Cell Strategic Plan: Reducing Risk, Building Resilience, and Facilitating Inclusive Economic Growth*, Washington: USAID.

Vilcan, Tudorel (2016) *Hollow Politics of Resilience: The Case of Flood Governance in England*, PhD thesis, University of Southampton.

(2017) 'Articulating Resilience in Practice: Chains of Responsibilisation, Failure Points and Political Contestation, Resilience: International Policies', *Practices and Discourses* 5, 1: 29–43.

Vrasti, Wanda (2013) 'Universal but not Truly Global: Governmentality, Economic Liberalism and the International', *Review of International Studies* 39, 1: 49–69.

Walker, B., C. S. Holling, S. R. Carpenter, and A. Kinzig (2004) 'Resilience, Adaptability and Transformability in Social–Ecological Systems', *Ecology and Society* 9, 2. Available from: www.ecologyandsociety.org/vol9/iss2/art5/ [Accessed 15 December 2013].

Walker, Jeremy and Melinda Cooper (2011) 'Genealogies of Resilience: From Systems Ecology to the Political Economy of Crisis Adaptation', *Security Dialogue* 42, 2: 143–60.

Walters, William (2012) *Governmentality: Critical Encounters*, Abingdon: Routledge.

White House (2011) *National Strategy for Counterterrorism*, Washington DC: The White House.

(2013) *Presidential Policy Directive – Critical Infrastructure Security and Resilience: Presidential Policy Directive/PPD-21*, Washington DC: The White House. Available from: www.whitehouse.gov/the-press-office/2013/02/12/presidential-policy-directive-critical-infrastructure-security-and-resil [Accessed 18 April 2017].

(2015) *Presidential Policy Directive/ PPD-8 (2015) National Preparedness*, Washington DC: The White House. Available from: www.dhs.gov/presidential-policy-directive-8-national-preparedness [Accessed 18 April 2017].

Whitman, Richard (ed.) (2006) *Normative Power Europe: Empirical and Theoretical Perspectives*, Basingstoke: Palgrave.

Wight, Colin (2006) *Agents, Structures and International Relations*, Cambridge: Cambridge University Press.

Wildavsky, Aaron (1988) *Searching for Safety*, New Brunswick NJ: Transaction Press.

World Bank (1997) *World Development Report 1997: The State in a Changing World*, New York: Oxford University Press.

(2014) *Building Resilience: Integrating Climate and Disaster Risk into Development. Lessons from World Bank Group Experience*, Washington, DC: World Bank.

World Resources Institute in collaboration with United Nations Development Programme, United Nations Environment Programme and World Bank (2008) *World Resources 2008: Roots of Resilience Growing the Wealth of the Poor*, Washington, DC: World Resources Institute.

Youngs, Richard (2010) *The EU's Role in World Politics: A Retreat from Liberal Internationalism*, Abingdon: Routledge.

Zanotti, Laura (2005) 'Governmentalizing the Post-Cold War International Regime: The UN Debate on Democratization and Good Governance', *Alternatives* 30: 461–87.

Zebrowski, Chris (2013) 'The Nature of Resilience', *Resilience: International Policies, Practices and Discourses* 1, 3: 159–73.

(2016) *The Value of Resilience: Securing Life in the Twenty-First Century*, Abingdon: Routledge.

Index